AT THE MERCY OF THEIR CLOTHES

MODERNIST LATITUDES

Modernist Latitudes
Jessica Berman and Paul Saint-Amour, Editors

Modernist Latitudes aims to capture the energy and ferment of modernist studies by continuing to open up the range of forms, locations, temporalities, and theoretical approaches encompassed by the field. The series celebrates the growing latitude ("scope for freedom of action or thought") that this broadening affords scholars of modernism, whether they are investigating little-known works or revisiting canonical ones. Modernist Latitudes will pay particular attention to the texts and contexts of those latitudes (Africa, Latin America, Australia, Asia, Southern Europe, and even the rural United States) that have long been misrecognized as ancillary to the canonical modernisms of the global North.

Barry McCrea, *In the Company of Strangers: Family and Narrative in Dickens, Conan Doyle, Joyce, and Proust*, 2011

Jessica Berman, *Modernist Commitments: Ethics, Politics, and Transnational Modernism*, 2011

Jennifer Scappettone, *Killing the Moonlight: Modernism in Venice*, 2014

Nico Israel, *Spirals: The Whirled Image in Twentieth-Century Literature and Art*, 2015

Carrie Noland, *Voices of Negritude in Modernist Print: Aesthetic Subjectivity, Diaspora, and the Lyric Regime*, 2015

Susan Stanford Friedman, *Planetary Modernisms: Provocations on Modernity Across Time*, 2015

Steven S. Lee, *The Ethnic Avant-Garde: Minority Cultures and World Revolution*, 2015

Thomas S. Davis, *The Extinct Scene: Late Modernism and Everyday Life*, 2016

Carrie J. Preston, *Learning to Kneel: Noh, Modernism, and Journeys in Teaching*, 2016

Gayle Rogers, *Incomparable Empires: Modernism and the Translation of Spanish and American Literature*, 2016

Donal Harris, *On Company Time: American Modernism in the Big Magazines*, 2016

AT THE MERCY OF THEIR CLOTHES

*Modernism, the Middlebrow,
and British Garment Culture*

Celia Marshik

Columbia University Press   New York

Columbia University Press
Publishers Since 1893
New York   Chichester, West Sussex
cup.columbia.edu

Copyright © 2017 Columbia University Press
Paperback edition, 2022
All rights reserved

Library of Congress Cataloging-in-Publication Data
Names: Marshik, Celia, author.
Title: At the mercy of their clothes : modernism, the middlebrow, and British garment culture / Celia Marshik.
Description: New York : Columbia University Press, [2016] | Series: Modernist latitudes | Includes bibliographical references and index.
Identifiers: LCCN 2016022756 (print) | LCCN 2016034823 (ebook) | ISBN 9780231175043 (cloth) | ISBN 9780231175050 (pbk.) | ISBN 9780231542968 (e-book)
Subjects: LCSH: English literature—20th century—History and criticism. | Clothing and dress in literature. | Fashion—Social aspects—Great Britain—History—20th century. | Clothing and dress—Social aspects—Great Britain—History. | Modernism (Literature)—Great Britain. | Identity (Psychology) in literature.
Classification: LCC PR478.C58 M37 2016 (print) | LCC PR478.C58 (ebook) | DDC 820.9/3564—dc23
LC record available at https://lccn.loc.gov/2016022756

COVER DESIGN AND PHOTOGRAPH: Jenny Carrow

In memory of Kenneth Marshik

Contents

List of Illustrations ix
Acknowledgments xi

Introduction: At the Mercy of Their Clothes   1

1. What Do Women Want? At the Mercy
   of the Evening Gown   25

2. Wearable Memorials: Into and Out
   of the Trenches with the Modern Mac   66

3. Aspiration to the Extraordinary:
   Materializing the Subject Through Fancy Dress   102

4. Serialized Selves: Style, Identity,
   and the Problem of the Used Garment   145

   Coda: Precious Clothing   178

Notes 185
Bibliography 221
Index 231

Illustrations

1.1. Kenneth Beauchamp, "Poor Clara" 26
1.2. The label of Mrs. Neville 31
1.3. Dressed to be threatened in Kathlyn Rhodes, "The Harvest of Folly" 38
1.4. Overexposed in "The Harvest of Folly" 39
1.5. Mourning dress made by Mrs. Neville 41
1.6. Black and gold woven metal thread and velvet evening dress, worn by Lady Ottoline Morrell 56
1.7. "An unusual photographic study, in the Goya manner, of Lady Ottoline Morrell" 58
2.1. Women's mackintoshes sold through the *Harrods General Catalogue* 73
2.2. "A member of the Women's Volunteer Reserve" 80
2.3. Detail of an advertisement for Phosferine 81
2.4. Advertisement for Aquascutum military and civilian coats 83
2.5. "Special Values in Weathercoats," *Harrods Weekly Price List* 89
2.6. Detail of notices of men "Killed in Action" or "Died of Wounds" 91
2.7. Advertisement for "The Famous 'Aquascutum' Storm Coats" 96
3.1. George J. Nicholls dressed as a side of bacon 104
3.2. Cover of *Fancy Dresses at Harrods* 110
3.3. Lady Arthur Paget dressed as Cleopatra 112
3.4. Lady Abdy dressed as "sea mist" 113
3.5. Arthur Watts, "After the Fancy-Dress Ball" 119
3.6. Celebrants at the "Alice in Wonderland" party 129
4.1. Secondhand-clothing shop in London 150
4.2. Poster issued by the National War Savings Committee 151
4.3. A. Wallis Mills, "War Economy" 151
4.4. Bert Thomas, "The New Poor" 153

Acknowledgments

The debts one accrues when writing a book are impossible to repay. Nevertheless, it is a pleasure to acknowledge the many colleagues and friends who supported this work. My early research was funded by a grant from the Faculty in the Arts, Humanities and Social Sciences (FAHSS) initiative at Stony Brook University, and work with the Messel Family Dress Collection at the Brighton Museum & Art Gallery was supported by the Dean's Excellence Fund. Many archivists helped to make that work fruitful, but Greta Pawlowski (formerly of Aquascutum), Martin Pel (Royal Pavilion & Museums, Brighton & Hove), and Sebastian Wormell (Harrods) deserve special thanks for the welcome and guidance they offered. As I completed the manuscript, I was provided with crucial release time by my then dean, Nancy Squires, and chair, Eugene Hammond. I thank them for investing in my project in a way that was as timely as it was generous.

The initial (and evolving) ideas behind this book were tried out at a series of conference presentations where I benefited from the suggestions of Melissa Bradshaw, Anne Fernald, Christine Froula, Randi Koppen, Karen Leick, Ilya Parkins, Paul Saint-Amour, Lily Sheehan, Carey Snyder, Julie Vandivere, John Young, and many others. Drafts of chapters were vetted by writing partners and groups who provided support, feedback, and friendship that made the work a little less lonely. I thank Bonnie Gordon for helping hone my early research questions, Adrienne Munich for inspiration, Susan Scheckel for convivial writing sessions, Jane Garrity for sharing her insider's knowledge of Virginia Woolf and fashion, and Jessica Burstein for her patience with repeated e-mail exchanges. This book might still be in embryo were it not for Allison Pease and Laura Frost, lunch dates extraordinaire whose humor leavened their criticism. Writing our second books together lifted the load considerably, and I am honored to follow in your footsteps.

An American working on British garment culture could have no better friends than I found in Ann and Hugh Yendole, my hosts during some of my longest trips to London. They provided companionship at the end of days in the archives and introduced me to the delights of Pimm's, *The Great British Bake Off*, and Sundays in the garden. Ann, there was a moment in the (now closed) newspaper library at Colindale when I unpacked the lunch you made for me and almost wept at your kindness. My love to you and to Rosie and Audrey, whose good cheer enlivened recent visits.

Back at Stony Brook, I benefitted from research assistants whose efforts on my behalf helped maximize writing and research time. I thank Kathryn Klein for preparing bibliographies of scholarship I cite here, Kathryn and Ula Klein for spending a summer perusing *Punch* for cartoons about garments, Emma Brinkmeyer for plumbing New York City libraries for periodicals and encyclopedia entries from the 1920s and 1930s, and Katharine Perko for batting cleanup as I finished this manuscript. Katharine, I deeply appreciated your patience and speed as you verified quotations, proofread, and reformatted. To all of you, I look forward to the time when I'll hold *your* books in my hands.

I am fortunate to have had the opportunity to work with Jessica Berman and Paul Saint-Amour in their capacity as editors of the Modernist Latitudes series. Their early interest and encouragement, and their questions about and feedback on early drafts, helped me see how to make these garments speak to a wider audience. Philip Leventhal has been a model of calm from our first coffee to production, and I am grateful for his attention and guidance.

Mark Bowen has been my steadfast companion throughout the time it took to complete this project. Only he knows the twists and turns that form the backdrop to every sentence, and only he knows how to cheer me up when the scholarly life—and life in general— seems more granite than rainbow. Thanks for making sure that I never bought a mackintosh, for extracting me from my office and desk, for fixing my Photoshop failures, and for finding the ham man. Your curiosity and creativity consistently inspire me to take risks, secure in the knowledge I can talk them through with you.

During the years I worked on this book, we lost my father, Kenneth Marshik. I learned that the price of having a great dad is the grief that follows his death. This book is dedicated to the memory of his unbounded patience, support, and love.

AT THE MERCY OF THEIR CLOTHES

The commodity becomes our uncanny double, evermore vital as we are evermore inert.

Hal Foster, *Compulsive Beauty*

Introduction

At the Mercy of Their Clothes

Readers of modernist fiction find few characters more marginalized and abject than *Mrs. Dalloway*'s Doris Kilman. Highly educated and deeply religious, the all-but-unloved and -unlovable woman tutors Richard and Clarissa Dalloway's daughter, Elizabeth, and "year in year out" wears "a green mackintosh coat."[1] As Clarissa Dalloway speaks to Elizabeth before her daughter embarks with Kilman on a shopping expedition, she senses Kilman's presence:

[O]utside the door was Miss Kilman, as Clarissa knew; Miss Kilman in her mackintosh, listening to whatever they said.
   Yes, Miss Kilman stood on the landing, and wore a mackintosh; but had her reasons. First, it was cheap; second, she was over forty; and did not, after all, dress to please. She was poor, moreover; degradingly poor.[2]

In this brief description, Virginia Woolf makes evident the gendered expectations and economic realities that Kilman negotiates through her clothing. While readers often feel little sympathy for this controlling, self-pitying character, the short rationale for her attire concisely captures her lack of means, increasing age, and refusal (or inability) to meet the standards of fashionable, feminine dress. Or, rather, it is Kilman's mackintosh that encapsulates everything wrong with her social position: at one glance, it communicates her lack of style, impoverished state, and increasingly peripheral status.

This much is evident. Kilman's mackintosh, however, engages much more than a twenty-first-century reader might initially perceive. In the 1920s, fashion designers began to offer the mac in a range of colors, cuts, and fabrics. While few could afford the coats reimagined by Elsa Schiaparelli and Leda-Maria La Tour, colorful, inexpensive macs were available through mass-market retailers.[3] Kilman's garment is thus out of step with what *Mrs. Dalloway*'s initial readers would have seen on the London streets; instead, the novel connects her mac with an earlier moment in which the coat was a de-individuating garment worn by people who could not rise above their class or condition to assert a distinctive self (children, servants, the poor, and soldiers). After World War I, the older style of mackintosh was associated with violence and death, and interwar writers repeatedly placed it on the backs of characters who cannot control their circumstances or ends. Our readings—and the way Woolf handles her female character—gain depth and nuance when we see that the author cloaks Kilman in a garment that positions her among the most downtrodden of masses. In fact, the mac's history makes pointed Woolf's choice of an anachronistic version of the coat for Doris Kilman.

In the fiction of Woolf's contemporaries, garments dynamically engage social history, working with assumptions, tones, and trajectories no longer familiar to us. Think of Stephen Dedalus in *Ulysses*, distracted from his meditations in "Proteus" by thoughts about his secondhand footwear: "His gaze brooded upon his broadtoed boots, a buck's castoffs *nebeneinander*. He counted the creases of rucked leather wherein another's foot had nestled warm. The foot that beat the ground in tripudium, foot I dislove."[4] If Kilman cannot rise above her coat, no more can Stephen escape his dependence on secondhand clothing, and readers have long understood that this passage provides evidence of the character's poverty. But Stephen's dependence is all the more mortifying for occurring at the precise historical moment when new clothing had become the norm and castoffs less an expected part of a wardrobe than a tainted reversion to older sartorial practices. Stephen, like the wearers of secondhand clothes in other texts from the 1920s and 1930s, finds that the castoffs he wears trouble the boundaries between him and the original owners of his pants, boots, and other used garb. Buck Mulligan's boots aren't only "rucked" (creased and worn); *Ulysses* imbues them with Buck himself, and they become capable, despite Stephen's best efforts, of remaking the artist in the image of his uncouth friend.

Such examples operate in texts aimed at other reading publics as well. Consider, for example, the nameless protagonist's shame in Daphne du Maurier's *Rebecca*. Dressed in a fancy-dress costume inspired by a portrait of one of her husband's ancestors, the young nobody engages in a sartorial form that was pervasive from the 1900s through the 1930s. At a time when choosing a unique and flattering costume was a yardstick of cultural competence, she descends the stairs of her husband's manor convinced that she *finally* looks a credit to her wealthy and cultured spouse, Maxim de Winter. When the narrator joyously reveals herself, however, her dress evokes a furious response. "What the hell do you think you are doing?" Maxim demands, and then orders her to "go and change."[5] A moment of triumph becomes personal tragedy as du Maurier's character discovers that she has unwittingly replicated a costume worn by her husband's deceased first wife, Rebecca. Anyone can see her mistake, but when this example is read alongside others, the power of fancy dress to remake those who wear it becomes clear. After taking on the appearance of Maxim's ancestor and (unwittingly) Rebecca, the protagonist can no longer return to her old self; even after the costume comes off, her appearance and behavior remain altered.

The donning of an evening gown, a mackintosh, a fancy-dress costume, or a pair of secondhand boots has far-reaching consequences in British fiction: garments can place a new lens over a purportedly known personality; they can stake claims to ideas and values that turn out to be inappropriate moments later; they can inscribe individuals in groups that strip them of specificity; and they can infuse a wearer with someone else's identity. Some of these "powers" may sound like truisms, but the act of labeling an idea as commonplace has prevented analyses of fictional moments that are stranger than we think. In the early twentieth century, such experiences were often cast as very peculiar indeed, as becomes clear though linking fiction to advertising, fashion journalism, film, dress history, and surviving examples of the garments themselves. By reading across a range of period texts, we see garments emerge as a means of getting at the difficulty of becoming a person—a singular self—in the early twentieth century, the precise historical moment when the proliferation of consumer goods suggests that the process of individuation should have been getting easier. At times, garments hint that there is nothing to selfhood at all—that clothes may make a person into a thing.

In these works and many others, modern British literature foregrounds the inscription of and resistance to history through a range of garments. I use the words "garments" and "clothing" advisedly. While fashion plays an important role in this study, many of the characters and people I discuss were not consciously participating in a fashion system; that is, their choice of clothing was not driven by the hope to be stylish or up-to-date. While all clothing is, to some degree, influenced by new designs and changing tastes, I reserve the term "fashion" for individuals who actively engage with, and garments that reflect, the styles of the moment. Through representations of clothing, fiction of the period offers subtle commentary on stubborn class boundaries, the difficulty of reimagining gender roles, the relationship between the individual and the masses, and the lingering trauma of World War I, among other issues. To detect this engagement, however, we have to stop taking the "stuff" of the early twentieth century for granted and remember that particular garments, and the characters who wear them, emerged in a historical moment not our own.[6] Clothing, one of the everyday vectors through which people engage with material culture, becomes an acutely conscious arena in which to consider the capacity for individual choice vaunted by modernity. As my readings throughout this book demonstrate, few choices of "what to wear" turn out to be neutral; many such choices, however deeply planned and executed, result in unpredictable plots and actions.

As philosophers and historians have long noted, the modern world conceived of itself as offering unprecedented opportunities for individualism, for "singularity particularized without limit" in the words of Jürgen Habermas.[7] By the early twentieth century, the industrial revolution had purportedly placed within everyone's reach the materials that such singularity required, albeit in different qualities and at a range of prices. But garments provide ongoing and particularly poignant examples of encounters with a material world that was and is often unresponsive to human will and desires; in addition, they serve as touchstones for expressing values such as conformity (read more positively as "good taste") or transgression, for privileging psychology (interiority) or appearance (exteriority), and for registering a person's degree of interest in aesthetic pleasure. We can better understand what is at stake in literary and other texts, then, as well as a range of period cultural phenomena (including processes of democratization, changing gender roles, and formations of economic and social classes like the "new poor") through looking at what characters and historical figures wear, what happens to them in specific types of clothing, and how they feel about their dress, experience, and self.

In order to understand the range of meanings negotiated through references to specific types of garments, the pages that follow take the reader through a capacious archive. Canonical modernists like Joyce and Woolf feature prominently, but we cannot understand the dynamic relation between clothing worn on the street and that figured in literature by looking to high modernism alone. This book therefore ranges across the modernist and the middlebrow, categories that function less as binary than as shifting, overlapping, and open to intervention. While authors who self-identified as middlebrow often set themselves (or their characters) up in explicit opposition to "intellectuals," their work, as Faye Hammill and others demonstrate, shares important techniques and beliefs with modernism.[8] In the case of clothing—however different the narrative styles, political sympathies, and aesthetic aims of particular works may be—they agree on a fundamental tenet of the object world: garments impinge on, frustrate, and alienate wearers. By reading *Mrs. Dalloway* not only with *Ulysses* but alongside *Punch*, *Vogue*, *Rebecca*, and Lord Peter Wimsey mysteries, we notice affinities emerge among writers and artists who might seem to share little more than a historical moment. Garments thus become a tool for getting beyond and behind ideological distinctions that separated writers in the period and often continue to structure what we read and teach.[9]

Where modernist and middlebrow representations of garments diverge, however, they help to make plain ideologies of the self that are rooted in differences of reading publics or artistic projects. Although neither modernist nor middlebrow writers and readers belonged to discrete economic and social classes, a focus on reaching a wide audience—of achieving fame and celebrity[10]—meant that many middlebrow writers took in popular cultural phenomena and (particularly middle-) class experiences that are not widely treated in modernism. For example, in the interwar period, a class emerged that came to be known as the "new poor," a phrase that identified individuals and families whose standard of living had radically fallen in the years after World War I. This phrase, and the experience it encapsulates, is prevalent in both fashion journalism and popular fiction, particularly in relation to secondhand garments, which became the best option for many declassed women and men. Despite its currency, this expression never crosses the pages of British modernism, a strategy that isolates characters (one thinks again of Doris Kilman) whose circumstances declined during and after the war. While a range of texts contain figures who struggle in the economic climate of the 1920s and 1930s, the sartorial dimensions of that struggle are represented with sharply different emphases. Juxtaposing varied representations of castoffs, for instance, reveals modernism's dedication to a singularity of sartorial *and* literary style; middlebrow works, in contrast, often see the literal and figurative costs of this stance as too high for their characters and, by implication, many of their readers to adopt.

As my description suggests, in addition to literary texts, this study draws on fashion periodicals, advice columns, cartoons, advertisements in newspapers and magazines, biographies, letters, early films, and memoirs. These documents help to reveal the networks that surrounded the period's imaginative works, and they suggest how and why specific pleasures and perils accreted onto particular garments. In part, then, this book integrates aspects of cultural studies because I read across a range of texts to see how garments are articulated, never assuming that the voice that emerges is univocal. Instead, what becomes evident is how the period's literature—works as different as James Joyce's *A Portrait of the Artist as a Young Man* and Evelyn Waugh's *Vile Bodies*—intervenes in, departs from, or affectively mobilizes associations with and histories of particular garments.[11]

Although the materials this study assembles are wide-ranging, my archive is mainly British. This national optic allows me to remain attentive to networks constellated around specific garments—for example, to the ways in which a reader might link the illustrations in a Sunday serial to advertisements, fashion columns, and popular fiction in other publications on her nightstand. Moreover, I study a period when a great deal of everyday dress had a local character. The terminology associated with two of the garments I take up—the mackintosh and fancy dress—never became common outside Britain at any point in the twentieth century. The fact that names for clothing, in these cases and others, remained distinct even in a period of international travel suggests that assumptions about specific garb did not always cross oceans, even when the individuals who wore those garments did. In part, this stubborn regionalism comes out of distinctly British class structures, national events, weather, local customs, and newspapers and magazines.[12] British *Vogue*, unlike its American counterpart, could counsel readers that "no Englishwoman who spends her money on a really attractive wet-weather wrap will ever have reason to deplore lack of opportunity for its use."[13] The national inflection of British garb has been taken up in such volumes as C. Willett Cunnington's *English Women's Clothing in the Present Century* (1952), Christopher Breward, Becky Conekin, and Caroline Cox's *The Englishness of English Dress* (2002), and Alison Goodrum's *The National Fabric: Fashion, Britishness, Globalization* (2005); as these titles suggest, dress history, while attentive to the ways in which styles and fabrics cross borders, also sees reason for examining clothing in the space in which material most often circulated: locally and nationally. In the case of secondhand clothes, we can trace this circulation quite literally as garments moved from London to Glasgow, Devon to Edinburgh, and Birmingham to Swindon after a brief stop in Cornwall, where the secondhand dealer Robina Wallis bought and sold garments. At a time when a local seamstress or tailor was as likely to make one's dress or pants as a factory worker, and in a place where (as Christopher Breward has noted) "few . . . could afford the new clothes in the shops,"[14] British garment culture was a national, and at times even regional, formation.

Such details also motivate my focus on the early twentieth century. Although my discussion of the garments begins with biographies that initiate at different points—the mackintosh was patented in 1823; fancy dress emerged as respectable in the 1840s—my literary examples are bookended by the 1890s and 1940s. Some garments clearly have had long afterlives in which they became all but unrecognizable: in the second half of the twentieth century, for example, the mac came to be associated with "flashers" (perhaps best "immortalized" in the opening to *The Benny Hill Show*) instead of with poverty, war, and social immobility. Longitudinal study remains provocative, but I focus on decades when innovations in the manufacture, advertising, and purchase of clothing excited authors and ordinary citizens alike. And the innovations were many: *Vogue* was founded in 1892; *Women's Wear Daily* appeared in 1910; the mac became widely affordable in the 1890s; and Selfridges opened its doors in 1909. This historical window also witnessed an explosion in fashion (if not the more prosaic clothing) theory; thinkers ranging from Georg Simmel to Thorstein Veblen to J. C. Flügel to Walter Benjamin turned their attention to territory that was not virgin (witness Thomas Carlyle's *Sartor Resartus*, first serialized in 1833/1834) but largely unexplored.[15] Only the advent of World War II, which upended the manufacture and trade of garments, could put a halt to an exuberant proliferation of clothing and theories about it; in a climate of extreme material scarcity, which lingered long after the war, clothing reverted to a necessity. As rationing steadily tightened, British citizens went from being able to purchase one new outfit a year to devoting most of their coupons to one or two items, such as a wool overcoat. In the climate of total war, restricted access to garments made evening gowns and fancy dress the stuff of dreams. Even secondhand clothes became prized as individuals and families had to "Make-Do-and-Mend."

Woolf's *Mrs. Dalloway*, and particularly Doris Kilman's mackintosh, also underlines another power of garments: some items of clothing participate in processes that turn human subjects into objects. After Elizabeth and Kilman leave to go shopping, Clarissa Dalloway muses about "love and religion": "The cruelest things in the world, she thought, seeing them clumsy, hot, domineering, hypocritical, eavesdropping, jealous, infinitely cruel and unscrupulous, dressed in a mackintosh coat."[16] This description is at once a meditation on Kilman's values and a thought experiment that animates the mackintosh. The character fades through figurative language that makes the coat, and not the woman, incorporate qualities normally aligned with subjects. Kilman becomes both human *and* thing to Clarissa and the reader, a process that echoes Barbara Johnson's observation that "a person who neither addresses nor is addressed is functioning as a *thing*."[17] Texts often use the mackintosh and the other garments I discuss in this book to position characters as things: individual speech and subjectivity become muted by the assumptions strategically deployed when writers place particular clothing on a creation's back.[18]

Clarissa Dalloway's (and Woolf's) use of a material object to render a character as a thing resonates with many theorists and writers of the early twentieth century. Garments are regarded with a unique and thoroughgoing suspicion: writers of the period employ clothing to challenge the fantasy that the human subject is in control of or privileged in the material world. Authors repeatedly stage conflicts between subjects and garments to suggest that clothing *damages*, *reduces*, and even *erases* subjects.[19] While a reader may assume that any garment can wield this power, and there are certainly isolated examples of other garments that can dehumanize, I focus on four types of clothing that British writers figure as consistent threats to human wearers. The evening gown, mackintosh, fancy-dress costume, and secondhand garment were, I demonstrate, at the heart of extensive and wide-ranging concern. The cultural history in which these garments participated helps in part to explain why they repeatedly enacted the object's powerful capacities; they normally convey exceptionalism or abjection, and because they fall toward two extremes of sartorial experience, they are less easy to take for granted and make visible clothing's ability to confound subject and object status. Importantly, the economic range of these items—evening gowns and fancy dress could be astronomically expensive; macs could be, and castoffs were, comparatively cheap—demonstrates that the concern about the potentiality of things was not confined to a particular class. My work excavates the assumptions and histories accreted onto these types of apparel and then traces how and why writers use, revise, or challenge them to thwart characters' desires, plans, and even lives in creative productions of the early twentieth century. By appearing to act with the kind of agency normally ascribed to humans, and by positioning humans as objects, these garments emerge as a labile trope to figure anxieties about individuation and the self.

This description may recall the work of Elaine Freedgood, who in *The Ideas in Things* performs "metonymic readings" in which "the object is investigated in terms of its own properties and history and then refigured alongside and athwart the novel's manifest or dominant narrative—the one that concerns its subjects."[20] I find Freedgood's work evocative, but my project suggests that in the early twentieth century, the "manifest or dominant narrative" does not concern only human subjects: clothing behaves as quasi-subject and positions human subjects as quasi-objects. Modern garments are *animate* in a manner that mahogany and calico curtains (two of Freedgood's central examples) are not. Moreover, I challenge Freedgood's conclusion that modernism, unlike Victorian realism, operates on a model of "more meaning from within the novel, less from the reader."[21] There are certainly differences between the Victorians and the novelists of the twentieth century, who often frame the relationship between persons and things as competitive and dangerous.[22] My study proposes, however, that British fiction continued to engage with a reader's knowledge of the world outside the novel long after the death of Victoria. I recover the associations that would have informed early-twentieth-century readers' understanding of particular garments that are rendered strange, but are *not* explained away, by the books that mobilize them. Instead, the texts I examine seem interested in complicating and exploring the relationships among garments and human subjects—in getting a reader to think along with them about what objects mean and in what ways humans, too, are objects.

The late nineteenth and early twentieth century was a time of intense preoccupation with the ontological status of things. Herbert Spencer's

The Principles of Sociology, for example, explored the "fetichistic conception" among "primitive" peoples that "each person's nature inheres not only in all parts of his body, but in his dress and the things he has used."[23] Although Spencer connected this theory with the "Yncas" and "Coast Negroes," his study suggests that some Western concepts (such as perfume and exhalation) originated in the idea that human spirits could transmute objects into animate things.[24] The decades after Spencer published his work saw increasing artistic and theoretical interest in the relationship between humans and the material world; in the 1910s, "objects and things are newly engaged by (or *as*) the work of art for Pound, Marcel Duchamp, Williams, Gertrude Stein," and in the 1920s, "things emerge as the object of profound theoretical engagement in the work of Georg Lukács, Heidegger, and Walter Benjamin."[25] Such interest suggests that objects in the early twentieth century cannot be entirely understood as commodities; instead, it is the non-commodity (or extra-commodity) aspect of things that period texts invite us to consider.

As my vocabulary and range of references has already signaled, my work on garments is indebted to the field of thing theory. This body of work offers vocabulary and strategies of reading that can teach critics to patiently examine the ways in which subjects and objects (including texts) behave, take action, and are acted on. Theorists such as Barbara Johnson, Bruno Latour, and Alfred Gell urge us to rethink the firm divide between subject and object and instead posit a continuum between the two, any point of which both humans and things can assume. In *Persons and Things*, for example, Johnson attunes her readers to the fact that figurative language depends on personification and other techniques that collapse subjects with objects—that *language* tends to facilitate dehumanization.[26] Her work thus serves as a reminder that the very tools available to writers—and even the ordinary language we use every day—blur the boundaries between subject and object. Literature therefore provides a rich venue for exploring the borders between persons and the material world and for expressing concerns about those categories, ontological distinctions on which the claim to modernity was based.[27] More important for my purposes, Johnson argues that humans *see themselves and others* as objects; in the conclusion to her study, she states that as she worked on *Persons and Things*, she realized that "people *wanted* other people to be things so that they could be dealt with."[28] My work builds on Johnson's own by examining how garments, which she does not take up, help authors (and readers) to deal with characters.

Latour, in contrast to Johnson, works in the context of sociology and, more recently, philosophy. In *We Have Never Been Modern* (1991), *Reassembling the Social*, and his many other works, Latour is not interested in literary language per se. Instead, what he offers is a model for tracing how objects participate in the formation of social relationships and the social world. Latour also enjoins us to think about what happens when objects interfere with this process: "[I]in addition to 'determining' and serving as a 'backdrop for human action,' things might authorize, allow, afford, encourage, permit, suggest, influence, block, render possible, forbid, and so on."[29] The readings that follow take Latour's injunction to heart, and I reveal the many ways in which British texts were figuring objects as things (and behaving as things themselves) *avant la lettre*. Latour also offers a helpful distinction between objects and things; the former "transports meaning or force without transformation" while the latter "transform, translate, distort, and modify the meaning of the elements they are supposed to carry."[30] I demonstrate *why* "input is never a good predictor of . . . output"[31] in the case of certain attire—why, that is, some garments frustrate or damage the human input that went into their manufacture, advertising, selection, purchase, and care. "Context stinks!" remains a mandate throughout this book, serving as a reminder that one cannot simply invoke the abstraction "culture" or "society" to explain a given phenomenon.[32] Instead, I aim to provide scrupulous attention to the avenues that frame and position particular garments in streets and homes as well as between the covers of a book; I carefully trace how categories of clothing mediate—and at the most extreme, enrich, damage or queer—human characters' interactions and sense of self.

To understand why and how this process works, I draw on the work of Gell, an art historian and anthropologist whose ideas have been taken up less often by literary critics than by dress historians. In his posthumously published *Art and Agency*, Gell argues that agency depends on where a person or thing "stands in a network of social relations."[33] Like Latour, then, Gell places subjects and objects on a continuum and argues that both exercise degrees of agency. As Gell insists, this claim is not "a form of material-culture mysticism"[34] but a way to address how objects express and mobilize intentionality. In his view, objects are not simple vehicles for human will and desire; instead, objects and things "distribute" people (their personae, identities, and intentions) unpredictably. In Gell's words, humans "suffer . . . from forms of agency mediated via images of ourselves, because, as social persons, we are present, not just in our singular bodies, but in everything in our surroundings which bears witness to our existence, our attributes, and our agency."[35] Gell's immediate example is volt sorcery—spiritual practices that involve models of individuals or body parts such as nail clippings—but the principle is generalizable, and I use it to explain how garments become things when they modify an individual's intention, sexuality, gender identity, or sense of self.

In donning an evening gown that turns out to be wildly inappropriate—for example, as in the cases of Ottoline Morrell and of Virginia Woolf's Mabel Waring discussed in chapter 1—a woman can be stuck in a distributed version of her persona that does not fit a given social situation. In this case and others, the distributed person goes awry as garments concretize a persona at a moment in time—materialize a temporal gap—that makes the wearer ultimately "the victim of his own agency, by a circuitous causal pathway." Gell observes that such "vulnerability stems from the bare possibility of representation, which cannot be avoided."[36] This comment points to the important role of representation in confounding subject–object distinctions; in the early twentieth century, such representations proliferated by means of "new" technologies (photography, film, mass-market publications) as well as older forms (the novel, painting), which made images of the self at once easier to generate and harder to control.[37] Garments like the evening gown and fancy-dress costume—which were often illustrated in advertisements, fashion journalism, and gossip columns—thus offered the opportunity for spectacular representation of the self *and* the danger of making a negative spectacle. More quotidian clothes, like the mackintosh and secondhand garment, also distributed selves in unpredictable ways; as a range of fiction suggests, the distributed self that a garment carries might be at odds with the individual who wears it, rendering him or her victim of the agencies of others.

While Johnson, Latour, and Gell provided the inspiration for my reading of garments in literature and culture, Bill Brown's work paved the way for examining things in the literature of the twentieth century. His monumental A *Sense of Things* raises, among its many avenues of inquiry, one question that animates some of my own work: "How are things and thingness used to think about the self?"[38] His conclusion, which he fleshes out through a reading of Henry James's *The American Scene*, suggests that writers often resist the opposition of persons and things; James, for example, gives voice to buildings to "re-enchant modernity's disenchanted world of objects. Within the illogic of projection and introjection, the animate and the inanimate, like the subject and the object, become indistinct. And this lack of distinction can be cast as an elaborate obstruction of that modernity which insists on an ontological distinction, arbitrary and artificial, between inanimate objects and human subjects."[39] This reading of James is in parallel with many of the texts that I examine in this study—and I, like Brown, trace moments when writers blur ontological boundaries. I part ways with him, however, in attending to the moments when such "re-enchantment" *threatens* the human subject; when the writers discussed in this book animate garments, it is generally part of a process that diminishes or frustrates the human. At such moments, a given subject does not use garments to come to terms with selfhood: characters find themselves at the mercy of their clothes, and it is not clear what is using what. As J. C. Flügel writes in *The Psychology of Clothes*, if a garment "is liable to behave in a way that is not in accordance with the wishes of the wearer, it is apt to seem a troublesome foreign body rather than an agreeable extension of the self."[40] Here, Flügel figures the thingly quality of the object as "troublesome" and "foreign" in its resistance to the desires of the human subject who wears it. Modernity thus emerges less as disenchanted than as haunted;[41] through representations of clothing, I (in contrast to Brown) argue that a range of writers were concerned about what might happen if modernity's founding principle of the subject/object binary were to collapse.

While the terms and tools of thing theory have been helpful to my work, this book seeks to complicate previous studies of things in three ways. First, my focus on garments runs counter to the examples on which most thing theory proper relies. Theorists often prioritize mechanical or technical objects that malfunction; in Latour's words, such objects become "easily visible" as things through "accidents, breakdowns."[42] Latour's use of the *Columbia* shuttle disaster, and Gell's frequent references to his car, prioritize the thingly behavior of what we might think of as "hard," mechanical objects.[43] My study intends to show that soft technologies like clothing emerge as thingly even when they do not rip, stain, or otherwise "break down." As I will demonstrate, most garment-things are perfectly functional at the very moment that texts represent them as most threatening; although clothes seldom malfunction, they become visible as things through figuring and positioning the self incorrectly. My focus on clothing also marks a difference from literary studies' use of thing theory, which tends to prioritize things that are around, but not *on*, the body; Freedgood, for example, works on furniture and tobacco, while Brown examines billiard balls, lumps of iron, and bric-a-brac. While the field of fashion studies *has* brought together thing theory and clothing, such work tends to be conducted for the early modern period or used to examine the contemporary experience of getting dressed.[44]

Second, my work departs from previous studies of things in arguing that many texts posit an economy or a conservation of subjectivity. As garments are animated (rendered thingly), one can easily imagine a scenario in which subjectivity multiplies, where the world is re-enchanted and more widely populated by animate beings. Indeed, this is precisely Brown's argument about *The American Scene*. In contrast, when garments become things—when, in Brown's words, consciousness is "reconceived as something dispersed throughout the material world"[45]—modern literature depicts *human* subjectivity as diminished. It is as if, echoing the scientific law of conservation of mass, texts speculate that the object world can gain power and will only when the human subject has *lost* power or disappeared. George Orwell's memoir *Down and Out in Paris and London* provides one of the many concrete examples of this experience. When a promised position fails to materialize after his return to London, Orwell decides to store his best clothes, sell the rest, and live on the proceeds. In the cheap attire that he acquires from a Lambeth rag shop, Orwell finds himself another person: "I stayed in the streets till late at night, keeping on the move all the time. Dressed as I was, I was half afraid that the police might arrest me as a vagabond, and I dared not speak to anyone, imagining that they must notice a disparity between my accent and my clothes. (Later I discovered that this never happened.) My new clothes had put me instantly into a new world."[46] Orwell's experience underlines the power of clothing to take away the very traits that individuated him: his speech, his prospects, his education, his sexual desirability, and his social class are swallowed up by a shabby secondhand coat, trousers, scarf, and cap. As Orwell concludes, "Clothes are powerful things."[47] This explicit testament to the power of secondhand clothing underlines a fundamental premise of this study: although Orwell *voluntarily* exchanged his good clothes for the tramp's suit, it is not his own choice or power that he recalls. Instead, this passage highlights the supremacy of garment-things, which reconfigure his identity and shape his self-understanding. Orwell discovers that he is not *in* the clothes of a tramp; he *is* the tramp, and nothing else, because of his secondhand garments.[48]

Such conservation of subjectivity leads me to the third manner in which I build on previous studies of things. As this book demonstrates, representations of the self-reflexive and self-constructive aspect of garments make them central to, and even able to disrupt, the purportedly interior (non-thingly) processes of psychic development and maintenance of an adult sense of self. Because they cover the body and let one conceive the self as coherent and whole, garments can highlight the difficulty (and, at times, *impossibility*) of selfhood in modernity. As sociologist Anthony Giddens has observed, "Appearance, to put the matter bluntly . . . , becomes a natural element of the reflexive project of the self."[49] While it is by no means the *only* aspect of this project—Giddens also discusses "demeanor" and "sensuality"—garments and accessories are among the factors that become "particularly important with the advent of modernity."[50] As a result, the *resistance* of clothing to individual desires, the thingly behavior of particular garments, receives particular attention.

Even theorists who focus on subjectivity note the import of the things closest to us in developing a sense of self—that garments "are closer than they appear" and permeate who we are. For example, the formulation of the mirror stage—Jacques Lacan's well-known analysis of the role of reflection in a child's development of a coherent self—is contemporary with the period covered by this book. Although the final version of his essay was published in 1949, Lacan first presented his ideas in 1936, at the Fourteenth International Psychoanalytical Congress, in a paper titled "Le stade du miroir."[51] The earlier version of this seminal work has not survived, but Lacan's later argument that the mirror stage marks an "*identification*" or a "transformation that takes place in the subject when he assumes an image"[52] posits a foundational moment in psychological development when the child apprehends him- or herself as an image and thus as a thing.[53] At a time when so many writers were figuring objects as active and animate in their fiction, one of the emerging giants of psychoanalysis was describing the obverse process: the moment when the ego comes "to love itself as an object, in that adorable *other* who presents it with the mirage of its own omnipotence."[54]

This "mirage" is, importantly, constructed through the aid of objects. Lacan mentions the *trotte-bébé* (baby walker), which may support the child in front of the mirror, and his antecedents detail many others. Scholars have pointed out that Lacan's coinage of the term "mirror stage"—and his 1936 and 1949 versions of the essay—are grounded in the work of thinkers whom Lacan does not cite.[55] They position Lacan's essay in what Darian Leader calls a late-nineteenth- and early-twentieth-century "major research programme" into "imitative mechanisms."[56] For example, Charles Cooley, an American sociologist, had posited a "looking-glass self" in 1902.[57]

Cooley's "looking-glass self" not only seems uncannily familiar to those who have read Lacan but, more important for my purposes, reconstructs the social scene that surrounds the young child as he gazes into the mirror:

> In a very large and interesting class of cases the social reference takes the form of a somewhat definite imagination of how one's self—that is any idea he appropriates—appears in a particular mind, and the kind of self-feeling one has is determined by the attitude towards this attributed to that other mind. A social self of this sort might be called the reflected or looking-glass self.... As we see our face, figure, and dress in the glass, and are interested in them because they are ours, and pleased or otherwise with them according as they do or do not answer to what we should like them to be; so in imagination we perceive in another's mind some thought of our appearance, manners, aims, deeds, character, friends, and so on, and are variously affected by it.[58]

The difference between Cooley's and Lacan's foci is obvious: Cooley writes about a conscious thought process in adults, whereas Lacan theorizes a stage of unconscious psychological development in children. Despite this distinction, Cooley's observation that "we see our face, figure, and *dress* in the glass" should remind Lacan's readers that the child who looks in the mirror does not see only her body; the physical body in front of the mirror is, for many infants, a *dressed* body, and the child thus identifies the self with a *clothed* image. In Lacan's words, the "virtual complex" in the mirror reduplicates a compound reality composed of "the child's own body, and the persons and things around him."[59]

Garments thus participate in a process of self-recognition and self-consolidation that is always already fraught. When a reflection meets our expectations, the "virtual complex" synthesizes the person and things in the mirror. As Elizabeth Wilson optimistically posits in her influential study *Adorned in Dreams*, "Fashion . . . substitutes for the real body an abstract, ideal body; this is the body as an idea rather than as an organism. The very way in which fashion constantly changes actually serves to fix the idea of the body as unchanging and eternal. And fashion not only protects us from reminders of decay; it is also a mirror held up to fix the shaky boundaries of the psychological self."[60] Wilson's formulation positions fashion in place of Lacan's mirror; in offering an ideal that stabilizes the self, she claims, it provides a permanence that anneals the woes of physical bodies, mortality, and psychic insecurity. This model equates being clothed with being whole, and it, like Lacan's argument, indicates that a "self" is not an interior state but a composite assemblage of body and things. To read fashion theory, and psychoanalysis, against the grain is thus to discover, as Jessica Burstein argues, that "the possession of a psychology—that most interior of terrains—is constructed by fashioning the psyche along the lines of, and indeed as the result of, an external environment."[61] Burstein's reading of Freud, and my reading of Lacan, thus locate flat ontology—the absence of distinction between subjects and objects—at the heart of the so-called self.

This line of thought illuminates why the project of the self is so precarious in much of the literature that my study takes up. It allows us to see, for example, that Wilson's argument ignores the fact that reflections can, and often do, fall short of expectations—that garments (whether explicitly fashionable or not) can undo as well as "fix" the self. In many of the examples that follow, readers will encounter characters who are confused and shamed by selves that do not measure up to a coherent ideal. They feel, like the character in a cartoon I discuss in chapter 1, "at the mercy of their clothes." Of course, Lacan (unlike Wilson) argues that the individual can *never* achieve what is, after all, a fictional state; in this respect, garments may serve the self by providing a clear object to blame—by accounting, through a multitude of reasons, for the irreducibility of the individual to its ideal self. Indeed, garments that fail the self may keep alive the hope that one will achieve the ideal, in the future if not at present.

This is precisely the promise on which the fashion industry has always operated. As clothing options proliferated in the early twentieth century, buyers could find themselves paralyzed by their choices. In British *Vogue*, Paul Poiret, like many other designers, promised to help, exhorting readers: "[D]on't dress like everybody else: don't wear a uniform. Wear a Poiret dress."[62] The *Daily Telegraph* published similar advertisements for mass-market retailers, including Selfridges, that assured readers that its dresses conferred the "charm of individuality" and that each model was "an original."[63] In its connection to the self, in its potential to confer particularity, the fashion system—and garments more generally—pledged to aid modern subjects as they negotiated the relationship between the particular and the group *and* between the image in the mind and that in the mirror. That clothing hindered as often as it helped—and that writers more often focus on the disappointments than on the triumphs—points to the power of garments to arrest attention and, in so arresting, to underline the relationship between materiality and the will of individuals or collectives.

* * *

At the Mercy of Their Clothes begins with the evening gown, a garment that had, by the turn of the twentieth century, a long history of use by the women of the upper and middle classes. I trace the gown's emergence as a specific type of evening wear as well as the cluster of associations that gathered around it, associations that worked to reinforce ideas about femininity and class that were under pressure at the beginning of the twentieth century. As women's political, economic, educational, and sexual rights increasingly became topics of private and public discussions, the evening gown began to seem strange, a bizarre remnant of a time when marriage and motherhood were the only occupations for women of leisure. Representations of the gown in the popular media render it as threat and problem, a thing that overexposes women's bodies and thus their sense of self. Reading across fashion and advice columns, advertisements, serial fiction, and early film, I demonstrate that the evening dress is often figured as a resistant thing that impinges on women's bodies, leaving them open to scandal and, in one extreme example, to murder. I link discussions of the gown to tropes of death and mourning and trace the proximity of evening and mourning dress; together, these literary and sartorial forms position the gown as not opposed to (or a respite from) the violence and death that characterized so much of the early twentieth century but as contiguous with experiences of danger and loss.

Chapter 1 then examines the gown in the work of three professional women writers: Virginia Woolf, Rebecca West, and Jean Rhys. They animate the gown in their fiction and nonfiction, but what is most curious about their works is the amount of sadness and regret that darken feminist depictions of conventional dress. Surprisingly, the evening gown itself becomes something to be mourned, an outmoded form of habiliment that nevertheless offers women a promise of tactile gratification and aesthetic play. Abandoning this particular type of dress may be personally or politically liberating, these writers suggest, but the evening gown's passing also forces them to recall as pleasure what they would seemingly prefer to dismiss as false consciousness. I conclude the chapter with an examination of Ottoline Morrell, the Bloomsbury hostess and patron who became infamous for her unusual dress. Using several of

Morrell's extant evening gowns as examples, I argue that she exercised a modernist design sensibility when creating her gowns; at the same time, the uses to which those gowns were put in romans à clef penned by Morrell's contemporaries demonstrate that sartorial experiment could be represented as folly. As Morrell's painstakingly designed gowns become alienating things in the satirical novels of her former friends, women's evening dress emerges as a harbinger of a larger fear: that even clothing amenable to personal taste and design can effect a decrease in agency.

Tracking down the economic scale, chapter 2 considers the mackintosh, a utilitarian and (for many decades) decidedly unfashionable raincoat. Because it was far from stylish, the mac was associated with groups of people who could not (afford to) choose what to wear: servants, children, the working and lower-middle classes, and soldiers. As the coat became increasingly ubiquitous, it was appropriated by fiction writers to highlight the tension between groups—the masses who bought and were clothed in the coat—and individuals. In the first three decades of the century, writers such as Elizabeth Bowen, Rebecca West, and Beatrix Potter examined how the mac freezes wearers in youthful or insufficiently gendered subject positions, a pattern that suggests that to put *on* the coat is to put *off* claims to self-determination, singularity, and maturity. The mac thus became a marker of diminished agency; if the wearers of evening dress sometimes felt their intentions and will muddled by the gowns they had selected, the mac suggests that mass-market and ubiquitous garments could pose an even greater threat to a wearer's individuality.

I then trace the mackintosh's role in World War I—the garment we now call a trench coat was a mackintosh cut on military lines—to demonstrate that advertisers emphasized the garment's de-individuating qualities, allowing buyers to "wear the war" in a manner that expressed national cohesion but muddled singularity. Wearing the coat, as Helen Zenna Smith's *Not So Quiet . . . Stepdaughters of War* (1930) portrays, could lead to civilians being mistaken for soldiers. Smith's middlebrow work, one of the raft of war novels published in the decades that followed World War I, underlines the transformation of the mackintosh by its role in the conflict. Although it continued to be a necessary component of British closets, and while new materials and designs meant that some postwar mackintoshes were fashionable, the coat materialized a negative history. Associated with catastrophe and loss, Smith's mac is mirrored in the work of a range of writers of the 1920s, who repeatedly represent the coat as de-individuating, abject, and threatening rather than protective.

Even in works that are *not* set in or are not "about" World War I, including Virginia Woolf's *Mrs. Dalloway* (1925), James Joyce's *Ulysses* (1922), and Dorothy L. Sayers's *Unnatural Death* (1927), the coat becomes a perambulating reminder of threats to the human body, through both war proper and the institutions that mobilize men and women to fight it. By refusing to forget the histories linked to this garment, texts turn the mac into a trope for the diminished safety and subjectivity of individuals who choose, or are required, to wear it.

Climbing back up the economic ladder, chapter 3 takes up fancy dress, a category of clothing intended to be worn to a popular form of pre- and postwar entertainment: the costume party. Like the evening gown, this type of garb was normally donned by members of the upper and middle classes, and it appeared to offer wearers the opportunity to exercise a high degree of choice. The *OED* defines "fancy dress" as "a costume arranged according to the wearer's fancy,"[64] which suggests that the ensemble is limited by only the wearer's imagination and originality. Fancy-dress costumes could be rented, purchased at major retailers (such as Harrods), or bespoke, and men and women could adopt a popular type (such as Pierrot), a historical character, a place, an era, or an abstract idea. I begin the chapter by tracing the available options; as articles and advertisements in fashion periodicals and newspapers suggest, fancy dress seemingly offered people a wide range of lenses to place over their normal identities—to enhance, but not disguise, their everyday appearance and persona. In the press of the day, fancy-dress costumes emerged as the supreme sartorial form for projecting an idealized self, one that would be free from the quotidian demands of work and practicality that governed most garments.

In memoirs, letters, cartoons, and novels of the period, however, fancy dress appears to be complicated and challenging attire, placing as it does the wearer's originality and sense of self under a microscope. Or, rather, fancy dress goes "wrong" by reinscribing selfhood: most representations of fancy dress intimate that garments cannot transform but only reinforce a self. Costumes thus fortify ontologies of the subject that locate personality and identity within individuals.[65] Characters who wear aspirational fancy dress find their desires thwarted; moreover, the tension between self and fancy dress demeans those who had hoped to become something or someone else, if only for a night. A wide range of texts figure fancy dress as less spectacular than spectacularizing, a genre of clothing particularly liable to negative outcomes. Publications as diverse as *Punch*'s cartoons, Evelyn Waugh's fiction, and Daphne du Maurier's *Rebecca* (1938) repeatedly depict characters as being shamed or let down by fancy dress that refuses to be transformational.

At the same time, a few novels revel in the possibility that selfhood may be no more than a costume. After tracing Woolf's experiences of fancy dress, which she relished as an opportunity to abandon her usual self, I argue that *Orlando* (1928) configures a model of selfhood based on fancy dress: a character who becomes whatever she wants through dressing the part. The novel's presentation of an ontology of surfaces makes it unique in the high-modernist canon, but I demonstrate that *Orlando* has company in the unexpected form of Dorothy L. Sayers's *Murder Must Advertise* (1933). Together, Sayers and Woolf celebrate the exceptional character who is no more or less than what he or she wears. Reading Lord Peter Wimsey in light of Orlando also reveals a point of significant agreement across the spectrum of interwar fiction: only the very wealthy and talented individual can afford to construct a self from moment to moment. Woolf and Sayers offer the most positive vision of being at the mercy of one's clothes; while most characters feel alienated and shamed by fancy dress, the modern British version of the "1 percent" reaches its pinnacle through mastery of this sartorial form.

Again descending the economic scale, chapter 4 turns to secondhand clothing, a category of garments that figures conservation of subjectivity as well as cultural disparities among novels targeted at different readerships. Selling and buying used clothing was commonplace until the mass-production of textiles and clothes made "ready-to-wear" widespread; the trade in "castoffs" became more shameful (and less normal) as manufactures and vendors increased new clothing options at a range of prices. Yet the idea that dress was "democratized"—a theory popular among many period observers and recent dress historians—occludes the ongoing trade in secondhand clothing, particularly in the decades after World War I. I bring to light the increasing reliance of the "new poor," an economic class defined by its straitened postwar circumstances, on selling its old clothes and occasionally buying others' castoffs. By excavating an extensive secondhand trade through advertisements, the archive of a dealer, and dress histories, I demonstrate the demand for used clothing as well as the circumstances that made castoffs acceptable (or the obverse) to consumers. Because it throws into relief assumptions about who could access what garments pre- and postwar, secondhand attire helps us understand the impact of a radically evolving economic situation on many British citizens between the wars.

Popular novels of the interwar period emphasize one model of the secondhand trade: the manner in which circulating one's castoffs distributes the self. Whether characters sell or donate their old clothes, they often find themselves in the humorous position of giving themselves away through items that communicate private information, such as shoe size, economic position, or taste. Such exchanges are often tinged with comedy, both in the sense of conveying obvious humor and in the sense of portraying human struggle positively. If one were only to read these types of representations of secondhand attire, one might think that distributing the self through clothing was a relatively untroubling necessity. Although it exposes characters to jokes, often at their own expense, it emerges in most middlebrow texts as a matter to take lightly.

In contrast, self-consciously experimental work, including fiction by James Joyce and Jean Rhys, depicts clothing's capacity to distribute the self as alienating and even threatening. If characters must wear secondhand attire, they can tolerate the experience if the clothing comes to them through brokers, who as intermediaries recommodify other people's castoffs. But if characters must wear secondhand attire that is given to them— or if they see their own castoffs rejected by the market—the garments become predatory, capable of muddling a character's personality or taking away that personality. In texts like *Ulysses* and "A Solid House," used clothing accrues important aspects of the person who first wore it. As I demonstrate, other secondhand items are not regarded in the same light; clothing alone carries with it threatening aspects of the first owner. The contrast between comedic and tragic treatment of castoffs points to the curious fact that, at the same historical moment, writers could agree that things distribute the self while holding completely different views about the process. As I suggest, this difference maps onto attitudes toward the artist: works that prize artistic innovation, singularity, and defiance cast secondhand clothing as akin to adopted styles and reject it accordingly. By treating the thing and the literary form in a similar fashion, such writers draw attention to significant cultural tensions; if authors agreed on the function of garment-things, they disagreed on the affective experience of the distributed self.

The conclusion takes a brief look at garments during World War II. As rationing rendered new clothing increasingly hard to access, and as the "Make-Do-and-Mend" campaign encouraged British citizens to wear their (and other family members') clothes longer, garments became rare and precious. Evening gowns and fancy dress became scarce; moreover, these types of attire were regularly framed as inappropriate in light of the suffering of soldiers and civilians during the war. In contrast, mackintoshes and secondhand clothing were increasingly valued: a good coat or a well-preserved pair of old trousers suddenly had virtues that they had not been assigned before the conflict. The restricted choices available to consumers made clothing doubly familiar—it was well worn *and* passed around families—and friendly; with human bodies directly threatened by aerial bombardment and possible invasion, British garments came to seem less capable of alienating the self and more capable of being trusted companions in difficult times. The absence of choice—the purported capacity for individual decision making that undergirded people's experience of clothing in the early twentieth century—defangs the garment-thing and positions it as treasured resource instead of animate object.

* * *

This book argues that we must recover the animation of garments in the early twentieth century; if we care to look, British writers figure material's capacity to carry history, to carry the self, and even to make that self. They also suggest that their contemporaries moved through a world in which clothing qualified the ideological and psychological process of the self, thwarting singularity, complicating relationships, and making visible a distinctly British culture in the midst of massive reorganization.

1 What Do Women Want?

At the Mercy of the Evening Gown

The sketch depicts a young woman in evening dress—shoulders hunched, eyes closed, head tilted in weariness. In the background, another woman confides to her male escort, "There's Clara. She's always so at the mercy of her clothes!" (figure 1.1). Clara is fashionably attired, her evening gown, necklace, and other accessories flattering and harmonious; yet both the observer's comment and Clara's facial expression suggest that she is "at the mercy" of something. Because Clara's clothing is her only visible attendant, the evening gown appears to impinge and impose on its wearer, oppressing a young woman who should instead be enjoying the party in the background.

This cartoon, published in *Punch*, was not alone in representing a woman "at the mercy of" her evening gown. Although many British women undoubtedly found aesthetic pleasure in wearing such attire, early-twentieth-century texts repeatedly represent women's evening dress as an assemblage in which humans, garments, and accessories work in concert but seldom in harmony. Reading across British mass-market fiction, modernist essays and narratives, and films as well as considering the experiences of historical figures, I demonstrate that the evening gown—a garment that had a long history of use by middle- and upper-class women—resists human agency and solicits harmful connections.

Young Woman. "THERE'S CLARA. SHE'S ALWAYS SO AT THE MERCY OF HER CLOTHES!"

FIGURE 1.1   Kenneth Beauchamp, "Poor Clara," *Punch*, May 1, 1929, 489. (© Punch Limited)

Representations of the gown often figure this material creation/object as a participant in events and actions that endangered individual women, rendering them vulnerable to murder, rape, and social stigma as well as to less dramatic (but still traumatic) moments of public awkwardness and shame. The gown, in the texts I analyze in this chapter, emerges as a silent actant that can motivate individual behavior, create opportunities, and make itself available to multiple interpretations. At home, in private, it could be the locus of much joy and aesthetic pleasure; in public, it could suddenly turn on its wearer, rendering her "at the mercy of her clothes."

A range of associations had accrued to the evening gown by the early twentieth century, associations that help to illuminate why Clara's creator—cartoonist Kenneth Beauchamp—may have selected *this* item of clothing for his sketch. As Elizabeth Grosz has argued about things in general, a "thing has a history: it is not simply a passive inertia against which we measure our own activity. It has a 'life' of its own, characteristics of its own, which we must incorporate into our activities in order to be effective."[1] In donning an evening gown, a woman like Clara had to adapt its "life" to her own—to put on not only a dress but also a set of practices and expectations that were undergoing radical challenge. In incorporating this material object, women often experienced a transformation beyond that achieved through any "extreme makeover": they found themselves in situations where the dress, and not its wearer, appeared to exercise helpful or harmful agency.

Popular and feminist modernist representations of women in evening dress explore a paradox: even though evening gowns were characterized by sumptuous materials and beautiful designs, writers of the period consistently choose to depict them in a negative, threatening, and even animate manner. There is variation among the texts, but there is striking unanimity about the gown's role in producing negative experiences that range from unwilled labor to stabbing. Moreover, some of these texts figure the garment as producing a kind of postsubjective sexuality, in which desire is not grounded in an individual but is mobile and unpredictable. Less inert than involved, the evening gown possesses a nonpurposive (but effective) agency that can queer gender identity and sexual orientation. As my readings will indicate, the evening gown often works in tension with humans; at moments, it even seems to speak and emote.

While a variety of authors share the general sensibility that women are "at the mercy of" evening dress, they part ways when modernists pay greater attention than do popular writers to the emotional appeal of the garment. Virginia Woolf, Rebecca West, and Jean Rhys figure the gown with intense longing;[2] in their work, the dress solicits desire and calls into being emotional bonds that keep women in thrall to a conservative and regressive garment. This profound yearning for evening dress betrays these women's ambivalence about the relationship between embodied forms of aesthetic practice and the gendered coding of sartorial genres. The evening gown thus emerges as a point of contact between different kinds of fiction *and* a place where attitudes toward conventional dress diverge: animate objects threaten women, but only feminist texts weigh in on why such objects cannot simply be left behind. For Woolf, West, and Rhys, evening dress lingers precisely because it has the potential to offer bodily pleasure and to serve as an aesthetic medium, however resistant.

Such resistance emerges most clearly by examining the evening dress of Ottoline Morrell, the aristocratic *salonnière* and patron whose fanciful garb was skewered by her contemporaries in letters, diaries, and romans à clef. Extant examples of Morrell's evening gowns as well as her design credo suggest that she might easily have been regarded as a fashion innovator—as someone *not* "at the mercy of her clothes"—rather than as the embodiment of bad taste. That Morrell instead became the butt of several writers' and artists' humor (a position little challenged by scholars until recently) helps us to understand a specific problem with evening dress in the early twentieth century. At a time when women's educational, economic, sexual, and political options underwent significant realignment, and when women's daytime dress evolved to reflect changing activities and roles, nonconformity in women's evening dress elicited profound and often nasty criticism. Morrell found her evening dresses and accessories extracted and assembled into fictional characters and plots over which she exercised no control.

As creators of texts that were also powerful objects, many early-twentieth-century writers configured the evening gown into a cautionary tale about the tension between material objects (and representations of those objects) and human wearers. In this particular historical window, representations of the evening gown depict women at its mercy; placing it on the bodies of their characters allowed writers to think about the resistance of the object world *and* to explore the way in which women, too, are objects. Representations of the dress defamiliarize a garment that is active and agentic, and the women who wear it discover that they could buy, but never truly own, the evening gown.

Evening Gowns as Particular Things

Even though a unique set of concerns and questions constellated around women's evening dress in the early twentieth century, the gown was not a new garment. As Jane Heglund writes, "There is a consensus among dress historians that evening dress materialized as a discrete category in the mid-1820s" when women's magazines began to identify garments in fashion plates with the label.[3] Although such categorization might suggest general agreement about the gown, Heglund notes that "there are surprisingly complex expectations related to appropriateness of fashionable dress for evening,"[4] suggesting that codification did not simplify the question of what a woman might wear. As *Vanity Fair* reported in March 1923, "There are several degrees of formality in evening dress. It is in just as bad taste to wear too elaborate a gown to a public restaurant as it is to wear too informal a frock to the opera."[5] In short, while evening dress as a category had existed for about seventy-five years by the turn of the twentieth century, the phrase pointed not to one kind of dress but to a range of garments suited—or ill suited—to such leisure pastimes as dances, court presentations, and dining. Unlike men's evening wear, which offered a formalized and limited set of choices, women's evening dress served as a mobile display of an individual's taste and social sense, demonstrating the wearer's comprehension of norms or her inability (or unwillingness) to follow them.

While a range of garments fall under the label "evening dress," the category collectively serves as a temporal, class, and gender node—a material confederation of time, privilege, and femininity. Twentieth-century evening dress, unlike its nineteenth-century ancestors, appeared in sharp contrast to the garments that women wore during the day. Quentin Bell observed, for example, that in the 1920s and 1930s "one style, that of futile exercise, is used for day wear; another, that of futile repose, serves for the evening."[6] Although Bell's use of the word "futile" appears to fudge the difference between day and evening wear, this opposition is further refined by dress historian C. Willett Cunnington, who quotes an unidentified fashion journal in support of his argument: "'The great variation between day and evening clothes is the result of the present-day liking for clothes designed for specific occasions.' For the day costume was, in effect, becoming almost an 'occupational' costume, designed primarily for that use and not for sex attraction."[7] This opposition between exercise/occupation and repose/sex attraction, an opposition that maps onto daytime and evening activities, defines the evening gown and manifests itself in the particular materials and cut of the gown from year to year. Although the general line of day and evening dress may be parallel at any one time (hobble skirts for walking and evening dress, for example), the cut, materials, and trimmings of evening dress distinguish it as a garment suited to times and places where daytime dress could, according to fashion norms, not go.

Its opposition to daytime, and particularly occupational, dress allows the evening gown to materialize class as well as temporality. Because of the sheer expense of such garments, they articulated a woman's economic status; in 1912, for example, a woman might pay 3.5 guineas for a summer suit and 5.5 for an evening dress, and in 1922, a "knitted woolen day dress" would cost 5 guineas, while an evening gown of velvet and georgette would cost 23 guineas.[8] As sociologist Georg Simmel argued in 1908, the expense of evening dress could mystify the qualities of those who wore it:

> Inasmuch as adornment usually is also an object of considerable value, it is a synthesis of the individual's having and being; it thus transforms mere possession into the sensuous and emphatic perceivability of the individual himself. This is not true of ordinary

dress which, neither in respect of having nor of being, strikes one as an individual particularity; only the fancy dress . . . , which gather[s] the personality's value and significance of radiation as if in a focal point, allow[s] the mere *having* of the person to become a visible quality of its *being*.[9]

Simmel's analysis suggests that evening dress enabled economic class to materialize social class; that is, the evening gown is not a dress that a woman owns but a stance and a position that she *becomes*. His argument foreshadows the profound interpenetration of human and thing that contemporary theorists sometimes refer to as an assemblage; in Simmel's formulation, a human body in evening dress foments a visible identity that is simply different from the same body in "ordinary dress."[10] The materials, construction, and design of a gown rendered a woman as not just wealthy but *finer* than her less privileged counterparts.

Although Simmel casts this process as a kind of mystification, British evening dress was less sartorial false consciousness than a means of constructing class differences that were increasingly under stress in the twentieth century. As the century unfolded, and particularly after World War I, more and more women entered the workforce and increased their purchasing power. As a result of the so-called democratization of dress, a greater number of women could afford evening gowns, and in the view of some observers, this meant that class differences were less visible than they had been. The democracy-of-dress theory is addressed in chapter 4, but one example can illuminate the general argument: "Fashion has now become a democratic expression instead of being, as it once was, the exclusive symbol of the upper class outlook."[11] The evening gown was not, however, a form that lent itself to ready-to-wear and mass-production, and thus it served to synthesize superior having and being long after other garments had become available at a range of prices. For example, in his discussion of evening fashions of 1933, Cunnington writes that "as the skin-tight dress called for great skill in cut and fit[,] the cheaper models found it a difficult fashion to follow with success."[12] Even uncomplicated styles of evening dress were not easy for the middle and working classes to emulate. In 1929, the *Encyclopaedia Britannica* noted that when patterns became "quite simple" in 1924, dressmaking firms "began to make false jewels to match models and even to make perfumes to agree with the lines and colours of their models."[13] As Gilles Lipovetsky argues, evening gowns remained markers of "social distinctions and social excellence" through

FIGURE 1.2 The label of Mrs. Neville, a London dressmaker patronized by Maud Messel. (Courtesy of the Royal Pavilion & Museums, Brighton & Hove)

sumptuous, elaborate designs characterized by distinctive labels, shapes, and fabrics (figure 1.2).[14] In short, some types of garments were less "democratic" than others; the evening dress continued to require a great deal of disposable income throughout the first half of the twentieth century.

While the evening gown thus materialized time and class, it was, most importantly, a means of assembling gender and emphasizing what was presumed to be heterosexuality. As Heglund observes, it is "a special form of dress that amplifies a woman's femininity and often proclaims her desirability."[15] It specifically "draws attention to a woman's body and serves to define her gender, establishing her as an object to be gazed upon by her audience."[16] Through emphasizing a woman's body and producing her status as an object, the garment facilitated British courtship rituals, which required young women to wear the gown when "coming out" and older women to wear it for socializing and chaperoning. Elizabeth Wilson explains how carefully such dress positioned and pitched the cause of the women who wore it:

> The dress of the ... virgin on the marriage market had ... subtly to convey family status as well as personal desirability: seductiveness, albeit virginal; along with apparent submissiveness and a willingness to obey, the ability to run a household should be suggested; the ethereal qualities of the Angel in the House must somehow be combined with the suggestion of sufficient health and strength to bear a large family. And in a society, or at least in a class, in which women outnumbered men, the importance for a woman of distinguishing herself from her rivals should not be overestimated.[17]

It is difficult to imagine such a complicated assemblage, balancing as it would spiritual and moral qualities with suggestions about the wearer's reproductive capacity. Wilson's prose endows the dress with almost mystical powers, and the passage implies that a young woman wearing such a gown could be silent, so loudly would her garment "speak." Dressmakers had to negotiate the tensions between the body and the gown carefully; Lady Duff Gordon, better known as the couturier Lucile, recalled that her dresses for debutantes were often controversial: "Matchmaking mothers would stare anxiously at their daughters when I had dressed them in something that showed every line of their lithe young bodies and murmur: 'Are you quite sure, dear Lady Duff Gordon, that it does not look too suggestive?'" She dismissed such suspicions, but showing the "line" of bodies was precisely the purpose of her designs and of the evening gown generally.[18]

Later in the century, commentators became willing to admit that the purpose of evening dress was to showcase the female body. In 1941, Cunnington baldly described evening dress as "a type of costume in which sex attraction is always a powerful motif."[19] The styles of the 1920s and 1930s had made this motive impossible to ignore. In the 1930s,

> the conspicuous features of sex appeal were confined to the evening, when the "nudity principle," carried on from the late Twenties, was further developed by moulding the dress to fit the body "clinging like a wet cloth." This was achieved by cutting the material on the cross, and for the first half of the decade a thinly veiled anatomical demonstration, accentuated by the lavish display of bare backs, left nothing to the imagination.[20]

At such moments, the evening gown emerged as a means of hyper-genderization; emphasizing the body, femininity, and beauty, it positioned women as clothed and yet exposed in designs that demanded increasing levels of physical fitness and slimness.[21] The bias cut, or "cutting the material on the cross" in Cunnington's words, emphasized the wearer's breasts, waist, and derrière, while a close fit suggested that a woman's shape was not molded by foundation garments.

Throughout the early twentieth century, the evening dress materialized time, class, and gender in a surprisingly consistent manner. Although particular styles came and went—the S-shaped silhouette, flapper line, and bias cut looked quite different from one another—the function of evening dress was to produce a woman for leisure activities in which courtship and heterosexual attraction were the important, and often the main, features. Even World War I, which so altered women's daytime pursuits and the ratio of men to women at dances, dinners, and other entertainments, little affected the garment. Some couturiers closed their ateliers for the duration of the conflict, and the Standard Dress movement briefly offered patterns that may have obscured class differences.[22] Styles, however, continued to evolve and kept the gown's function intact. Even commentators who want to suggest that the war altered the form ultimately imply that it was surprisingly resilient. Cunnington argues that in 1917, "owing to war conditions the evening dress . . . declined into almost a makeshift affair." He continues, however, to observe that "the waistline, when apparent, is definitely higher than formerly,"[23] which suggests that the gown evolved in a recognizable manner. Unlike the mackintosh, which was uniquely transformed by international conflict, the evening gown emerged as, if not ahistorical, stubbornly resistant to radical change. Although the cut of such dress altered dramatically over time, the manner in which it framed and positioned women remained consistent: as a sartorial genre, it seemed less reflective of most modern women's lives than, for example, the sportswear that was increasingly popular for daytime attire.

For this very reason, commentators regarded British women's evening dress as a particularly *conservative* form, and the twentieth century threw this tendency into high relief. Because the role associated with the garment was precisely the role challenged by many women in the period—and because other clothing evolved rapidly during the same time frame—evening dress could be, for the first time, perceived as a throwback. As Cunnington observed in 1941,

> It seems to be a rule that while sport has gradually done much to break down social conventions as regards the body, the evening dress has done nothing; this is due, of course, to the difference of the underlying motive, the one being a radical breaking away from sex-attraction and the other a conservative clinging to it. If we want to see modern dress design at its best with genuine inspiration we turn to the sports costume; if we want to see it at its worst, without inspiration and feebly imitative, we find it in the evening dress of today.[24]

As this passage demonstrates, dress historians regarded the garment as less socially significant and interesting than other garb that expressed changing attitudes toward women's bodies and pursuits. Breaking away from the motive of "sex-attraction" was "radical" and resulted in innovative designs, materials, and styles; the evening gown, while changing from year to year, allowed for less experiment. It thus plays a comparatively minor role in some period dress histories. As the *Encyclopaedia Britannica* enthused in 1929, "The evolution of modern feminine dress, corresponding closely to the emancipation of women at the beginning of the 20th century, provides one of the most captivating pages in the history of modern civilization."[25] The entry illustrates "evening costume," but the section on modern dress concludes by emphasizing "the influence of sport" on women's clothing.[26] Thus the emancipation of women would not spell an end to the evening gown, but it would highlight the garment's relationship to dated versions of femininity.

Given this "life" of the evening gown, in which it served to materialize leisure, privilege, and femininity, it seems little wonder that so many feminist writers expressed a profound unease with and distrust of evening dress. But the garment is also represented in British popular culture of the period in surprisingly ambivalent ways. While we might expect that the evening gown would be an object of desire in films, fiction, and serials addressed to a popular audience—that such texts would convey images of enviable upper-class luxury—it instead emerged as a key player in assemblages that endanger women. The gown thus seems less desirable than risky, less enviable than an example of the limits of human control.

Overexposed: Evening Gowns in British Popular Culture

A woman in evening dress is threatened with violence and death; recollections of accidents are constructed around descriptions of evening gowns. Popular forms such as films, fashion magazines, and memoirs suggest that the sleeveless, décolleté styles of the early twentieth century correlated with a social exposure that threatened to ruin women in fashionable evening wear. In part, this seems a matter of simple titillation: if the sight of a woman in danger is exciting, a well-dressed woman in danger might increase one's visual pleasure. But many representations of the evening gown in popular narratives go beyond mere titillation: fashion journalism points to the evening dress as the (unwilled) mirror of mourning clothes, and memories of a gown destroyed by total war suggest that the garment models the potential fate of the person who once wore it. In a range of cultural formats during the period, the gown looks less like a pleasurable object to consume than a material constellation of dangerous situations and painful memories to avoid.

The biograph film *A Ballroom Tragedy* (1905), for example, depicts a woman who is punished with the participation of her evening wear. Biographs offered a popular form of visual entertainment in the years before longer films—and the cinemas that showed them—were technically possible. Placed in or near seaside promenades, arcades, shopping areas, and other spaces where people congregated for leisure, biograph machines offered sixty seconds of moving pictures for a small fee. A viewer inserted his or her coin into a slot and then leaned into the machine, gazing through an eyepiece to watch the flickering image. There was a voyeuristic pleasure to watching these pieces, a pleasure captured in their nickname: "What the Butler Saw" machines.[27] The films themselves were often suggestive, and a viewer expected to see shameless behavior of some kind.

The plot of *A Ballroom Tragedy*—if one can even call it a plot—is straightforward.[28] Two couples meet and exchange partners, but when one couple takes advantage of their apparent seclusion to kiss, the gentleman's original partner returns and exacts murderous vengeance. The titillation of this short film clearly depended on the characters' transgression of gender norms and expectations. A viewer might anticipate that the original male escort of the woman in white, who enjoys the stolen kisses, will demand satisfaction from her partner in animal lust, but it is (seemingly) a female rival who instead murders her counterpart. More radically, the viewer could read the scene as a closeted lesbian drama: perhaps the murderer slays not a rival but an unfaithful lover. The lesbian's apparitional quality (as Terry Castle has theorized)[29] would account for the killer's simply leaving the scene of the crime, with no notice taken of her disappearance. This reading highlights a fact that period fashion commentators elided: the sexual attraction mobilized by the evening gown was not necessarily *heterosexual* (a point I return to in my discussion of Jean Rhys's "Illusion").

While the woman in white is murdered in response to her behavior and not to her gown, on closer inspection, behavior, body, and attire emerge as inextricable—as an assemblage. It is clear that we are meant to distinguish between the film's female protagonists through their garments.

The two men in the film are all but indistinguishable from each other because their evening dress is so similar. Although the man who kisses the murder victim wears a white waistcoat, in contrast to the black waistcoat of the other man, the men's clothing is otherwise identical: black ties, tails, and trousers. Men's evening wear does not signal anything special about the wearer; in *A Ballroom Tragedy*, the men are only the backdrops to more meaningful sartorial forms.[30]

The evening gowns of the female characters, however, construct their roles before the sexual transgression and murder take place, and their dresses emerge not only as frameworks for human interaction (as texts) but as opportunities for action (as tools). The murder victim wears a far more revealing dress than does her counterpart. Although a long feather boa swathes part of her neck and shoulders, her white gown's half-sleeves cover only her lower arms, and the tops of her breasts are clearly visible when she faces the camera. Moreover, the gown is largely backless, and the woman's exposed back is precisely where the knife enters her flesh. While satin or silk would offer little resistance to a blade, the fact that the main character is literally stabbed in the back points to a correlation between her exposure and her murder—it suggests that the cut of her gown *encouraged* a particular assault. As the woman in white transforms from subject to object, human to corpse, in front of the viewer's eyes, her dress emerges as quietly volitional: it does not kill its wearer, but it provides a literal and figurative opening (even, perhaps, an invitation) to the woman with a knife.

In contrast, the murderer's dress covers her body. The satin gown has half-sleeves that conceal her upper arms, and a modest neckline exposes only her throat and upper sternum. This dress is less striking than that worn by the woman in white, and it proclaims the wearer's comparative propriety. The dress might also serve to conceal her weapon; viewers have no way of knowing whether her attack was premeditated, but her more voluminous draperies could conceal a knife or dagger. *A Ballroom Tragedy* thus uses the evening gown to illuminate how the garment *participates* in events instead of serving as inert matter. The film revolves around gowns that project the wearers' sexual mores and collaborate in producing particular actions. Without the specific dresses worn by each character, the women's values would remain illegible and the plot of the brief film less feasible.

In film and mass-market fiction, images of women in evening dress threatened with violence present gowns as a menacing sartorial genre, as garments that expose not only women's bodies but their lives. "The Harvest of Folly" (1928) by Kathlyn Rhodes, serial fiction published in the *Sunday Graphic*, provides representative examples of a type: the woman in a fashionable evening gown who is vulnerable to a specifically (in this case, hetero-) sexual violence. The story, which chronicles the attempt of Lesley Chester to retrieve a letter documenting a "youthful folly," is illustrated by images of the main female characters in sumptuous gowns whose low necks and lack of sleeves correlate with a social exposure that threatens to ruin them. For example, when Lesley pleads with Lord Thirsk, a much older roué, for the return of the letter, she wears an evening gown, "the light shining on white neck and white shirt front."[31] The text highlights the contrast between women's exposure and men's composure: Thirsk's "shirt front" may be visually parallel to Lesley's neck, but his garments cover him, while hers expose her body and, seemingly, her past. Although Thirsk offers to give Lesley the letter if she will marry him, the illustration suggests that he menaces her with rape instead. As she clutches her hands to her chest and presses her knees together—strategies that work to compensate for the gown's revealing cut—the caption reads, "Lord Thirsk . . . I want my letter more than anything in the world, but I can't pay your price for it," a line that implies that Thirsk has asked for a sexual, instead of a marital, payment (figure 1.3).

In this image and others in "The Harvest of Folly," the gown—and the flesh it bares—positions the female character as open to unwelcome advances because of the very absence of boundary between body and world. Instead of working *with* the human body it clothes, the gown works *against* that body in a kind of negative-feedback loop that increases the garment's power as the character's agency diminishes. Although Thirsk obligingly dies of a heart attack and frees Lesley from this first threat, the rest of the story follows Lesley and her cousin Rosemary as they are "terrified," offered (potentially drugged) Eastern cocktails, and otherwise imperiled while wearing white, pink, and black evening dresses (figure 1.4). In most of these illustrations, the characters place a hand on their neck (thus covering décolletage) or press their knees together, bodily responses to specific dangers and to a dress that provides little protection. Through illustrations and plot, "The Harvest of Folly" frames British evening gowns as conventional fashions that uniquely (no one is threatened in a tennis frock) and persistently expose upper-class women to negative experiences. It is as though the revealing styles of evening fashions in the 1920s made what women offered—and stood to lose—most clear to

FIGURE 1.3   Dressed to be threatened in Kathlyn Rhodes, "The Harvest of Folly," *Sunday Graphic*, March 4, 1928, 16.

readers of the *Sunday Graphic*. Although the advice columns in the paper suggest that few readers could afford the kinds of dresses worn by the characters in Rhodes's story, the evening gown helps to assemble types of women whose virginity and reputation hold a high value.

Films and popular fiction suggest, then, that the evening gown imperiled women in the first three decades of the twentieth century. While *A Ballroom Tragedy* and "The Harvest of Folly" were largely aimed at working- and middle-class audiences, even the upper class, which regularly bought and wore evening gowns, used complementary images for the dress. In such cases, it became a physical imperative to mourn, its implication less of present danger than of recent or impending loss. In 1920, the British women's magazine *Eve* observed that the current craze for the tango was accompanied by a narrow sartorial style at seeming odds with the dance itself: "[W]e *do*, p'raps, take our tango with an *arriere* tang of melancholy. We are faintly funereal, and there is certainly something

FIGURE 1.4 Overexposed in "The Harvest of Folly."

somewhat mute-like about the black and white garb of our dancers."[32] Thus dresses defined women as melancholic and silent; presumably, some women enjoyed the tango and accompanying parties, but this column described the fashions worn to them as formulating a general look of sorrow. Two years later, the *Gentlewoman* reported,

> [B]lack no longer is the decree issued by Paquin [French designer]. It is with a sigh of relief that one hears the reign of black has ended. Our functions and parties were becoming positively funereal. Everywhere black. It was deadly and uninteresting, and though, I admit, exceptionally smart for occasions, it was certainly being overdone. Well, now it's ended. Dame Fashion can now work one of her dramatic miracles that please her so much, and switch the world of mourning into a world of hope and spring.[33]

This striking passage points to the way in which some writers framed fashion as a form of foreign sovereignty that painted evening entertainments in a monotone. It would take a "miracle" to alleviate the "world of mourning" described in the column. Although the writer identifies a specific source for the color of evening gowns in the name of Jeanne Paquin, she also gestures toward intangible social forces in the personification of fashion and thus vacillates between causal explanations for the escape from the funereal. But "Dame Fashion" proved to be fickle, and later that decade, Jean Patou, in just one such example, was promoting a dress called Fugue in British *Vogue*. Constructed of sheer black tulle and black beaded fabric, the dress brought the "positively funereal" back into fashion—but, of course, the color had never left.[34]

The "world of mourning" and melancholy repeatedly described in the British fashion press of the 1910s and 1920s seems counterintuitive. If women did not like the black gowns offered by designers, surely they could have purchased dresses in other colors. But British women were repeatedly called on to wear mourning in the early decades of the twentieth century, a practice that extended to evening dress. After the deaths of Queen Victoria in 1901 and King Edward in 1910, for example, many British citizens, especially those in the upper class who could afford to do so, dressed in mourning. As Juliet Nicolson observes, Queen Mary, to provide just one (admittedly elevated) illustration, was obliged to wear mourning dress five times in a fifteen-year period.[35] Magazines like the *Ladies Field* illustrated mourning evening dress for women in the court,[36] and the *Times* published many advertisements for "Court and General Mourning," including at least one placed by Maison Paquin.[37] The Messel Family Dress Collection archives many black evening gowns and capes worn by Maud Messel that date from 1910 to 1914. Their sumptuous trimmings and materials included silk chiffon, sateen, and taffeta as well as jet beads, velvet ribbon, Guipure lace, braid, and sequins, all in black (figure 1.5; see figure 1.2). Some of these dresses were made by Mrs. Neville, a London designer, which demonstrates that mourning was not anti-fashion but resulted in the incorporation of black into garments, including the evening gown.

In addition to royal deaths, many women had private reasons to don mourning clothes during World War I, as a result of the influenza epidemic of 1918 and 1919, or after isolated deaths from natural causes. Vanessa Stephen wore such an evening dress in 1897 after the death of her half-sister Stella. Her dressmaker "concocted a dress that suggested mourning yet was also fashionable and pretty: transparent black material sewn with tiny silver sequins hung over a white underdress."[38] Her

FIGURE 1.5 Mourning dress made by Mrs. Neville, ca. 1911 or 1912. (C004170; courtesy of the Royal Pavilion & Museums, Brighton & Hove)

biographer's description of the dress as "pretty" but also fitting within the codes of mourning illustrates the way that this specific evening dress synthesized the wearer's loss *and* her ability to remain fashionable and desirable. Moreover, women who once purchased mourning attire sometimes continued to wear black; as the *Illustrated London News* observed in 1910, black "is . . . becoming to a great many women who have, perhaps, seldom allowed themselves the opportunity of seeing themselves attired in exclusively black until national feeling required the change."[39]

Although mourning dress gradually fell out of favor during the twentieth century, it did not become rare in Britain until the 1950s.[40] Fashion columnists' laments about the prevalence of black in evening dress—and their characterization of such dress as melancholic and funereal—point to a specific period when such garments were a form of mourning. It seems little wonder that the funereal would itself become fashionable in a period when so many women were called on to observe social rituals of mourning. Surprisingly, however, columnists repeatedly lamented that black dresses *themselves* materialized emotional states, and they represented women as unequal partners with gowns that assembled negative affective experiences long after mourning proper had ended.[41]

Such gowns could also lead women into situations that would require mourning. The "fate" of specific dresses recalled in memoirs positions the evening gown as a victim of the violence, death, and destruction so widely visited on material of all kinds during and after World War I. The Viscountess Rhondda (Margaret Haig), who was active in the Women's Social and Political Union and was one of the founders (and later editor) of *Time and Tide*, used evening dress to capture the vulnerability of humans and garments to military threat. Although she seldom describes specific garments in her book *This Was My World*, evening gowns emerge as exceptions, and one provides a way back into the memory of the sinking of the *Lusitania*. As a young woman, Haig worked as her father's confidential secretary, which required an appropriate wardrobe: "In the evenings—almost every evening—we went out, either to the theatre or to dinner parties. With money supplied by my father, I bought a lot of frocks in which I fancied myself very much, particularly in one black velvet evening one."[42] To this point in her account, Haig's experience of evening dress seems positive, an example of such gowns working in a harmonious assemblage with, and not against, a wearer. After mentioning the black velvet gown—the *only* gown that she specifies in this section of her memoir—Haig describes the fate of this dress and others: "[T]hey all went down in the *Lusitania*."[43] Haig and her father survived, but her garments did not, and their watery fate highlights what might have easily happened to Haig herself. The writer no doubt lost many possessions in the sinking of the ship, but it is the loss of her evening dress, and especially the black velvet gown, that Haig recollects in her memoir, a choice that points to a particular linkage between woman and gown. While the evening dresses in *A Ballroom Tragedy* and "The Harvest of Folly" testify to the dangers of overexposure that the gowns permit, Haig's memoir singles out the black evening dress to represent her bodily exposure to military violence. Collectively, such texts reveal evening gowns as singularly cathected garments in fiction and memory—as a form of dress repeatedly chosen to construct and represent physical and emotional harm.

Instead of mobilizing a wearer's taste and social competence, the evening dresses in films, popular fiction, fashion journalism, and memoirs participate in terrifying events and conjure negative memories. Evening dress thus serves to trouble certainties, especially about mortality, and representations of it emphasize the ways in which sartorial forms subtend and complicate human (particularly women's) agency. Grosz, in assessing the relationship between human bodies and things, has argued that "the thing and the body are correlates: both are artificial or conventional, pragmatic conceptions, cuttings, disconnections, that create a unity, continuity, and cohesion out of the plethora of interconnections that constitute the world. They mirror each other: the stability of one, the thing, is the guarantee of the stability and on-going existence or viability of the other, the body."[44] As the representations addressed in this section suggest, however, the thing can *also* create discontinuity and disconnection—it can remind readers, viewers, and individuals that the body is not guaranteed an ongoing existence. In fact, evening dress often suggests that this particular thing can make a body *less viable*. The evening gown of the early twentieth century served to articulate this condition particularly well, in large part because of social practices and events peculiar to Britain. It helped to create and illuminate the exposure of women to revenge, assault, and even international conflict.

Although the evening gown was a form of conventional attire and undoubtedly provided pleasure for countless women, mass media and memoir did not naturalize the garment but instead highlighted its ability to construct particular kinds of subjects—murder victim, murderer, mourner, and survivor among them. Striking parallels emerge between such representations and those produced by professional writers, whom one might expect to reject the garment's conservative gender norms. And, indeed, the work of Virginia Woolf, Rebecca West, and Jean Rhys conveys suspicion of and anger toward this form of dress. These writers express more pointedly political reservations about the garment than we have yet seen, but their letters, stories, and essays also highlight the sensory pleasure that evening attire solicited. They thus articulate a profound uncertainty about a gown that beautified and crippled simultaneously and highlight the power and life of the garment. These complicated representations of the evening gown illuminate human–nonhuman relationships that are ubiquitous but uneasy.

The World's Worst Failure(s)

Given the evening gown's articulation of sex appeal and upper-class leisure, it seems little wonder that the fiction and nonfiction of professional women writers contain extensive meditation on the dress. What is unanticipated are the largely consistent ways in which these writers represent the evening gown: through figures of death, failure, mourning, and depression. Strikingly, feminist authors ascribe these emotions not only to women but to *the gown itself*, animating the garment with an affective life and the power to direct human behavior. Such representations of the evening gown are also tinged with melancholy—with admissions of attachment to and pleasure in dresses and styles that emerge as threats to the lives and careers that the writers painstakingly carved out for themselves. In part, the ambivalence stems from the history of the gown; as Diana Crane reminds readers, by the turn of the twentieth century, "fashionable clothing embodied gender ideals that no longer corresponded to the realities of women's lives, as women became better educated, entered the workplace in greater numbers, and participated in political activities."[45] It thus makes sense that feminists often highlighted the evening gown's regressive powers. At the same time, this critique threatened to make inaccessible an ongoing source of visual, auditory, and corporeal pleasure, rendering professional women frustrated and occasionally angry.

In August 1901, Virginia Stephen—not yet the famous writer Virginia Woolf—confessed her lack of success as a debutante in a letter to her friend Emma Vaughan: "Really, we can't shine in Society. I don't know how it's done. We aint popular—we sit in corners and look like mutes who are longing for a funeral."[46] The simile was clearly meant to amuse Vaughan, but the image of Virginia and her sister Vanessa attired in evening gowns but longing for (and sometimes wearing) a formal ritual of mourning is an acute example of Woolf's "frock consciousness." This feeling, which Woolf discusses in her memoir "Am I a Snob?," encompasses a painful sense of inferiority centered on her appearance in and purchase of clothing.[47] While Woolf was no more comfortable in casual than in evening dress, she writes about the latter both very early and late in her adult life; accounts of gowns feature in her letters and diaries as early as 1901, and she returned to evening dress in "22 Hyde Park Gate" (1920), "Old Bloomsbury" (1921–1922), and "A Sketch of the Past" (1939). In these texts, Woolf represents failures and transgressions achieved through the evening gown to mark her nascent challenges to traditional gender roles as well as to admit the compelling allure of a sartorial competence that she never achieved.

Her youthful letters capture the norms of adult female behavior as refracted through one particular act: donning an evening gown. The young writer was delighted by and interested in her debutante apparel. In a letter from 1901, she reports the delivery of several gowns that, in her words, "deserve to be shown."[48] Her appearance in such gowns must have been strikingly different from the images we now have of her, in which she is demurely covered to the neck by layers of fabric and lace. In "A Sketch of the Past," Woolf describes the process of donning her evening wear in a passage that provides a glimpse of how she may have looked in 1901: "At seven thirty we went upstairs to dress. However cold or foggy, we slipped off our day clothes and stood shivering in front of washing basins. Each basin had its can of hot water. Neck and arms had to be scrubbed, for we had to enter the drawing room at eight with bare arms, low neck, in evening dress."[49] Woolf's descriptions emphasize her body's exposure in evening gowns as well as the materials that went into making and accessorizing them; one dress was made of satin and ornamented with "long white gloves," "satin shoes," and a necklace of amethysts or pearls.[50] White satin and amethysts became tropes for evening dress in Woolf's memoirs; thus attired, Virginia and Vanessa would depart for the evening's engagements.

Although in hindsight Woolf would recall 7:30 as the time when "dress and hair overcame paint and Greek grammar,"[51] at the time she enjoyed the "thrill" of her evening gowns and the circumstances they enabled: "[F]or the first time one was in touch with a young man in white waistcoat and gloves; and I too . . . in white and gloves. If it was unreal, there was a thrill in that unreality."[52] The "white and gloves" serve as a reminder of the "road most traveled" for young women of the author's class at the turn of the twentieth century. In reading such descriptions, it becomes clear that she was, literally, outfitted in expensive garments that assembled her status as a potential, and traditional, wife and mother.

But Woolf felt that the gowns, gloves, and amethysts never quite fit. Or, rather, despite her apparent beauty, she felt herself out of harmony with objects through which she moved. Her confession that "we aint popular—we sit in corners and look like mutes who are longing for a funeral" thus marks a failure that is at once social and aesthetic. Although "mutes" might signal a literal silence, the conflation of the oral and the visual in this letter indicates that there was also something wrong with her "look": she *looked* like a mute. Instead of harmonizing with the attire that might have rendered her an attractive debutante, she appeared silent and mournful. Like the fashion press, then, these letters align the evening gown with the funereal even when that dress was not fabricated in mourning colors.

Later correspondence suggests that the young writer found the gown an alienating form because it required mastery over an object world that she seldom achieved. Subsequent public appearances in evening gowns were marred when Virginia Stephen, "all glorious without," scandalized bystanders as an undergarment—presumably her drawers, since she describes it as "not the one one talks about"[53]—fell to the floor. Such public humiliations serve as a reminder of the difficulty of coordinating the wearing of a gown, underclothing, and accessories before the invention of the zipper, elastic, or Velcro: each piece could misbehave and mar the "glory" that the assembled result was meant to convey.

Woolf's attempts to experiment with less conventional evening fashions were no more successful than her appearance in designer gowns. "A Sketch of the Past" chronicles an evening gown "made cheaply but eccentrically, of a green fabric, bought at Story's, the furniture shop. It was not velvet; nor plush; something betwixt and between; and for chairs, presumably, not dresses."[54] At once a trial balloon and an attempt by a wallflower to mimic the wall, to provide herself with better "cover," this dress made the wearer "apprehensive, yet, for a new dress excites even the unskilled, elated."[55] The green dress highlights the evening gown's ability to elicit pleasure—its potential to serve as a form of aesthetic expression and to create affective bonds between human and thing. This experiment, was, however, short-lived.

The author's half-brother and escort, George, rejected this gown, instructing her to "tear it up." This rejection, Woolf wrote, was based on the gown's "infringement of a code"[56]—its perceptual challenge to values that the evening dress traditionally communicated. The dress thus expressed, in material form, Virginia Stephen's desire to contrast with fashionable debutantes: it relayed, as an object, the young woman's nascent quest for a form of difference. That Woolf recalls the green dress *over three decades later* to illuminate a conflict with her half-brother, whom she characterizes as a "fossil of the Victorian age," suggests the import of this specific evening gown to her construction of personal history. This passage allows the author to highlight her eventual escape from the "fossil," but the upholstery dress, and its categorical rejection by George, leads into a metaphoric description of his violent response. George was, Woolf writes, a "machine" that "bit" into her "with innumerable sharp teeth."[57] Although her other half-brother liked the green dress, George's "teeth" kept her from wearing it again in his presence. The dress, which initially materialized the young writer's eccentric and creative take on the evening gown, thus came to represent her lack of agency in her turn-of-the-century, patriarchal household.

Woolf's evening gowns, then, are textually linked with mourning, embarrassment, and (failed) insurrection. Although many of her metaphors are infused with wit and irony, her sense that "the coffin of my failure" was firmly "nailed" by her inability to incorporate the evening gown signals an ambivalent response to her largely unwitting nonconformity.[58] By the time Woolf wrote "A Sketch of the Past" in 1939, the coffin of her social and sartorial failure could signal the fact that she was always destined to become the kind of woman who would marry Leonard Woolf, remain childless, and publish some of the twentieth century's most important novels and feminist polemics. And yet, we should not let the trajectory of Virginia Woolf's life obscure Virginia Stephen's sartorial mortification.

At the time they occurred, the young woman's forays in evening gowns left her conflicted. For all of her jokes, she confessed that she felt "all the pretty young Ladies far removed into another sphere."[59] And in her diary, she wrote that it was a really noble ambition" to merge one's behavior with an elegant appearance: "You have, for a certain space of time to realise as nearly as can be, an ideal. You must consciously try to carry out in your conduct what is implied by your clothes; they are silken—of the very best make—only to be worn with the greatest care, on occasions such as these. They are meant to please the eyes of others—to make you something more brilliant than you are by day."[60] We might be tempted to excavate Woolf's famous irony from these lines, but for a time she saw in the evening gown an "ideal" to which she might aspire. Her suggestion that such dress might make one "more brilliant than you are by day" echoes Simmel's claim that the gown assembles higher states of being than those achieved through ordinary dress; the writer, significantly, articulates the gown's activity in the same diction used for intellectual achievement—brilliance. Virginia Stephen's knowledge of Greek, grammar, and writing set her apart from other young women her age, but her admiration for an elegant appearance—and her frustration that she could not achieve it—is captured in the coffins and funerals with which she represents evening dress.

Like Woolf, Rebecca West understood the appeal and menace of evening dress.[61] In "The World's Worst Failure," West's titular disaster is embodied by women in evening dress, and the category encompasses those who make a successful appearance and those who are marred by various imperfections. The text asserts that the garment is incompatible with intellectual achievement; moreover, the piece suggests that material objects solicit affective bonds that motivate unworthy work—that "brilliance" at night (Virginia Stephen's word) comes at the cost of a dimming of one's talents by day.

West's narrator begins by describing a French woman who emerges as the perfect example of well-dressed femininity:

> Her body was not the loosely articulated thing of arrested and involuntary movements that serves as the fleshly vehicle of most of us, but was very straight and still, with the grace of flowers arranged by a florist, with a dress so beautiful that one imagined it hard and permanent like a jewel, yet so supple of texture that one could have crushed it into a handful. *It was the aim of her fragility to rouse such thoughts of violence.*[62]

"The World's Worst Failure" casts the woman in evening dress as neither self-willed nor entirely safe. West's metaphor of flowers that have been *arranged* by another frames the woman as less self-articulating than styled. Such figurative language also underlines the perishable nature of the woman in the gown; while her dress may have the permanence of a mineral, she herself provokes the desire to crush, assault, and destroy. West's use of the passive voice represents the woman as only partially responsible for arousing desire. To be elegant and well attired thus emerges as a sartorial expression of object status—the inorganic world ("like a jewel") impinges on the organic flower/body and renders it, too, a thing.[63]

As the essay continues, West represents the French woman in her gowns as on par with other items in the object world that take their meaning from interaction with human subjects. Noting the woman's boredom and loneliness, West ascribes her condition to a lack of use: "One perceived in her discomfort that there must be many sorts of pain of which no cognizance is taken in this world: the anguish of the chair on which nobody sits, the wine that is not drunk, the woman bred to please when there is no one at hand to be pleased."[64] West's comparisons liken the fashionable woman—and the essay aligns fashionability specifically with the evening dress—to an animal or object. While such a thing may feel pain, an emotional response that West credits and recognizes, the writer seems to set herself above or outside this object world, where she writes about but does not experience the impact of "the system of the *chic*."[65] The essay articulates an ontological binary (subject/object) but also begins to complicate objects by attributing emotional states to them; these are things that West thinks through but that also themselves think and feel.

As the piece continues, however, West suggests that there can be no simple rejection of the evening gown—no subject position above or outside the anguished object world. The narrator examines her own appearance in a mirror:

> And I—I was a black-browed thing scowling down on the inkstain that I saw reflected across the bodice of my evening dress. I was immeasurably distressed by this by-product of the literary life. It was a new evening dress, it was becoming, it was expensive. Already I was upsetting the balance of my nerves by silent rage; I knew I would wake up in the night and magnify it with an excited mind till it stained the world; that in the end I would probably write some article I did not in the least want to write in order to pay for a new one. In fact I would commit the same sin that I loathed in these two women. I would waste on personal ends vitality that I should have conserved for my work. And I was sinning for the same reason, for what could make me drape myself in irrelevant and costly folds of petunia satin, and what could make me forfeit my mental serenity at their defacement, if it were not for some deep and overlaid but sturdy instinct for elegance?[66]

The speaker is roused to anger—to "silent rage"—by her appearance; in the mirror, West apprehends herself as a damaged object far from the ideal that such a reflection might consolidate.[67] She, too, becomes a "thing" experiencing the kind of pain "of which no cognizance is taken in this world." The ink stain points to a bleeding of the narrator's professional (daytime) pursuits into her personal (evening) life, an exchange that travels in both directions: her literary pen mars the gown, and its replacement will mandate intellectual work of the kind she would otherwise avoid. The power of the pen is thus equaled by the power of "petunia satin," which might be "irrelevant" but also answers a desire—West calls it an "instinct"—for beautiful gowns *and* the fantasy of self-consolidation that such gowns may enable.

West's entire description expresses skepticism about sensual and aesthetic pleasure; it is "work," and not the garment, that the speaker values even as she knows that she will commit herself to the labor necessary to replace the dress. The passage thus illustrates West's acceptance of, in Kathryn Laing's words, "a variety of negative assumptions about femininity and the feminine,"[68] but it more importantly illuminates the push–pull of the object world, which alters West's career plans and trajectory. "The World's Worst Failure" deploys the gown to highlight both woman's status as thing (the French woman, the narrator in the mirror) and the garment's ability to direct agency, a power normally ascribed to human subjects. At this moment, woman and dress have an inextricable relationship in which the position of "primary" and "accessory" blur, and West thus draws attention to the evening gown's singular ability to complicate the subject/object binary. If the essayist acknowledges that pleasure ensues when dress and wearer work as a harmonious (if heterogeneous) assemblage, West can represent the pursuit of such pleasure only as folly: the essay concludes that the love of dress renders woman "the world's worst failure."[69] Replete with images of rage and disappointment, West's essay inscribes the evening gown as a material site of negotiation and struggle.[70]

Like Woolf and West, Jean Rhys examined the intimate relationship between women and evening dress that led to feelings of frustration, loss, and anger. Her short story "Illusion" (1927) animates the evening dress, thus building on the work of her contemporaries. It also portrays the tortured relationship between woman and dress as the result of a particularly British malady: a closeted desire for sartorial pleasure. Reversing West's optic and viewing a British woman, Miss Bruce, from the perspective of the unidentified Parisian narrator, "Illusion" suggests that there is something anti-British about fashionable evening dress and that the garment both suffers at the hands of women and makes them suffer.

The opening paragraphs of the story establish the main character, Miss Bruce, as a British artist living in the Latin Quarter. The narrator's descriptions position Bruce as an exemplar of British femininity: "One thought of her as a shining example of what character and training—British character and training—can do. After seven years in Paris she appeared utterly untouched, utterly unaffected, by anything hectic, slightly exotic or unwholesome."[71] Rhys's subtle irony casts Bruce's style as a form of sensible British habitus; her daytime attire is a personal uniform (serge dress in the summer and tweed costume in the winter), and when going out in the evening, "she put on a black gown of *crêpe de chine*, just well enough cut, not extravagantly pretty."[72] By the time the reader reaches the meat of Rhys's story, Bruce has been firmly established as a British woman in, but not of, Paris. She also has been established as a queer character; the narrator observes that Bruce speaks with a "thoroughly gentlemanly intonation" and "looks appraisingly" at pretty women when they pass her.[73] While Rhys's story does not go so far as to explicitly identify Bruce as homosexual—indeed, the character ignores the "worship of physical love" "going on all the time all around her"—readers in the know may have readily identified the character as queer or as a closeted lesbian.[74]

The plot of "Illusion" revolves around the narrator's exploration of Bruce's boudoir. Bruce has been hospitalized, and the narrator must prepare an overnight bag for her. Opening Bruce's wardrobe—"a big, square solid piece of old, dark furniture, suited for the square and solid coats and skirts of Miss Bruce"[75]—she makes a discovery: the tweedy Bruce collects exquisite gowns that she does not wear in public. The narrator finds a "glow of colour, a riot of soft silks": "In the middle, hanging in the place of honour, was an evening dress of a very beautiful shade of old gold: near it another of flame colour."[76] The evening gowns occupy a place of honor in Bruce's closet because they are the pinnacle of feminine fashion—the garment most able to produce an idealized class and femininity. Yet these gowns are never worn.

Bruce's decision to buy, but never publicly wear, her evening gowns results in two outcomes. It first reveals a surprising side to the queer, British Bruce, and here Rhys sounds a great deal like West writing a decade earlier. The narrator guesses that Bruce was tempted to purchase the gowns by "the perpetual hunger to be beautiful and that thirst to be loved which is the real curse of Eve."[77] Notably, the narrator imagines that Bruce *could* assemble a flattering look with her garments and makeup; the problem inheres in her unwillingness to venture outside her apartment when thus transformed. After donning a new dress and cosmetics, the narrator speculates, Bruce would "gaze into the glass at a transformed self" and think, "No impossible thing, beauty and all that beauty brings. There close at hand, to be clutched if one dared."[78] Unlike West's narrator, Rhys's character consolidates an ideal through the evening gown; the object, and the objectified reflection in the glass, enables a fantasy of unity and control that so few literary characters achieve through the garment. Despite this success, "somehow she never dared."[79] This passage casts Bruce as a closeted devotee of the chic who experiences profound pleasure in and desire for the kind of feminine display that the evening gown allows.[80]

Bruce never makes this display by wearing her gorgeous gowns to parties, perhaps because she has constructed a professional persona—"clean, calm and sensible"[81]—that she cannot reconcile with the daring, beautiful thing she perceives in the mirror. Moreover, her sexual persona, which might better be described as an *a*sexual persona, would be undone by a dress that emphasizes femininity. Invested in a form of depth ontology (surface/depth) that privileges masculine British character traits instead of feminine appearance, Bruce restricts herself to material assemblages that convey who she thinks she "really" is. As an artist, like the West of "The World's Worst Failure," she regards evening fashions as an indulgence for models (female objects) but not for painters (male subjects); the story concludes with her admiring another woman's hands and arms in a "gentlemanly manner."[82] Such behavior puts her dresses, and her desire for them, back in the literal and figurative closet.

In addition to revealing a repressed side of Bruce's, and Britain's, sartorial life, the narrator's descriptions of Bruce's wardrobe animate the gowns inside. She fantasizes about a new dress arriving and becoming all but articulate: "'Wear me, give me life,' it would seem to say to her."[83] But such life is seldom granted, and before she leaves Bruce's apartment, the narrator regards the dresses as locked up and aware of their imprisonment: the evening gown of old gold "appeared malevolent, slouching on its hanger; the black ones were mournful."[84] After animating the objects with this personification, the narrator further anthropomorphizes the gowns as she "felt a sudden, irrational pity for the beautiful things inside. I imagined them, shrugging their silken shoulders, rustling, whispering about the *anglaise* who had dared to buy them in order to condemn them to life in the dark."[85] Bruce's French-speaking dresses are, figuratively, buried alive. Endowing the dresses with speech, the narrator casts them as French subjects repressed by a British woman who dares not wear them. Once again framing Bruce's inability to wear the evening gowns as a peculiarly national condition, the narrator imagines the dresses not as objects but as things that may have desires for the future at odds with those of the woman who nominally owns them. But one has to consider the perspective of the object to see it as a thing—as more than inert matter—and Bruce seemingly does not adopt this view.[86]

Or perhaps she does. "Illusion" concludes with a recovered Bruce describing the contents of her wardrobe as a "collection" as she "carefully" stares over the narrator's head. Refusing to meet her friend's gaze, Bruce states, "I should never make such a fool of myself as to wear them. . . . They ought to be worn, I suppose."[87] Here, Bruce appears to concur with the narrator's compassion for the garments that will not be worn. "Illusion" echoes West's description of the "many sorts of pain of which no cognizance is taken in this world: the anguish of the chair on which nobody sits, the wine that is not drunk,"[88] and, Rhys might add, the evening gown that is not worn. The story reveals the repressed passion of Bruce and makes the reader pity her self-denial *and* depicts the death-in-life of the Parisian gowns that, like Bruce's desires, remain closeted. A dress, Rhys suggests, solicits a woman's purchase but, more importantly, *wear*; women who ignore the garment's vital objective run the risk of repressing the object world's needs *and their own*. The story thus encourages readers to listen to the thing, an activity that is not an abstract philosophical exercise: "Illusion" suggests that in the desires of the thing, one will find the desires of the so-called self.

The evening gown became a touchstone for Virginia Woolf's, Rebecca West's, and Jean Rhys's examinations of garments, traditional forms of femininity, and the lives of women artists. Because it reveals the body during evening entertainments far removed from professional achievement, it became a profoundly intense site of frustration, humiliation, and anger. Woolf's anguished experiences with evening dress convey her dismay at unwitting nonconformity *and* her resentment when thwarted in her attempts at fashionable experiment; West endows the garment with life by blurring the subject/object binary and by recording the dress's power to impinge on her profession; and Rhys maps such problems onto a British, national femininity and expresses the interpenetration of the life of the thing and that of the human. Together, such representations frame the garment as embodying conservative gender roles but also as expressing its own trajectory toward a public life. These texts complicate and question long-accepted assumptions about the object world's passivity, in part through unsettling the subject/object binary and in part through an affective response to things. Feminist writers cast women in the evening gown as at the mercy of their clothes; such representations uncover power sharing between people and garments that does not always prioritize human needs.

While Woolf and West viewed evening dress as the province of women who were not like them (Woolf's "pretty young ladies," West's French woman), it also becomes clear that, for these women, the gowns solicited desire even if such desire was "pathetic" (Woolf), a mark of "failure" (West), or an "illusion" (Rhys). The glimpses we get of sartorial pleasure—West's "petunia satin," Rhys's "riot of soft silks," and others—often recede into the background, but they do not disappear. The evening gown held out the possibility that it *might* give aesthetic pleasure to the wearer and *might* "make [a woman] something more brilliant than [she is] by day." It was this very possibility that Ottoline Morrell explored.

Making It Quaint: Ottoline Morrell's Experiments in Evening Dress

While Woolf, West, and Rhys generally purchased their evening gowns from dressmakers and couturiers, and thus did not wear their own designs, some of their contemporaries used the garment as a platform for aesthetic experimentation. One of them was Ottoline Morrell, an aristocrat, artistic patron, and society hostess whose unusual garb is one of the reasons she is so well remembered.[89] Her unconventional evening gowns were not, or not only, careless or gaudy but an artistic venture that should be placed alongside other modernist aesthetic experiments.[90] The way we read Morrell's gowns matters because we can then parse the negative representations of her appearance in the works of her contemporaries; if, as Alfred Gell has argued, "vulnerability stems from the bare possibility of representation" of the self in and as object(s),[91] Morrell provides an especially poignant example of how, when, and why evening gowns assembled a caricature. Morrell's fearless venture into an everyday aesthetic praxis was on a par with the goals of the Omega Workshops in its daring, if not in its eventual popularity, but the artists and writers who knew her insisted on inscribing her style as, at best, characterized by aristocratic excess and, at worst, a lamentable failure. Like the main character of Woolf's short story "The New Dress," which I will also discuss, Morrell's gowns served to complicate human agency in romans à clef and literary history.

So what *did* Morrell's garments look like? Many of her gowns that have been archived by the Fashion Museum in Bath date to the 1910s and 1920s and indicate the hallmarks of Morrell's mature style. When she wore sleeveless gowns, she often festooned them with wide lace collars, which would have concealed her upper arms.[92] Her gowns were either high-waisted or more daringly fashioned with a long straight bodice, dropped waist, and flared skirt. Such garments were the product of collaboration with her dressmaker, Miss Brenton, and occasionally with her daughter's lady's maid, Ivy Green. Morrell would provide the inspiration for the gowns, usually in the form of postcards or sketches, as well as the fabrics and trimmings for their construction. Brenton, for her part, weighed in on designs and assembled gowns quickly. As Morrell's biographer Miranda Seymour has noted, the gowns "seldom cost more than three guineas," a pittance for a woman who was the half-sister of the Duke of Portland. In Seymour's words, this low cost was due to rapid production: "[S]eams were skimped, lining was not used, fastenings were minimal, hems and turnings were often tacked into position."[93] Brenton sometimes would "stretch" materials to prevent the need to buy additional yards of costly silks and satins. In one gown, for example, a cuff was pieced together with scraps that would normally have ended up on the dressmaker's floor.[94] Seymour likens such garments to "theatrical props" and writes that "Ottoline's dresses were designed, not for comfort, but to stir the imagination of the viewer."[95]

Morrell's appearance was thus an expression of being not *in*, but in negotiation *with*, fashion.[96] Her attitude toward dress design is reflected in a letter to Morrell from Brenton, who lamented that "it is so difficult to keep *out of the fashions* as the narrow frocks do suit you so much . . . but we must make our things quaint and unusual by the colouring or embroidering."[97] Morrell and Brenton's design credo indicates that the dresses they produced were meant to resist, not follow, current styles; if a fashionable line suited Morrell, an evening dress would be made of unusual materials. The designs and fabrics thus worked in dynamic tension with one another. In a black velvet and copper print gown, for example, a modern pattern competes with pouf beret (melon) sleeves, a style popular in the 1830s (figure 1.6). The contrast between the historical allusion—or anachronism—and the modern materials makes this dress an example of that most modern of mantras: Pound's "make it new." Thus we might articulate Morrell's credo as "make it quaint" or "make it unusual"; in either case, her style was meant to flatter *and* to signal a departure from fashionable norms.

Such gowns underline Morrell's sense of tradition—in this case, fashion's traditions—and of the "historical sense" that T. S. Eliot, for his part, was defining as "indispensable" for modern poetry. Read, if you will, Eliot's famed treatise "Tradition and the Individual Talent" while imagining him not as the marmoreal author of *The Waste Land* but as a fashion columnist for *Vogue*:

> [T]the historical sense involves a perception, not only of the pastness of the past, but of its presence; the historical sense compels

FIGURE 1.6 Black and gold woven metal thread and velvet evening dress, worn by Lady Ottoline Morrell, 1930s. (Fashion Museum, Bath and North East Somerset Council / Bridgeman Images)

a [designer] to [create] not merely with his own generation in his bones, but with a feeling that the whole of the [history of costume] of Europe . . . has a simultaneous existence and composes a simultaneous order. This historical sense, which is a sense of the timeless as well as of the temporal and of the timeless and of the temporal together, is what makes a [designer] traditional. And it is at the same time what makes a [designer] most acutely conscious of his place in time, of his contemporaneity.[98]

While Eliot would, no doubt, be horrified to have his model of aesthetic praxis applied to Morrell's gowns, his argument—not only here, but generally—usefully helps us frame the designs, materials, and effects of Morrell's dresses as a careful blending of stylistic allusion with innovation, and of traditional and modern materials into something new. With a silk-taffeta gown, Morrell balanced the fabric's modern print with handmade lace, which adorns the collar.[99] Paired with staid colors or prints, the lace would have seemed a traditional trimming for a British aristocrat's gown, gesturing toward generations of bespoke clothing, high-quality materials, and refined dress. Tacked to the neckline of a gown constructed of fabric with an unusual print, however, the lace positions the dress in relation to the "standards of the past" (Eliot again) and stakes a claim for the innovation of the gown and, by association, its wearer.

Such designs attracted the attention of two major fashion photographers and the fashion press. Morrell was repeatedly photographed by Baron Adolf de Meyer, the first fashion photographer to be officially appointed by American *Vogue* and a contributor to Alfred Stieglitz's *Camera Work*. Although his photographs of Morrell were not, to my knowledge, featured in *Vogue*, she was twice profiled in that magazine.[100] In 1928, Morrell's personal sense of style was celebrated in a full-page photograph taken by Cecil Beaton, the most famous fashion photographer of his day (and one of the best-known such photographers of all time) (figure 1.7). The identification of Morrell in the photo's caption underlines one of the reasons that she was a particularly appropriate sitter for *Vogue*: she embodied the balance the magazine tried to strike among coverage of high fashion, the avant-garde, and Britain's social elite.[101]

Beaton's photograph and *Vogue*'s caption displays Morrell at her sartorial zenith. There is ample allusion to history in Morrell's style, including her pearls, her favored beret sleeves, and the brocade pattern of the gown's fabric. The reference to her "Goya manner" similarly locates Morrell historically; her appearance works in a tradition of high-art forms that *Vogue*'s readers were expected to recognize. At the same time, Morrell's fan is decidedly modern, almost futurist, in design, adding a piquant counterpoint to the traditional elements of the costume. Finally, the off-the-shoulder cut of the gown balances the historical and the contemporary, alluding both to the 1820s (Goya's final decade) *and* to the influence of Spanish art on postwar fashion, particularly between 1921 and 1925.[102] Morrell's "Goya manner" was thus of the past and the present, an assemblage of inspirations, styles, and forms that made her unique.

Through the lens of Beaton, and in the pages of *Vogue*, Morrell emerged as a significant practitioner of a unique style, one that combined traditional and innovative elements and took its place among both the fashionable and the avant-garde. Despite this celebration, Morrell was

FIGURE 1.7 "An unusual photographic study, in the Goya manner, of Lady Ottoline Morrell, who is a Cavendish-Bentinck and half-sister of the Duke of Portland," *Vogue*, May 16, 1928, 60. (Cecil Beaton / Vogue © The Condé Nast Publications Ltd.)

well aware of the occasions when her sartorial experiments failed. In her memoir, Morrell recalled a trip to stay with "established people" when she found her own clothing inappropriate: "I packed my best dresses, which somehow, when shaken out and worn, seemed absurdly fantastic and unfitting for the company and the surroundings. These that at home I was so proud of and thought so lovely would suddenly be transformed into tawdry 'picturesque' rags, making me feel foolish and self-conscious in wearing them."[103] As Morrell's reflection indicates, new surroundings could alter her affective relationship to a garment as the object world impinged on and reconfigured it. This description neatly captures the dynamic relationships among the body in a gown, the gown itself, and the physical environment around it; had Morrell felt comfortable in her dresses, it seems likely that she would have ignored the role of things (dress and surroundings) in assembling that state. It is instructive to compare Morrell's reflections with those of her feminist contemporaries. While Morrell, unlike Woolf, West, and Rhys, aligned evening gowns with artistic expression, her dresses' construction and challenge to fashion's emphasis on the new rendered them as alienating as West's ink-stained petunia satin gown and Virginia Stephen's green dress. The perceptual changes triggered by relocation—the affective bonds broken in a new setting—rendered Morrell's gowns unstable and shameful.

Equally significant, Morrell understood her ideas and values on such occasions as parallel with her gowns: "All my own feelings and enthusiasms, like my dresses, I felt sure, would seem absurd and fantastic if I allowed them to be seen."[104] While Morrell could choose to conceal her passionate opinions—could forestall speech-acts that would isolate her from or set her in opposition to others—her dresses materialized decisions and commitments that she had made earlier and rendered her nonconformity *visible*. Morrell's example illuminates the ways in which sartorial assemblages become disruptive when they reflect decisions made at an earlier time.[105] Morrell might decide to remain silent, but she could not quiet, alter, or explain away a gown once she entered a room wearing it.

Morrell's sense of "unfitting" company *and* surroundings resonates with Virginia Woolf's short story "The New Dress" (1924), in which the main character, Mabel Waring, attends Mrs. Dalloway's evening party in an "old-fashioned silk dress."[106] Although the character recalls profound pleasure in commissioning the dress, and even regards herself as "a beautiful woman" when she first tries it on,[107] Waring quickly realizes that the dress that "looked so charming in the fashion book" did not look well "on her, not among these ordinary people."[108] The story pivots on the contrast between Waring's positive feelings about her dress and herself before she enters the Dalloways' drawing room and her self-loathing and rejection of the dress, which she comes to see as a "penance," afterward.[109] Although Waring wonders why she could be thus "whipped all round in a second by coming into a room full of people," her experience, like that of Morrell, positions nonconformist evening dress as pleasurable to create but humiliating to wear.[110]

In "The New Dress," Waring's gown (like West's petunia satin) has the power to render the character a thing. As Jessica Burstein observes, "The first revelation of self [in Woolf's story] is brought about by a mirror, or more precisely a series of mirrors, which appear in the anxiously breathless first sentence of the story."[111] After catching glimpses of her dress—Waring thinks, "How much humiliation and agony and self-loathing and effort and passionate ups and downs of feeling were contained in a thing the size of a three penny bit"—the narrator asserts, "What was still odder, *this thing, this Mabel Waring*, was separate, quite disconnected."[112] In parallel with other examples, the dress and reflection do not consolidate a coherent (if fictive) self but *disrupt* Waring's fantasy of personal unity and control. The dress, which impinges on Waring's status as agentic human subject, separates Waring from the other characters at the party, rendering her "solitary" and "self-centered" at the very moment when she should be connected to others in the room.[113] Woolf's story emphasizes the perils of taking creative liberties with evening dress, suggesting that woman's participation in social events (events assembled of multiple persons and things) depends on a sartorial conformity that becomes particularly visible when transgressed.

The parallels between Morrell and Waring remind readers that experiments with evening dress were no simple matter of exercising personal agency in regard to taste; as these examples indicate, the impersonal agency of a gown intervenes in a complex social setting that depends on the careful calibration of human and nonhuman objects. Morrell came to know this all too well. Writers and artists whom she had befriended savaged her appearance in letters, diaries, and, as Sean Latham has argued, at least ten romans à clef.[114] For example, although Morrell's styles had a great deal in common with those produced by the Omega Workshops, and she herself partially inspired Omega's dress production,[115] Morrell's use of color and elaborate trimmings were criticized by many in Bloomsbury. Leonard Woolf, for one, claimed that Morrell "looked like an enormous bird [with] brightly and badly dyed plumage."[116] Virginia Woolf made similar remarks about Morrell's evening dresses of "garish" "pink plush"[117] and of "tea kettle taffeta, all looped & scolloped [sic] & fringed with silver lace."[118] Although, for a time at least, the Omega Workshops were adopting similar shades in its clothing, the Woolfs' comments suggest that when Morrell wore such colors, she was unnatural and self-seeking. Moreover, her use of trimmings like "silver lace," which may have articulated her aristocratic status or family's wealth, was simply dismissed as an example of her "definite, rather bad, taste."[119]

Such remarks point to Morrell's inability to control how representations of her gowns, which are themselves things, circulated. While the scorn that Bloomsbury heaped on her attire was confined to private letters and diaries during Morrell's lifetime, other writers mocked her dresses in published works, rendering their judgments more painful. Aldous Huxley's roman à clef *Crome Yellow* puts Priscilla Wimbush, the Morrell character, in "a purple silk dress with a high collar and a row of pearls. The costume, so richly dowagerish, so suggestive of the Royal Family, made her look more than ever like something in the [music] Halls."[120] Wimbush's ensemble seems to be an evening gown, even though it is worn during the day. *Crome Yellow* suggests that part of the character's, and thus Morrell's, nonconformity stems from wearing evening dress at inappropriate times, but Huxley's novel equally mocks her dress at night. At a later evening event, she wears a "pale sea-green dress; on the slope of her mauve-powdered décolletage diamonds twinkled."[121] Wimbush's excessive ornamentation and use of color caricatures Morrell's evening wear, painting her in such broad strokes that she is rendered vaudevillian by the narrator. *Crome Yellow* thus solicits a reader's negative perception of Morrell through strategic representations of the evening gown and its accessories.

If Huxley's caricatures of his former friend's attire were hurtful, those by Osbert Sitwell were savage. In his first fictional work, *Triple Fugue*, Morrell is cast as Lady Septuagesima Goodley, whose clothes, bystanders speculate, "had been bestowed upon her by a charitable theatrical costumier."[122] Sitwell's novel, like Huxley's, exaggerates Morrell's use of color and ornamentation, as well as her apparent penchant for wearing evening dress and its accessories during the day. In a quasi-epic catalog, Sitwell's narrator offers a lengthy lost-property notice of items that Goodley mislaid while walking in the neighborhood of her country home, including

Seven herons' plumes set in brilliants.
A green ostrich-feather fan with tortoiseshell mount.
An Elizabethan whale-bone [skirt] hoop.
One crimson shoe-heel with cairngorm inset.
A tartan shawl.
A Japanese embroidered bag, with panels of flying storks worked in salmon pinks and rose silks.[123]

While Sitwell's text does not represent Goodley's dresses in any detail—they seem to stay on her—his generalizations about her appearance, and this list, castigate the character for crossing the countryside in assemblages that feature evening-gown accessories, including the plumes, fan, ornamented shoe, and embroidered bag. Morrell was thus caricatured for dressing in an excessive, rococo style and for not discriminating between day and evening dress, one of the primary distinctions that a fashionable woman of the period would be expected to make.[124] From our historical remove, it is impossible to know whether this latter charge is true, but Sitwell's novel demonstrates that Morrell's experimental, quaint dresses and accessories were vulnerable to, and perhaps even encouraged, representations that elicited a reader's negative judgment.

Sitwell's *Triple Fugue*—and the many other romans à clef that model characters on Morrell—repeatedly refashions experimental dress in ways that encourage readers to see the woman wearing it as asinine. These novels also position such garb as, paradoxically, queering her. W. J. Turner's *The Aesthetes* aligns Morrell's sartorial excess with gender violation:

> Virginia Caraway [the character based on Morrell] as we know her is merely a by-product of thwarted sex. Her hats, her cloaks, and her zebras are merely the coxcomb, spurs and ruffles of desire *rampant*—blue-blooded lust expressing itself heraldically. Moreover, since we know it is unusual for the female animal to display these insignia of sex—such ornamentation and vivid colouring being reserved throughout history for the male—it suggests that Virginia Caraway is more masculine than feminine.[125]

Turner misrepresents the history of couture in aligning "ornamentation" with human males, but his text effectively burlesques Morrell's appearance and queers the character who represents her. If evening gowns had long been associated with femininity, Morrell's attire demonstrates that, carried to an extreme, elaborate sartorial assemblages can cross an invisible line, and the body in a dress can be read as trans. Dress enacts a form of postsubjective sexuality in Turner's novel: desire and identity are queered by the things on, not in, the character—and, by association, Morrell.

Morrell was, of course, not the only historical figure to find herself embarrassed by fictional translations of her appearance, but she *was* uniquely popular as a figure of fun. Turner's novel provides insight into the reasons for her vulnerability, which was entirely tied up in her appearance. One character opines that Lady Caraway "is like Switzerland, or the Elizabethan drama, or the Russian ballet. It is probably because no one has ever lived with her. She is known only to tourists or sightseers. They look at her and go away—and write books about her."[126] It is precisely this "to be looked-at-ness" that inheres in the evening gown as a thing: under ordinary circumstances, it solicits attention because of its materials, style, and revelation of the female body; under extraordinary circumstances, such as with Morrell's experimental dresses, it invites the perception of assembled person and thing as an abject monument or event that encourages viewers to "write books about her." If public figures are always vulnerable to unflattering representations of themselves, Morrell's sartorial decisions made such vulnerability pervasive.

We might think of Morrell's evening dresses, then, as a site of accidents, albeit not the kind that produce crumpled vehicles and bodies. Memoirs, diaries and letters, and romans à clef represent her gowns as powerful affective catalysts that intervene in the wearer's sense of self *and* the responses of others. They thus highlight the potential of evening dress to serve as a type of "connector," which Bruno Latour describes as a system (his examples are law and religion) that traces and forges associations between entities that would otherwise remain separate.[127] Ordinarily, evening wear works as a material actant that links individuals who share styles, materials, and norms. Morrell's gowns instead become *dis*connectors; they impede rather than create bonds or, rather, they create bonds only among writers who enjoyed parodying Morrell. Her evening gowns serve as illuminating examples of things that produce harmful effects; like Mabel Waring's gown in Woolf's "The New Dress," her dresses express a form of material agency that diminishes human fantasies of power and control.

Today, with Morrell long dead and her gowns the very fabric of an archive, scholars can reconsider her designs and materials and are no longer dependent on the representations of her detractors. Such revision is necessary in order to perceive her contemporaries' surprising suspicion of sartorial nonconformity and the ways in which they ensured that her dresses would *become* Morrell; in a negative version of Simmel's theory of adornment, Morrell's *having* of experimental evening dress was synthetized into a type of cartoonish *being*. As Roger Fry noted about reaction to the Omega Workshops, "It's natural that people should dislike it when you try to do something new, but I'm always a little surprised at the vehemence and the personal antagonism that it stirs up."[128] There is ample evidence of the personal antagonism that Morrell stirred up, an antagonism that is articulated through mockery of her dress and that outlines the perils of experimenting with the evening gown.

What Woman Wants

In his analysis of early-twentieth-century women's fashion, C. Willett Cunnington blames female psychology for the continued popularity of traditional forms of decoration: "No doubt trimmings and added surfaces are very uneconomic, harbor dust, and are impractical for modern daily life. Yet for the purpose of sex-attraction, as in the evening dress, they are not to be despised. They obliterate the flatness so often seen, giving gradations of depth to the picture so that the eye is tempted to linger and study the composition. After all, is not this what Woman wants?"[129] Cunnington's query, which unwittingly echoed Freud's unpublished letter to Marie Bonaparte, expresses a widely held assumption about fashion: it responds to the desires of "Woman" as a collective, if not as an individual. In Cunnington's study, this belief is articulated in his discussion of the evening dress, a garment that does not have to tailor itself to particular weathers or occupations. The gown, according to Cunnington, exists solely to enable (a) woman's desire to present a "picture"—to assemble herself as a beautiful object that bystanders might contemplate. Sex attraction, here and elsewhere, emerges as the evening gown's raison d'être.

And yet a range of British texts—including films, fiction, memoirs, and diaries and letters—represent the evening gown as giving "Woman" precisely what she *does not want*. Even when allowing for variation in treatments of the gown, there is a surprising consensus that this garment is not an inert object but an animate thing. Moreover, the evening-gown-as-thing regularly diminishes the agency of the women who wear it: it exposes flesh that becomes vulnerable to blades and scandal; it cloaks women in colors that inculcate a world of mourning; it solicits desires that career women find themselves unable to resist; and it transforms carefully constructed assemblages into the (queer) stuff of satire. It might be tempting to bracket these reactions as punishment for commodity fetishism—for what John Frow calls the "strongest version" of the story of "the bad enchantment of the world of things"[130]—but such an explanation will not suffice. Evening dress was certainly most readily available to members of the upper and middle classes, and along with other luxury goods, it mystified the relationships between the garments and those who wore them, as Simmel and others observed. What is most striking, however, is that the texts addressed here do not naturalize or mystify *representations* of evening dress. Instead, the gowns are analyzed, recalled, mocked, and reevaluated in light of women's changing social roles, bids for artistic autonomy, and imbrications within wider historical events (including World War I and the deaths of monarchs). The textualized evening gown, then, makes it impossible to take the garment for granted.

It seems that the gown could not be naturalized at a time when it stood in sharp contrast to daytime clothing that reflected women's changing educational and professional opportunities. As Crane has argued, "'Closed' texts, garments with fixed meanings, were typical of class societies. 'Open' texts, garments that continually acquire new meanings, are more likely to appear in fragmented societies, because different social groups [and individuals] wish to express different meanings using the same type of garment."[131] In the first few decades of the twentieth century, the evening gown evolved from a closed to an open text. This shift was partly due to the increasing pressures put on the British class system, but it was more importantly a result of the fragmentation caused by the women's movement, which challenged the conservative gender roles previously written into the dress. Even women who were not suffragettes saw their clothing altered by the increasing popularity of sports, which generated a range of new garments and styles but did little to alter evening dress. As a result, evening gowns could no longer be taken for granted, and the women who wore them (and the authors who write about them) became newly attentive to the gown's capacity to produce both helpful and harmful effects.

Poor Clara—the *Punch* cartoon character "always so at the mercy of her clothes"—thus emerges as less an unusual case than an exemplar of a range of women who felt the particular pressure of evening dress. The gowns solicited affective ties, resonated with surroundings, and provided literal and figurative openings for events over which individuals exercised varying degrees of agency. As a mediator, it participated in an "on-going process" of forming "uncertain, fragile, controversial, and ever-shifting ties."[132] And it regularly dissolved those fragile bonds, reminding the women who wore them, and the readers of texts that represent them, that humanity was and is assembled by garments that are sometimes acted on and sometimes act in ways that surprise, delight, or torment.

2 Wearable Memorials

Into and Out of the Trenches with the Modern Mac

While evening gowns feature much more prominently in fashion histories than do prosaic, everyday garments, the ordinary occasionally gets its due. In *Why Women Wear Clothes*, C. Willett Cunnington observes that ordinary garb may, paradoxically, facilitate social recognition:

> Surely that is the absolute finality of fame, to cease to be a Person and to become a—thing; from having been the Duke of Wellington to turn into—*a pair of boots*. And of all these curious names attached to wearing apparel the student, after laborious researching, finds that some never had corporeal existence but were only fictitious characters drawn from books and plays. To add to his confusion he finds that proper names have been attached not merely to actual garments but also to styles and methods of construction....
>
> There seems no logic in the selection of such names as have been thus transfigured. Galoshes and mackintoshes, both made of a similar substance, suggest two eminent Scotsmen; but you will search in vain north of the Tweed—or elsewhere—for a "Mr. Galosh."[1]

This playful meditation on the naming of garments after people (or fictional characters) suggests that becoming a thing, in Cunnington's terms, need not be an alienating process. Wellington and Charles Macintosh have had their legacies enhanced through clothing that serves as material futurity, one in which ubiquitous, workaday attire points (however obliquely) to the men whose careers inspired it. The vagaries of naming might be confusing for "the student," as Cunnington modestly calls himself, but they do not confound or shame the person who has become the thing. No doubt these men hoped to leave a more prepossessing inheritance, but their fame is partly secured through the garments they wore or designed.

Contrast Macintosh, however, with characters who become *his* thing in novels of the early twentieth century. In the "Hades" episode of James Joyce's *Ulysses*, the reporter Joe Hynes takes down the names of those who attend the funeral of Paddy Dignam. Hynes asks Leopold Bloom,

—do you know the fellow in the, fellow was over there in the . . .
—Macintosh. Yes, I saw him, Mr Bloom said. Where is he now?
—M'Intosh, Hynes said, scribbling, I don't know who he is. Is that his name?[2]

The mysterious figure, henceforth known as M'Intosh, appears throughout *Ulysses*, known only by the coat that confers a spurious identity. The character's personal history is seemingly a tragic one: he eats dry bread, a clear sign of poverty; he purportedly "loves a lady who is dead," a mark of mourning and loneliness; and he is identified by medical students as suffering from "trumpery insanity," a sign of ill-health.[3] Joyce's M'Intosh is no man and unmanned throughout *Ulysses*, a perambulating reminder of the fragility of individual identity when a person becomes a thing.

At the opposite cultural pole of *Ulysses*, one finds P. G. Wodehouse's short story "Jeeves and the Dog McIntosh" (1930), in which Bertie Wooster takes care of his Aunt Agatha's beloved Aberdeen terrier. Wooster's canine charge is accidentally given away, but his indefatigable valet, Jeeves, manages to substitute another terrier in his place. As Jeeves explains, "One Aberdeen terrier looks very much like another Aberdeen terrier, sir."[4] To put it another way, one McIntosh looks much like another. In quite different ways, Joyce's and Wodehouse's texts emphasize the ubiquity of the mackintosh *and* of the creatures associated with the coat. Instead of reaching "the absolute finality of fame," M'Intosh and McIntosh find themselves de-particularized through the mac. Becoming a thing, such novels imply, can be much more alienating than Cunnington suggests.

In novels targeted at a variety of readerships, the mackintosh, under its various incarnations, repeatedly turns persons into things. It foments loss of individual identity; it cloaks the unscrupulous, deadly, and cruel. Moreover, the mac seems to have a bull's eye on it, protecting against the elements but attracting the violence of technological warfare. It turns people into units—particularly into uniform entities like soldiers—and into corpses, and it is therefore associated with forms of commemoration. The irony of such activity is increased by the garment's very ordinariness; it was commonplace on the streets of major cities and in the wardrobes of people of all conditions and histories. Although the mackintosh was commercially and popularly aligned with positive traits—including technological innovation, protection, value, and perseverance—writers of the period persistently animated it as enacting violence, anonymity, and the paralysis of characters dwarfed by economic and social structures they could not transcend. While the evening gown demonstrates the way that a bespoke item became acutely problematic in light of changing gender norms, the mackintosh suggests that writers were equally troubled by a mass-produced garment that turned persons into things, making individuals indistinguishable from one another. Evening gowns could and did shame when their wearers failed in bids to achieve singularity, when they failed to become unique and ideal objects; wearers of the mackintosh, I will demonstrate, could seldom aspire to the singular and instead became themselves undifferentiated and threatened material.

Literary scholars have examined representations of the mackintosh in individual novels and have explained what the garment signifies about particular characters, the limits of interpretation, and the social and ethical dimensions of each work.[5] In contrast, this chapter looks at macs across a spectrum of fiction to demonstrate that this most British of garments came to signal the power of clothing to gather connotations and to foment outcomes that individual wearers could seldom control or manipulate. If we consider the mac through the lenses of industrial and military history, children's literature, fashion columns, and advertising *as well as* novels, it becomes clear that the garment was either too innocent or too guilty for an adult to wear. The mackintosh became a mute participant in histories of industrial production and class divisions, in assumptions about which types of people could act on individual volition, and in a historical cataclysm that, until World War II, was unprecedented.

Given the presence of the mac in such locations, it is little wonder that writers deployed it as a symptom of—and, eventually, that it became a kind of shorthand for—negative qualities and narratives.

Before turning to a brief biography of the mac, I want to clarify my use of the term throughout this chapter. I subsume a number of words under "mackintosh," including "raincoat," "trench coat," "weather all," and "mackintosh" proper, in part because Charles Macintosh was the first commercial maker of the garment, and the word thus became the British catch-all term for raincoats. According to the *OED*, the mackintosh was "originally: a full-length coat or cloak made of waterproof rubberized material. Subsequently: a rainproof coat made of this or some other material."[6] Manufacturers and retailers did not always differentiate between different kinds of raincoats; the *Harrods General Catalogue* of 1928/1929, for example, does not distinguish between coats made of different textiles, indexing and identifying all raincoats with the term "mackintosh." The *OED* demonstrates the word's universalizing function with an example from *Noblesse Oblige: An Enquiry into Identifiable Characteristics of the English Aristocracy* that follows the definition of "mackintosh": "*Burberry* and *raincoat* are of the same genre, *macintosh* or *mac* being normal." In *Noblesse Oblige*, a footnote to this definition reads, "This use of *Burberry* no doubt arose because, even before 1914 . . . this was a good and expensive kind of macintosh."[7] This description explains the use of differing terms as an attempt by manufacturers and consumers to assert and maintain class hierarchies in the face of the garment's ubiquity, but "mac" was considered the "normal" term for a waterproof garment.[8] There was, however, nothing "normal" about this garment's deployment in a range of literature, which collectively uses the coat to think about the associations between, and blending of, persons and things.

Making the Mackintosh

The commercial history of the mackintosh indicates why negative connotations would gradually accrue to a garment that was (and is) quintessentially British. Charles Macintosh (1766–1843) invented a means of waterproofing fabric and patented it on June 17, 1823. Macintosh's process involved sandwiching rubber, softened by naphtha, between layers of cotton cloth.[9] Although the coats succeeded in keeping out water, they were unattractive and uncomfortable. Nineteenth-century macs were a drab green, long and shapeless, and hard to maneuver. The original material could not be tailored closely to the body because the rubberized fabric did not breathe, and a tight-fitting mac was a prescription for perspiration.[10] The coats themselves also smelled unpleasant. As early as 1839, "*The Gentleman's Magazine* remarked that 'a mackintosh is now become a troublesome thing in town from the difficulty of their being admitted into an omnibus on account of the offensive stench which they emit.'"[11]

Mackintoshes were unique in that they were an early artifact of British mass-production. In a period when most street clothing and outerwear was either home- or custom-made, the production requirements for macs, which had seams that necessitated chemical proofing, meant that "the mackintosh industry was one of the first clothing trades to be substantially carried out in factories."[12] Workers made individual parts of the garment, which was then assembled elsewhere on the premises, rendering the mackintosh a pre-Fordist exemplar of mass-production. Because they were not made to measure for individual customers and were manufactured far away from where they were bought and worn, mackintoshes foreshadowed the eventual popularity of "ready-to-wear" clothing. The coats were thus an emblem of modernity, but they were also marked by a lack of exclusivity, as mass-production rendered mackintoshes inexpensive. In 1893, the *India Rubber Journal* asserted, "Now the servant girl out of her slender means can procure a really stylish and serviceable waterproof for a mere trifle."[13] Manufacturers and servant girls were no doubt pleased that the coat had become so affordable, but such comments led to a growing sense that mackintoshes were cheap, and thus second-rate, articles.

The mac was a particularly British garment, in both its construction and its manufacture. Early in the coat's development, it became traditional to line the mackintosh with tartan cloth; as Sarah Levitt explains, "There was a fashion for all things Scottish" in the nineteenth century, and tartan linings "were especially appropriate in view of Macintosh's Caledonian Origins."[14] The coat continued to reference its national genesis—a British, if not English, patrimony—long after the vogue for tartan faded. Such linings persist in contemporary mackintoshes (as most Burberry advertisements make plain) and remain an oblique reminder of the coat's origins. Moreover, even though the American Goodyear Tire & Rubber Company developed its own version of the mac, in the early twentieth century "the entire British production supplied ninety percent of the world market."[15] British domination of what we might call the mackintosh sector means that the coat was and is aligned with a specific national identity; even today, British brands like Traditional Weatherwear (the descendant of Macintosh's original operation) remain popular in overseas markets because a British mac is "the real thing" according to many consumers.[16]

The first—and, over the long term, best—customer for the mackintosh was the British Army. When other manufacturers entered the market with different means of waterproofing cloth, they too found the army to be their best market. Ordinary soldiers wore mass-produced mackintoshes, but officers wore Aquascutums during the Crimean War and, later, Burberry waterproofs.[17] These companies offered tailor-made mackintoshes, but the cut and color of the garments they produced followed military specifications, making the coats of the officer class visually uniform. Even as the quality of a mac quietly expressed its wearer's social and economic status, the coat became a de-individuating garment worn by members of an institution that functioned because of group behavior, experience, and history. The mac thus substantiates Georg Simmel's argument that clothing can amalgamate individuals: "[S]imilarly dressed persons exhibit similarity in their actions."[18] While Simmel contends that fashion simultaneously facilitates "individual accentuation and original shading of the elements of" stylish garb,[19] the mac's utilitarian nature (and largely unfashionable history) rendered, as we shall see, individuality and originality extremely difficult.

It is illuminating to contrast even the upscale mac with the evening gown; while both garments were made to measure and costly, the synthesis of "having" and "being" that Simmel theorizes as characteristic of evening finery could only with difficulty pertain to a Burberry or an Aquascutum coat. A consumer would know that he had bought an expensive garment, but the casual observer might not. A comic story in *Punch* hinges on this very point. In "Personal," the narrator offers an account of her purchase of a "McIntosh," the product of "the celebrated British firm" that costs "the extra guinea." After she has the coat repaired, she is dismayed to discover that an unscrupulous tailor removed the McIntosh tag and sewed it into another raincoat, which promptly sold on the strength of the label. "Personal" thus suggests that the difference between a "McIntosh" coat and a cheaper garment is not always visible.[20] One mackintosh seemed very like another, and the coat thus helped to construct British masses, whether they were soldiers, officers, "servant girls," or simply ordinary consumers.

Early advertisements for the mackintosh tended to promote it to two types of consumer: sportsmen (and, to a lesser extent, women) and servants. In other words, the upper echelons of British society would wear their macs while participating in extraordinary leisure activities, while those in the working class would wear the same raincoats while performing their ordinary, workaday jobs. During the nineteenth century, Macintosh touted its waterproofs as a necessary implement for the sporting life, particularly for dangerous sports. In an advertisement published in the *Illustrated Sporting and Dramatic News* in 1890, a man and a woman wear the coats while yachting in rough seas.[21] This advertisement was no doubt intended to display the protective qualities of the mac—the couple is endangered but not wet—but it paradoxically aligns the garment with exciting pastimes that verge on the perilous.

If members of the yachting class wore mackintoshes when in danger of being washed overboard, they purchased these garments for their servants to wear when occupied in the routine tasks of driving carriages, opening doors, and carrying packages. Early Harrods catalogs depict mackintoshes as suitable for coachmen and footmen. While thus attired, they could escort their employers around town with the sheltering aid of umbrellas. These catalogs make plain why no woman of fashion would have worn a mackintosh when paying calls or going to evening entertainments: in 1912, the coats were still voluminous, chin-to-foot affairs (figure 2.1). Before the war, the coats were thus associated with the military, sports, and the working class. They were utilitarian garments that were connected mainly with de-individuating activities such as army or household service. They were appropriate for select leisure activities, but in contrast to the evening gown and to fancy dress, they positively interfered with making a distinctive, stylish appearance.

Sartorial Shorthand: The Mac, Children, and Poverty

In literature of this period, writers consistently align the coat with sport and protection but also with de-individuation. These qualities emerge most clearly in books written for children, who, like servants and soldiers, do not choose what they wear, and in depictions of working-class characters, who are treated as objects by those higher up on the social scale. Both groups are clothed in macs for pragmatic reasons, but when adults wear the coats, the garments come to represent—and even

INTO AND OUT OF THE TRENCHES WITH THE MODERN MAC   73

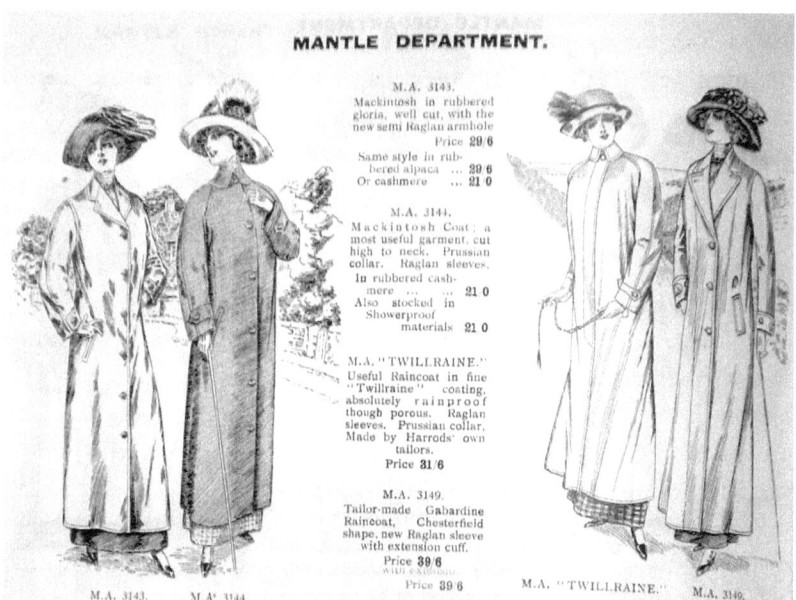

FIGURE 2.1 Women's mackintoshes sold through the *Harrods General Catalogue*, 1912. Although the women in the illustrations wear fashionable hats, the voluminous coats were labeled "useful" and did not constitute fashionable street wear. (Courtesy of the Harrods Archive, London)

to invite—a peculiar form of non-progression. These depictions of mackintoshes suggest that the coat became a trope to neatly figure the circumscription of personal choice by age or class. If the evening gown rose (and, as we have seen, often fell) because of the range of choices it mobilized, the mac renders adults a thing by highlighting a *lack* of choice: it turns a human subject into a type, an object that does not exercise agency and can be dealt with by more fortunate others.

For children, the mackintosh poses few problems. Beatrix Potter's *The Tale of Mr. Jeremy Fisher*, a sequel to her famous *The Tale of Peter Rabbit*, depicts the mackintosh as sound garb and, in fact, as nothing short of life preserving. In Potter's illustrated story, the title character, a frog, dons a mackintosh before going out to fish in the rain. The mac would have been regarded as appropriate sporting wear, so this choice seems unremarkable, a specific instance of Potter's general tendency to dress her animal protagonists in human clothes.[22] As the tale progresses, predator becomes prey, and a large trout swallows Fisher. Lest Potter's young readers fear, however, the narrator quickly reassures them: "[T]he trout was so displeased with the taste of the macintosh, that in less than half a minute it spat him out again." Fisher then pulls himself out of the water, "his macintosh all in tatters."[23] Potter pairs this description with an illustration that depicts the mackintosh with vertical tears, perhaps caused by the trout's sharp teeth. Although Potter avoids overt moralizing, the lesson of the tale seems clear: when venturing out, children should listen to adults and wear a mackintosh. It will protect them from rain and, perhaps, the larger dangers of the natural world.

The valorization of the utilitarian mackintosh for youth was reflected more broadly in illustrated newspapers of the early twentieth century. Older children wearing macs were depicted as having the plucky resolution to "carry on" in the face of Britain's notoriously wet weather. The *Sunday Pictorial* of November 21, 1926, included a photograph captioned, "Modern Gumboot Girls Don't Care: They Despise Rain's Dreary Drip." The accompanying text reads, "Rain doesn't frighten the modern girl—she just puts on [a] sensible raincoat and gumboots and 'doesn't care if it snows.' Here is a typical group at the women's hockey match."[24] Although the individuals pictured could be young women, the newspaper twice calls them "girls," a term that emphasizes youth, sport, and a cheerful attitude. Such news items, together with Potter's *The Tale of Mr. Jeremy Fisher*, frame the mac as eminently practical when worn by children or young adults. Fisher experiences a violent attack while wearing it, but the coat shields him from harm. More prosaically, the "gumboot girls" are protected from rain and snow. This protective quality, however, vanishes in representations of the mac worn by adults, who purportedly enjoy freedom of choice when it comes to attire. A practical coat becomes an object that de-individuates, a coat that only adults enslaved by common sense, and unable to be more subject than thing, would wear.

Rebecca West's novella *The Return of the Soldier*, for example, uses the mackintosh as shorthand for one character's poverty, which motivates her sartorial choices. In West's book, a British officer, Chris Baldry, forgets his adult life as the result of shell shock. His cousin Jenny, the novella's narrator, enables Baldry's daily visits with Margaret Grey, a woman living in suburban poverty whom Baldry loved in his youth. Grey's appearance is marked by her continual wearing of a "yellowish raincoat," which leads Jenny to reflect, "It would have been such agony to the finger tips to touch any part of her apparel."[25] Grey seems relatively untroubled by her appearance—if she recognizes her dowdiness, she is used to it—but the upper-class women in the book project characteristics and emotions such as "unpardonable" and "sick" onto her mackintosh.[26]

Grey's raincoat deftly captures her poverty and personal limitations, and through Jenny's descriptions and diction, West neatly illustrates the snobbery of her well-meaning narrator. According to Jenny, Grey "was repulsively furred with neglect and poverty, as even a good glove that has dropped down behind a bed in a hotel . . . is repulsive when the chambermaid retrieves it."[27] Later, Jenny describes Grey as "not so much a person as an implication of dreary poverty," a characterization that evacuates Grey's persona and history and makes her (and her coat) a perambulating, degraded figure for the class that would have been excluded from the luxurious world of Baldry Court before the war.[28] Like the glove that Jenny uses to signal Grey's physical decay, the yellowish mackintosh becomes "unpardonable" in part because it is out of place. As a result of the disruption caused by World War I, such dismal objects invade the world of the upper class, where servants might wear such garments but not visitors to the house.

While West clearly aligns the mackintosh with the dreary practicality that poverty necessitates, she also uses the garment to illustrate how upper-class women view those below them on the economic scale. The mackintosh prevents Jenny from perceiving Grey as an equal or, indeed, as human. During her most positive assessment of Grey's appearance, the narrator comes to see her shabbiness as akin to "the untidiness of a child who had been so eager to get to the party that *it* had not let the nurse fasten *its* frock."[29] Jenny's (or, rather, West's) choice of the word "it" instead of "she" is tactical: even though Grey displays superior understanding toward the end of the novella, her appearance and being are figured as less than fully feminine—indeed, as nonhuman—because of her mac.[30] In fact, the coat may be the cover that allows Margaret and Jenny to kiss (in the novel's famous line) "not as women, but as lovers do";[31] like the evening gown, the mackintosh has the power to queer those who wear it, subsuming gender and sexuality, however temporarily. At the end of the novella, when Baldry recovers his memory, Grey is reduced to a "figure mothering something in her arms."[32] She will have to return to her life of respectable poverty, a "figure" instead of a person. West's depiction of the yellowish raincoat constellates the mac with poverty and the ontological slide from person to thing. The mac works to anonymize and serialize Grey, an activity it will perform in novels throughout the next two decades.

Twenty years later, in his novel *Brighton Rock*, Graham Greene's murdering main character (alternately identified as "Pinkie" or "the Boy") watches as Rose, an impoverished waitress, approaches. Pinkie arranges to marry Rose after the unwitting young woman witnesses events that could incriminate him; Greene's male protagonist has no affection for his future wife—indeed, for anyone—and plans to kill her after he covers up a previous murder. As Pinkie "watched the girl as if she were a stranger he had got to meet," the narrator observes that Rose "had tricked herself up for the wedding, discarded the hat he hadn't liked: a new mackintosh, a touch of powder and cheap lipstick."[33] In this brief description, Greene makes evident Rose's desire to please her future husband. Her "touch of powder and cheap lipstick" signal an attempt to appeal to him even as they underline her poverty and unfamiliarity with makeup. It is, however, her "new mackintosh" (worn to a wedding!) that economically communicates her lack of style, impoverished state, and increasingly endangered position.

As Rose walks toward her future husband, the narrator observes that she has "tricked herself up" in the new mac. This phrase points to Rose's conscious decisions and actions—to her self-conscious effort to dress as well as possible. Greene's narrator, however, quickly shifts away from Rose's agency to how others, particularly Pinkie, see her: "She looked like one of the small gaudy statues in an ugly church: a paper crown wouldn't have looked odd on her or a painted heart: you could pray to her but you couldn't expect an answer."[34] Greene's language positions her, both for the reader and for Pinkie, as a tacky object; in figuring Rose as a statue, Greene strips her of movement, speech, and all trace of human agency. In her mac, she becomes less young woman than thing. This kind of process echoes Barbara Johnson's observation that "a person who neither addresses nor is addressed is functioning as a *thing*,"[35] a form of being that becomes clear as Greene's novel continues. Later, when Pinkie's lawyer asks, "And what is the little lady thinking?" it comes as no surprise that "she didn't answer him."[36] Rose remains silent after the wedding, letting her new husband speak for her and dictate her actions.

Although, in contrast to Margaret Grey, Rose is not regarded by upper-class characters, she is viewed through the lens of working-class men who consider themselves superior to her female sex, innocence, and greater poverty. Her mackintosh, like Grey's raincoat, becomes a focal point for human subjects who want to deal, not interact, with her. The mac thus captures and communicates an atmosphere of limited horizons, of problems of economic privation so acute that the poor seem less humans than objects. This type of representation of the coat remained prevalent right up to the outbreak of World War II. As late as 1939, George Orwell's *Coming Up for Air* aligns the mackintosh with the domestic hardships of the lower-middle class. At the conclusion of Orwell's novel, the protagonist, George Bowling, returns to a home pervaded with and characterized by the odor of the coat: "I fumbled with the key, got the door open, and the familiar smell of old mackintoshes hit me."[37] Bowling is soon enveloped in a spat with his wife, Hilda, and in the novel's final pages, the character (who also serves as the novel's narrator) returns to the smell of mackintoshes *four times*. Although no one in the scene wears a mac, the garment suffuses the family home, suggesting that the coat not only is a discrete object but confers a diminished way of being. As Bowling bids goodbye to the political speculation and the nostalgic memories of his childhood home that have consumed him for most of the novel, he concludes, "The old life . . . was fading out, all fading out. Nothing remained except a vulgar low-down row in a smell of old mackintoshes."[38] Here, the mackintosh does not turn a specific character into a thing, but Orwell's novel suggests that the coat comes to stand for the kind of life that Bowling and his ilk lead—the "common man's [and woman's] passivity and helplessness."[39] Along with West and Greene, Orwell implies that the mackintosh somehow infiltrates the homes, lives, and persons of those who live in or near poverty; instead of a garment that one might put on and take off, the coat creates an atmosphere in which characters find their choices so restricted that they hardly seem—or feel—like agentic beings.

Such examples deploy the mac to express the lack of choice faced by particular characters and, in Orwell's novel, in particular settings. The coat becomes a way to represent, and thus to think through, the de-individuating experience of poverty in Britain, which renders characters passive and vulnerable to the actions of others. Surprisingly, when an author places the garment on a privileged character, the coat's evacuation of agency similarly pertains. In *The Last September*, Elizabeth Bowen's novel about the waning days of the Protestant Ascendancy, the mackintosh at first seems simple and utilitarian. Lois Farquar, the young British ward of Sir Richard and Lady Naylor, wears the coat when driving and walking in the rain.[40] Because Lois is on the brink of coming of age, childish apparel seems appropriate. That she wears a mackintosh in the Irish countryside, and while driving and walking, also makes her seem to be properly attired, given the coat's history as a garment worn for sport.

As the novel continues, however, the mackintosh signals a kind of arrested development in its protagonist and the society that she represents.

As Jed Esty has noted, Bowen's novel depicts Lois's "balky nonprogress to adulthood" and portrays her as "frozen in her youth, stuck between cultures, hopelessly virginal."[41] Glamorous and mature characters, such as Marda Norton, get drenched in rainstorms and are chastised for going out without a mackintosh.[42] Marda, who moves into adult society and married sexuality when she leaves the Naylors' home, is the kind of character who does not wear a mackintosh; Lois, on the contrary, wears a coat that protects her from the rain but also embodies her lack of (hetero-)sexual passion and her refusal to become, or act as, an adult.[43]

In contrast to the childish mac that Bowen's "overgrown juvenile" wears, soldiers and Irish insurgents in her novel wear trench coats. This distinction, which is unique to Bowen, serves to highlight the contrast among the moribund Protestant Ascendancy, British soldiers, and Irish nationalists. Unlike Lois and the others in her set, characters in trench coats are purposeful; early in the novel, Lois hears "branches slipping against a trench-coat. The trench-coat rustled across the path ahead to the swing of a steady walker. She stood by the holly immovable . . . and there passed within reach of her hand . . . some resolute profile powerful as a thought."[44] The figure is unidentified, abstracted to the point that the coat alone seems to take action. Although a human body wears the coat (there is a profile), garment and wearer are inextricable, assembled as *one* thing. "It must be because of Ireland he was in such a hurry," Lois speculates; the trench coat thus underlines the abstraction of individual identity under the politicized violence dividing the country, where it is the cause (and not the man) that matters.[45]

The novel does not specify which side of the struggle this ghostly figure supports. Although Lois suspects that this trench coat cloaks a rebel, Bowen's novel pointedly depicts armed men—or, rather, armed coats—on both sides of the conflict. Later, Lois encounters another animated object: "[A] trench-coat flickered between the trees, approaching."[46] On this occasion, the man wearing the coat is particularized as Gerald Lesworth, a British soldier, but the coat moves and acts before Lesworth does. Indeed, Lois initially stares in the direction of the coat, unable to differentiate between Irish insurgents and British soldiers from a distance. A great deal rests on this distinction, given the violent attacks that take place at the novel's periphery, but through the trench coat, the novel constructs both soldiers and rebels as more alike than different. The soldiers and the insurgents are militarized, armed, and capable of violent acts. And both groups dispossess the Anglo-Irish: the insurgents bury guns on estate property and burn the great houses, but the soldiers constitute an "army of occupation" and are not entirely welcome. As Sir Richard opines, "This country . . . is altogether too full of soldiers."[47] Or, to follow the diction that Bowen uses elsewhere, it is altogether too full of trench coats—of men who function as things instead of as individuals.

Bowen's novel thus demonstrates the different ways the mackintosh transformed persons into things in the 1920s. In *The Last September*, the mackintosh confers a juvenile innocence, a child-like passivity, onto a character who might put on other garments and qualities. While West's, Greene's, and Orwell's characters cannot afford better outerwear, a woman of Lois Farquar's class could make different sartorial choices, and Bowen uses the coat to figure her protagonist's shortcomings. Arrested development is not the only quality put on with the mackintosh in *The Last September*, however; the coat also confers the anonymity inherent to military service. If they do not always efface the particular identity of individuals, mackintoshes trouble that identity by blurring distinctions between persons and even between the opposing factions of British soldiers and Irish insurgents. Although Lesworth briefly rises above his coat to exercise a degree of individual agency, the irony of *The Last September* is that readers have always known him to be on the losing side of the struggle the book represents. When Bowen's novel was published in 1929, the anonymous insurgents had already secured their aims with the establishment of the Irish Free State in 1922. The book thus suggests that it is occasionally *better* to be a thing than a person: the anonymous, resolute coat (unlike Lesworth and the other British soldiers in the novel) walked steadily to independence.

The Mackintosh at War

Bowen's use of the mackintosh in *The Last September* reflects her historical position, writing in the decade after the end of World War I. When macs were tailored and marketed for use at the front during the war, the biography of this garment took a dramatic turn; although waterproof coats had long been worn by soldiers, they had never been as ubiquitous—or as abundant—as they became between 1914 and 1918. One of the necessary items in any officer's "kit" was the trench coat, a long belted mackintosh cut differently for each branch of service.[48] Ordinary soldiers and female volunteers also wore such coats, though the cut and quality of individual examples varied, depending on the wearers' financial wherewithal.

The pervasive presence of trench coats during the war is well known, but at our historical remove, it is difficult to imagine the visual impact of the sheer proliferation of these garments. People saw men and women in mackintoshes everywhere: in the streets, at railroad stations, and in the newspapers. On December 24, 1916, for example, readers of the *Sunday Pictorial* would have seen the photograph of a member of the Women's Volunteer Reserve guiding soldiers, each figure attired in a mackintosh (figure 2.2). While there is some variation in appearance among the individuals, the coherence of their attire creates a group identity, one enhanced by the newspaper's decision not to provide names for either the volunteer or the soldiers. In their coats, they could be everyman (and everywoman)—or, at least, any British citizen of a certain age in 1916.

FIGURE 2.2 "A member of the Women's Volunteer Reserve acts as guide to the returned warriors," *Sunday Pictorial*, December 24, 1916, 1.

FIGURE 2.3 Detail of an advertisement for Phosferine, *Daily Telegraph*, July 5, 1917, 4. This promotion features a soldier in a mackintosh in the background as well as a picture of the man whose testimonial is quoted.

The trench-mackintosh reached iconic status as the coat appeared in advertising for products both associated with and far removed from the war. A promotion for war bonds in the *Daily Telegraph* on January 10, 1918, included a line drawing of a soldier in a trench coat "standing to" that pulled patriotic heartstrings and encouraged readers to give to the cause. Similar images also encouraged people to buy prosaic consumer products. Phosferine, a patent medicine for "nerves" and general conditioning, used a picture of a soldier in a mackintosh in a July 5, 1917, advertisement in the *Daily Telegraph* (figure 2.3). Although the text accompanying the photograph claims that Phosferine helped Private W. G. Amatt recover from shell shock, the advertisement depicts the very environment—and garment—associated with incurring this malady. Readers of advertisements would thus have seen the coat not only associated with protection, common sense, and grit, but also aligned with shell shock, wounds, and the violence that caused them.

While newspaper illustrations and advertisements for an array of products helped to connect the mac with the war, the firms that manufactured the coats were most responsible for keeping them in the public eye. These companies targeted their marketing to soldiers and civilians, and in so doing followed a nineteenth-century advertising tradition. As Brent Shannon has demonstrated, in Victorian advertising, "the most masculine—and therefore most popular—male figures were athletes and soldiers, and their presence was used to make even ostensibly gender-neutral products masculine and appealing to male buyers."[49] Soldiers thus helped to promote consumer goods by gendering them male, but the use of soldiers in advertisements that ran during the war had an additional effect. With coats marketed to and by officers and soldiers, consumer products generated a sartorial blending of home and front. This no doubt made wearers feel that they were materially aligned with the war; as Jennifer Craik has argued, uniforms are essential when nations and cultures want to emphasize group identity.[50] While trench coats were not identical, they were stylistically similar to one another and ubiquitous, thus producing a cohesive national style. In this respect, they were quite different from the evening gown: if it promised access to a singularity without limit, the wartime mackintosh offered a selfhood supported and mediated by a collective identity—a psychic structure premised less on individuation than on identification with others. To return once more to Simmel, the trench-mac demonstrates how omnipresent garments construct an "inner world" that reflects "the aspects of the external group governed by" the attire.[51]

The marketing of these coats helped to produce this national style by framing the same garments and makers as appropriate for both soldiers and civilians. In 1916, for example, the front page of the *Daily Mail* touted goods sold by Derry & Toms, including "Gentlemen's Raincoats," which are described as "suitable for military or civilian wear."[52] Such advertisements constructed a visual continuity between the trench and the city street through consumer goods. When Aquascutum described itself as "Military and Civil Tailors" in a Daly's Theatre program published in September 1916, readers would not have been surprised by the proximity of military and civilian models and modes (figure 2.4). The militarized

INTO AND OUT OF THE TRENCHES WITH THE MODERN MAC 83

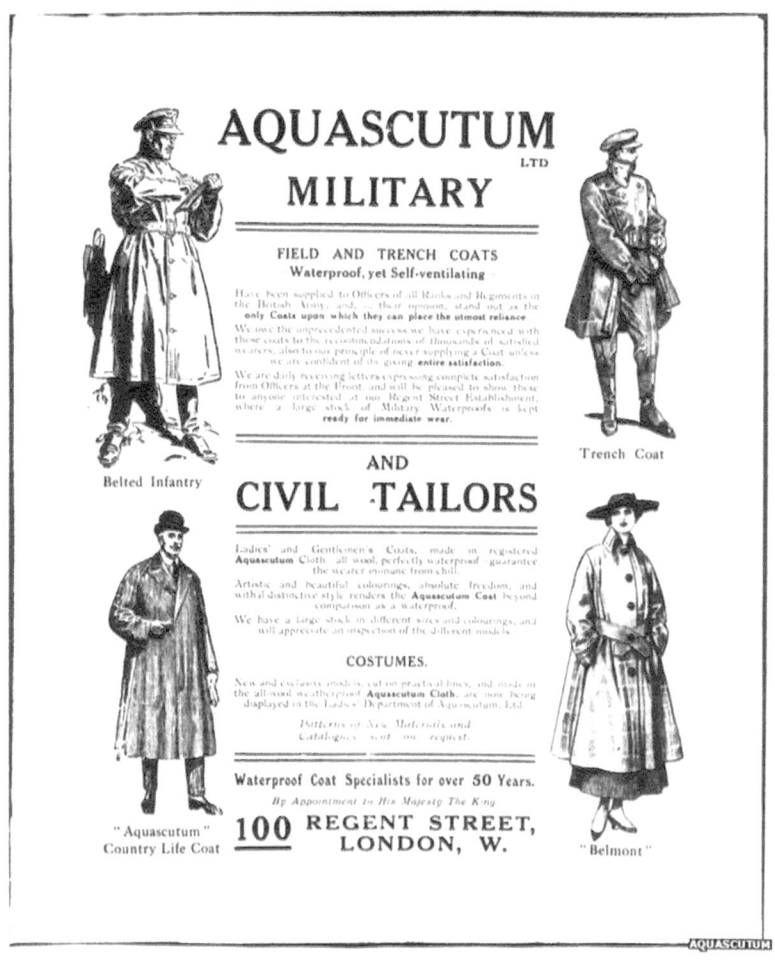

FIGURE 2.4 Advertisement for Aquascutum military and civilian coats, Daly's Theatre program, September 1916. (Courtesy of the Aquascutum Archive, London)

nation had a visual coherence created by clothing that aligned British bodies with one another.

Such conformity no doubt appeared unproblematic, the innocent desire of those back in Britain to model themselves on their "boys" and to look like they, too, were participating in the war effort. As Craik has argued, however, uniforms constitute one of the "central body techniques in the actualization of persona and habitus." Indeed, Craik sees this technique as so powerful that she questions, "Do people wear uniforms or do uniforms wear people?"[53] The marketing and wearing of the trench-mac conferred qualities otherwise aligned with officers and soldiers onto civilians. In retrospect, writers such as Virginia Woolf, James Joyce, Helen Zenna Smith (Evadne Price), and Dorothy L. Sayers would deploy the mackintosh to critique the militarism celebrated in such promotions; moreover, they would suggest that the coats themselves threatened the bodies and muddled the identities of those who wore them.

Each brand of military mackintosh had a range of strategies for promoting itself, but four general trends emerged during the war: firms celebrated the quality of the garments, cast the coats as suitable for all fronts and in all weathers, supplied testimonials that praised manufacturers for keeping men comfortable in the trenches, and suggested that the macs protected against all threats to the body of the wearers. In practice, these approaches often overlapped. I trace these advertising campaigns in some detail, in part because they are a component of this garment's history—what Elizabeth Grosz calls the thing's "'life' of its own"[54]—and in part to illuminate the narrative backlash against the mackintosh and its manufacturers after the war. Advertisements published in wartime aligned the coat with the very qualities, the very psychic processes, that writers would figure as dangerous in peacetime. If homogeneous appearance and protection from harm promised comfort and ease in a hostile environment, at peace, these qualities emerged as unappealing and as beacons of false promise.[55]

Because a number of manufacturers produced mackintoshes and trench coats, the firms vied with one another to position their garments as the best in quality. Burberry and Aquascutum, in particular, sought to create the sense that their coats were exceptional, worn by men of a certain caliber and class. Their promotional materials offer a glimpse of a world of privilege that some officers managed to enjoy even at the front. An Aquascutum ad that ran in *Punch* on April 18, 1917, quotes from a letter penned by an officer in German East Africa: "We are constantly having Tropical Rains, which wet one through in about two minutes. You will be pleased to hear that in spite of these awful storms, my 'Aquascutum' keeps me quite dry—when I am fortunate enough to have the native carriers near enough to get it."[56] This advertisement not only promotes the coat but aligns it with a class that enjoys "native carriers," whose burdens include the Aquascutum. Unlike the mackintoshes worn by children, child-like characters, and the poor in literary works of the period, this coat is worn by those who have servants to "do" for them. In the *Daily Telegraph*, Burberry similarly extolled its trench coats as maintaining "the highest Service tradition in point of smartness and distinction."[57] It might seem counterintuitive that looking stylish mattered to men four years into the war, but the advertisement positions the coat as a means to the end of an elevated, upper-class appearance. Burberry and Aquascutum were, and still are, invested in promoting themselves as distinctive, *luxe* brands, and wearing one of their coats communicated attention to sartorial detail under trying conditions.

These ads appealed to nonmilitary personnel as well as to soldiers because they present the garments as a class apart from more utilitarian mackintoshes. Although, as I suggested earlier, observers might not know that an individual was wearing a brand-name (and not a no-name) coat, the wearer himself would know, and the label thus served as a silent reminder of individual difference in a sea of conformity. A decade after the war, Helen Zenna Smith (the pseudonym of the popular author Evadne Price) would represent this association in *Not So Quiet . . . Stepdaughters of War*. Smith's text complements Erich Maria Remarque's *All Quiet on the Western Front* (1929) through a semi-biographical narrative about English women who work as ambulance drivers and cooks at the Western Front in France. Blimey, a working-class woman, buys a Burberry with her wages, and the coat plays a significant role in her personal transformation. For Blimey, a Burberry is a mark of her new earning power and class aspirations. The acquisition of a brand-name garment demonstrates that she has improved herself and can now aim for "distinction."

And yet, writing a decade after the war, Smith intimates that in putting on a Burberry, Blimey also puts on the generalized role of combatant. Even as the character selects a coat in a light shade to signal her individuality,[58] she purchases the same brand and type of garment worn by officers and other female war workers. This choice demonstrates the effective nature of Burberry's advertising, but the death that Smith metes out to Blimey implies that the coat materializes a particular fate along with the purported distinction it confers. The novel concludes with a horrific air raid in which bombs rain down on female volunteers as they shelter in a trench. In putting on a soldierly style, Smith suggests, Blimey also puts on a serializing identity that makes her vulnerable to a violent death. The narrator reports that "Blimey is bleeding from a wound in the arm . . . the blood is pouring from it." For her part, Blimey focuses on the marring of her coat and not on her injury: "'Now see wot's 'appened to me new Burberry, all covered in blood. Now see wot's 'appened to me new Burberry, all covered in blood,' she keeps muttering."[59] While these words are no doubt meant to communicate Blimey's shock as the result of a grievous injury, she focuses less on her wound (and impending death) than on the damaged commodity, which has facilitated and stands in for her wartime experience. When the narrator later reports her fate—"Blimey is unconscious from loss of blood. Her Burberry will never be any use again"[60]—the object's loss of "use" stands in for Blimey's loss of life. There is a human casualty here, but Smith's novel marks the terminal condition of the Burberry, a strategy that demonstrates the unity of person and garment (both so much material) in total war.

Not So Quiet. . . Stepdaughters of War deploys Blimey's Burberry to remind readers that the uniform identity materialized through such coats was hazardous. Although the character's final words (or, rather, her accent) remind readers of her individual history and working-class status, the novel's erasure of the distinction between (male) soldier and (female) cook reflects a broader truth about the way the coats were marketed. In addition to the emphasis on quality, other promotional campaigns conducted by the same firms suggest that the trench-macs erased individual identities, in part because numerous men (and women) in so many different places wore them. Advertisements thus aligned the mackintosh with the military and with the sacrifice of individuality required by military life. The marketing campaigns for trench-macs asserted that the same garment could be worn by anyone, anywhere, and thus this one coat might efface differences between the fronts, campaigns, and individuals fighting around the globe.

In these advertisements, illustrations work synergistically with text to represent the coat as universally needed and worn. In an ad in the *Times* on July 1, 1915, Burberry coats are said to "ensure advantages of the greatest value to Officers in France or Turkey."[61] This claim depicts the Burberry weatherproof as suitable for officers stationed on either front in any weather. The accompanying sketch shows a universalized soldier, whose face displays no remarkable features. Although he sports a small mustache, he is otherwise "any officer." This depiction allows readers to picture themselves in a Burberry, but it also points to a disquieting truth of military service: once at the front, officers and soldiers fill a place (occupy a coat), and it does not matter who or what they were before turning up with their war kits. The repetition of advertising images underscores this de-individuation. Each manufacturer had a limited number of illustrations it used to promote its coats in a given year; while the text of ads would change, the images would not, thus further effacing individual identities.

Such pictures also standardized "praise from the trenches" that manufacturers quoted from unsolicited letters. Most of the letter writers were not identified, though the advertisements promised that original documents to support the claims were available on request. While such letters asserted individual experiences and personalities, the illustrations accompanying them served to undercut the specificity of the writer's words. For example, a Burberry advertisement in the August 23, 1915, edition of the *Times* features a letter from J. K. Dunlop. Dunlop personifies his Burberry as "my best friend for some months in front of Ypres" because it both withstood "the rain and wind perfectly" and "seemed impervious to the filthy mud of the trenches."[62] Although Dunlop's testimony is replete with particulars of his time in the armed forces, there is no photograph to complement his words. Instead, the sketch that illustrates Dunlop's letter depicts an officer gazing stalwartly into the distance as he stands in a trench pelted with rain. The officer's face has nothing distinct about it—he may or may not look like Dunlop—and the coat therefore seems appropriate for *all* officers. In other words, the Burberry promotion works to homogenize individual experiences, which helps to cast its product as a garment that *any* officer on the Western Front could wear, a "best friend" to one and all in the trenches.[63]

Advertisements that feature "praise from the trenches" effaced differences among men, assembling identity through the clad body and advancing a collective, soldierly style. During wartime, the use of a satisfied, particular consumer to speak to and for the nation's combatants and noncombatants makes sense. As Jean Baudrillard argues, the uniform reflects "a structured, hierarchical society and seals like an emblem the ideological cohesion of a nation."[64] What is surprising, then, is that the same marketing strategies persisted after the war. In 1919, for example, readers of the *Illustrated Sporting and Dramatic News* were informed that the Aquascutum coat "kept out the rain during the blizzard at SUVLA BAY."[65] In postwar Britain, when ideological agreement was less consistent and widespread, dissident writers would seize on the garment as a sign of cohesion gone wrong.

During the war, the mackintosh could already be seen to track the costs of militarism. The collective struggle in which the coat displayed its merits was obviously a dangerous one. Because service at the front was uncomfortable and life threatening, the manufacturers of trench-mackintoshes touted the protective qualities of their coats. Burberry's advertisements must have been seductive, allowing consumers to fantasize that the right purchase might somehow help them beat the odds. The firm promoted its trench coats with language that casts the garments as a kind of armor. In an advertisement in the *Times* on July 16, 1915, for example, Burberry extolled its "Military Weatherproof" as "ALL-PROTECTIVE, no matter what the weather—rainy or cold, warm or temperate."[66] Although the immediate context for this claim is the weather, the advertisement suggests that the coat could protect against other dangers. Readers are told that the Burberry mac "ensures healthful security and comfort under each and every condition,"[67] a statement that, in retrospect, seems naïve about the conditions of trench warfare. As the war went on, Burberry dropped the "ALL-PROTECTIVE" claim, but other marketing campaigns contained similar rhetoric. On July 2, 1917, the *Daily Telegraph* published an advertisement that asserted, "From every front—from soldiers fighting in the desperate battles of France and Flanders, beneath the sweltering sun of Palestine and Mesopotamia, amongst the wind swept Balkan mountains, and in the miasmic depths of African jungle—comes the same consistent story of the perfect protection afforded by the Burberry."[68] This ad appears to acknowledge the difficult, and even deadly, conditions experienced by men at the fronts, but it promises "protection" in a context that covers not only weather but also "desperate battles." Purchasing and wearing a Burberry enabled consumers to materialize their wishful thinking. Buyers must have known that the coat could protect against only wet, dirt, and wind, but the desire for "perfect protection" against all threats was no doubt appealing.

Such advertisements made claims that would, over the course of time, come to seem incredibly disingenuous. And yet, other companies similarly promoted garments in terms that are shocking to the contemporary sensibility. The *Harrods Weekly Price List* for July 23–28, 1917, offered "Special Values in Weathercoats" named after battles. Both the "Somme," which was "cut after Cavalry pattern," and the "Meuse," a "Trench Coat, adapted for ladies, cut on service lines," were offered at sale prices (figure 2.5).[69] When one recalls that the Battle of the Somme, which was fought between July and November 1916, resulted in over 1.5 million casualties, and that Meuse is the department in France in which the Battle of Verdun (or "Meuse Mill"), also fought in 1916, took more than 250,000 lives, it seems incredible that a company would name coats after two of the bloodiest campaigns of the war. At the time, however, such names must have functioned like the "ALL-PROTECTIVE" claim; until people achieved historical distance from the war—a process in motion in the 1920s, when

FIGURE 2.5 "Special Values in Weathercoats," *Harrods Weekly Price List*, July 23–28, 1917. This circular features raincoats marketed to war workers who may have had contact with men wounded in the very battles these garments reference. (Courtesy of the Harrods Archive, London)

many novelists represented mackintoshes—such names and claims must have signified a determination to "carry on" despite the grim losses at the front. Advertisers banked on the emotional appeals of affording protection and of participating—if only through consumption—in the war effort. As Camilla Loew writes in her analysis of war posters, World War I was the first conflict in which women "had a right to . . . claim their experience as a part of war."[70] Harrods mackintoshes went even further and allowed women to *wear* the war: to lay claim to a kinship of experience that countered the purported incommensurability of men's and women's war work.

If the *Harrods Weekly Price List* and Burberry advertisements suggest that the mackintosh offered a mediated, material form of denial during the war, newspapers provided readers with ample evidence that the coat did not protect vulnerable bodies. On the same page of the *Times* of July 16, 1915, that carried the "ALL-PROTECTIVE" Burberry ad, readers saw several smaller classified notices for secondhand-clothing dealers. During the war, such dealers traded and advertised used uniforms, including, no doubt, trench-mackintoshes made by Burberry and Aquascutum. Used uniforms could have different provenances, but some of them undoubtedly came from bereaved families, who often received a loved one's kit after he died at the front. Vera Brittain's *Testament of Youth* describes reviewing her fiancé's belongings after they were returned after his death.[71] Many families kept their dead soldiers' garments as mementos, but given wartime shortages and economic necessity, garb in good condition was also sold to secondhand-clothing dealers or distributed among family friends. In other words, Britain's robust market for used clothing, as discussed in chapter 4, recommodified what may otherwise have remained family heirlooms. Brittain "never knew" what had happened to her fiancé's clothes,[72] but the classifieds suggested one possible destination for them.

Classified advertisements that ran throughout the war make the link between used coats and dead men even more direct. With the exception of the *Times*, these notices typically ran on the front page of daily newspapers, not toward the back, where they are located today. As a result, anyone picking up the paper would see these small announcements first. In many editions, advertisements for secondhand stores that dealt in used uniforms and trench coats were located, without evident irony, right next to the "Killed in Action" columns or appeals by charities that served wounded soldiers. The *Daily Telegraph*, for example, of January 5, 1917, published a call for used clothes by Salmon and Co. in the column next to "Killed in Action."[73] This unhappy juxtaposition was not unusual: on July 5, 1917, the *Telegraph* similarly put "Killed in Action" announcements right next to offers to purchase "Officers Uniform and All Effects" (figure 2.6). One might almost suspect the *Telegraph* of pacifism, but the newspaper was firmly conservative in outlook. Classifieds placed by Salmon and Co. and other secondhand-clothing dealers continued to promote their trade in officers' garments for years after the war ended, reminding readers of the business long after the armistice.[74]

Advertisements for trench-mackintoshes thus nestled cheek by jowl with reminders that such coats could not, in fact, defend against "all" the

INTO AND OUT OF THE TRENCHES WITH THE MODERN MAC 91

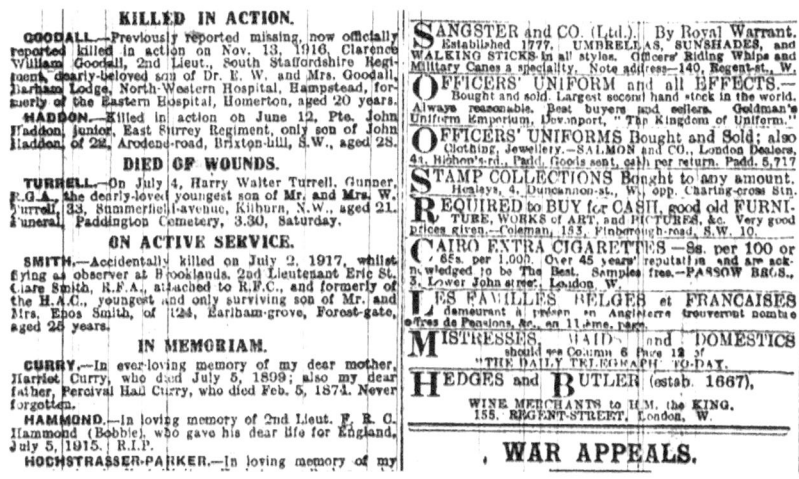

FIGURE 2.6 Detail of notices of men "Killed in Action" or "Died of Wounds" adjacent to advertisements for dealers in secondhand officers' uniforms, *Daily Telegraph*, July 5, 1917.

threats of the trenches. The garments could keep rain, wind, and mud at bay, but they could not shield against bullets, bombs, poison gas, and other weapons. In the years after the war, battlefield tourism and memorials helped to forge an association between violence and mackintoshes sold for use at the front; the garments themselves remained to testify to human bodies that lived and died wearing them. As Jane Marcus writes, "Blood-soaked ... coats are exhibited in the museum of World War I at Le Linge in Alsace."[75] The afterlife of such garments not only reminds museum visitors of the bodies that fought, were wounded, and sometimes died in their military macs, but also demonstrates that the object world often enjoys a permanence denied the human subjects who design, manufacture, purchase, and wear clothes. The mackintosh—in parallel with the black evening gowns that signaled mourning in the period—becomes a kind of memento mori in museums and in postwar texts, which frame the thing as *more* stable, *more* viable, than the human.[76] Although blood-stained coats lose their value as commodities—in contrast to secondhand garments, they are removed from circulation—they take on a new role as *muséal* objects and continue to have a use value denied their wearers. The death of Blimey, whose final words express horror at soaking her new Burberry with blood, serves as a fictional mirror for the men and women who died in macs that might memorialize but did not protect them.

Postwar Reflections and Transformations

The world of James Joyce's *Ulysses* seems a long way from Burberry advertisements, the *Harrods Weekly Price List*, and the battlefields of France. The novel, set as it is in Dublin in 1904, appears culturally and historically removed from World War I; Joyce's landmark aesthetic experiment seems equally removed from the war fiction of the 1920s and 1930s. As any student of modernism knows, however, *Ulysses* was written during the war and published less than four years after it ended. Joyce's man in the mackintosh (M'Intosh), who remains mistakenly identified throughout the book, has seemed to take no part in the text's historical moment, but his sartorial choice resonates with the slide from person to thing effected by the coat during the war.

Because the character is so oddly attired—he sports a raincoat on a sunny day during a drought—and because he is never identified by his proper name, M'Intosh has attracted the notice of many scholars. The arguments about this character are as heterogeneous as *Ulysses* itself, but they tend to fall toward two poles: those that claim that M'Intosh can be positively and correctly identified, and those that use M'Intosh as a lens into modes of understanding *Ulysses*.[77] Like the second cohort of critics, I do not think that Joyce's riddle can be solved. We can, however, explain why Joyce selected *this* garment for his character. Because the name of the garment *can* revert to a proper name—in Michael Sidnell's words, it is "an eponymous noun which is (unintentionally) made to revert to a proper one"[78]—the selection of the coat may appear self-explanatory. It represents a reversal of the process described by Cunnington at the outset of this chapter: instead of a person becoming a thing, a thing becomes a person. Or, rather, the name permits a person/thing assemblage, a character who is both a human (he has a history; he moves around the city of Dublin) and an object (it does not speak). Like the coats addressed earlier in this chapter, the mackintosh in *Ulysses* elegantly communicates the character's presumptive poverty: he eats dry bread, and his inexpensive garb manifests his limited means.[79] Most important, however, is a hitherto ignored reason that Joyce may have selected the mac for his silent, penurious mystery: the author uses the coat to suggest that the abstraction of human particularity enables men (and women) to be violently treated. If the savagery visited on Joyce's character is symbolic rather than literal, it is nonetheless striking and (within the world of *Ulysses*) permanent.

In "Circe," the dangers this garment poses to its wearer become most apparent. Leopold Bloom's wild fantasies of power and punishment include a group of sightseers who die after stating, "*Morituri te salutant.*" M'Intosh then appears through a trapdoor—a feature often used in medieval and Renaissance plays as a sign for a grave or hell—and accuses Bloom of being "the notorious fireraiser." When Bloom responds, "Shoot him! Dog of a christian! So much for M'Intosh!" he/it disappears with martial signs and rhetoric: "A cannonshot. The man in the macintosh disappears. Bloom with his sceptre strikes down poppies."[80] While the cannon shot does not apparently hit M'Intosh—he "disappears" but does not cry out or bleed—the character's appearance is juxtaposed with those who die saluting their leaders. In the aftermath of World War I, Joyce's representation of "cannonshot" and "poppies" (which were, of course, associated with the war dead because of the flower's prevalence in France) fuses the hybrid person/thing M'Intosh with World War I. Although Bloom thinks about the man in the mac later in *Ulysses*, M'Intosh disappears in this scene, which surely reminded readers in 1922 of the recent war and its attendant losses.[81]

As Robert Spoo has argued in his analysis of "Nestor," "Joyce's text, though ostensibly out of battle, is a neutral zone crossed and recrossed by rumors and phantoms" of the war.[82] The man in the mackintosh is one such phantom, his garment and "name" silent reminders of the militarism and death visited on millions of combatants. Equally important, M'Intosh speaks to the bizarre fusion of garment and wearer that the coat enacted; to wear the mackintosh, *Ulysses* suggests, is to give up individuation and human agency, however problematic and limited the latter may be. It is instructive to contrast M'Intosh with Leopold Bloom, who owns (but does not wear) a secondhand waterproof,[83] and with the epic's cast of characters who do not seem to possess a mac. By 1922, the garment must have seemed too threatening to wear, and Joyce's perambulating coat figured the way that individuals could disappear under the things they put on.

In the postwar period, when Joyce and the other authors I have mentioned wrote and published their novels, the mackintosh was making something of a comeback in serials that focused on fashion. The garment was still marketed to working-class customers as utilitarian; advertisements for this kind of mac generally emphasize its cheapness and value, as in promotions for John Blanford's inexpensive models in navy and fawn.[84] Although Mattamac, another firm that advertised mackintoshes, claimed that its coats were "identical in appearance with the usual five-guinea Weatherproof,"[85] the sales pitch for this class of coats focused less on quality than on low price.

If the working class had to make do with cheap mackintoshes, fashion columns demonstrate that those with money could look quite smart in their macs. These new coats, however, had to be carefully distinguished from the old mackintoshes. A striking number of columns acknowledge readers' preconceptions of the mac. *Eve* opened a discussion of "the modern conception of the old-time mackintosh" by observing, "Let us hope that history will not repeat itself, for it would be nothing short of a catastrophe to have to return to the drab, ill-fitting, evil-smelling garb of yore."[86] The rhetoric of history and catastrophe locates the mackintosh temporally, marking modern macs as distinct from previous iterations of the garment. And yet, this differentiating gesture was repeated on other dates and in other publications, indicating that the "old-time mackintosh" remained a vivid memory for many consumers. In 1929, the *Sunday Graphic*'s "Vogues and Vanities" column, which focused on upper-class society news as well as fashion, described the garment's transformation after first acknowledging its history:

> [T]hose of us who can remember the days when a waterproof was the last word in dowdiness were forced to "sit up and take notice" last week. On Wednesday it rained relentlessly at intervals on the Goodwood racing crowd. But . . . society merely slipped on its newest macintosh of rubberized velvet or silk in a gay plaid design, or a satin coat made rainproof by some secret process.[87]

In this column, the mackintosh is redeemed from being "the last word in dowdiness" through new fabrics, colors, and technologies. By distinguishing the coat from earlier incarnations, the mackintosh of the 1920s was cast as a fashionable, distinctive object.

In the 1920s and 1930s, then, the women's mackintosh was—with some labor—transformed at the level of consumer culture. At the same time, styles based on military coats continued to be popular for men *and* women. Even as the ready-to-wear and fashion industries framed some macs as stylish means of self-expression, there were reminders of the coat's alignment with World War I. In advertisements for mackintoshes modeled on military styles, allusions to the conflict could be indirect. The February 3, 1932, issue of British *Vogue*, for example, published a promotion for the "'Mosco' Mackintosh," which was "cut on the lines of a cavalry overcoat."[88] The reference to the cavalry in this advertisement signified perhaps no more than the style of the coat. In ads for Aquascutum weatherproofs, however, the war itself undergirded the brand; throughout the 1920s and 1930s, the firm traded on its garments' wartime "experience." An advertisement in the Early August 1923 issue of *Vogue* proclaimed that "in the Field of Sport women come to regard the Aquascutum Field Coat in the manners officers on Active service esteemed the Aquascutum Trench-coat—as a trustworthy bodyguard in worst of weather."[89] The personification echoes the description of trench coats as "best friends" during the conflict, positing an intimacy with material tested on the battlefield and subsequently available to all. The parallel between sports—specifically hunting, which would require a field coat—and war reminded readers of what men had worn at the front and advocated analogous garments for women's civilian use. An ad from the 1930s headed "The Famous 'Aquascutum' Storm Coats" similarly promoted military styles to men, particularly model G.9, which was "originally designed for the rigorous conditions created by trench warfare" (figure 2.7). More than a decade after the war, such language continued to align the mac with the front; the camion positioned in the background of the advertisement serves as a visual reminder that the coat, a *martial* thing, is uniquely available for civilian use. The Aquascutum coat thus emerges as a kind of sartorial monument: if women and men purchased it because similar garments had proved themselves during the war, daily acts of individual consumption were undertaken through a constellation of collective identity, trench warfare, and military technology.

Because consumers could buy everything from stylish velvet mackintoshes to storm coats in the decades after the war, writers of the 1920s and 1930s had a range of associations to choose from when clothing their characters in mackintoshes. And yet, very few authors chose to depict the coat—and the characters who wear it—as stylish, sporty, comfortable, or modern. More often, mac-clad figures look like *Mrs. Dalloway*'s Doris Kilman, who tutors the Dalloways' daughter, Elizabeth, and "year in year out" wears "a green mackintosh coat."[90] As Clarissa Dalloway speaks to Elizabeth, she senses Kilman's presence:

> [O]utside the door was Miss Kilman, as Clarissa knew; Miss Kilman in her mackintosh, listening to whatever they said.

FIGURE 2.7 Advertisement for "The Famous 'Aquascutum' Storm Coats," 1930s. A camion in the background visually references the history of this style, which had been designed for wear in the trenches. (Courtesy of the Aquascutum Archive, London)

Yes, Miss Kilman stood on the landing, and wore a mackintosh; but had her reasons. First, it was cheap; second, she was over forty; and did not, after all, dress to please. She was poor, moreover; degradingly poor.[91]

After Elizabeth and Kilman leave to go shopping, Clarissa muses about "love and religion," which she envisions as "clumsy, hot, domineering, hypocritical, eavesdropping, jealous, infinitely cruel and unscrupulous, dressed in a mackintosh coat."[92] The range of qualities that Clarissa projects onto Kilman—and specifically *into* her coat—points to the tutor's repulsive physicality, to Clarissa's upper-class distaste for the unfashionably dressed, and to Kilman's position as Clarissa's rival for Elizabeth's love and attention. If M'Intosh seems disembodied under his coat, Kilman's abject body is all too present, and her mackintosh underlines rather than disguises that abjection.

There are obvious reasons for Kilman to wear the coat, even if the weather makes it seem unnecessary. Like the characters penned by West, Greene, and Orwell, Kilman's poverty is materialized through the mackintosh.[93] She "could not afford to buy pretty clothes," so Kilman cannot make a striking, distinctive appearance. Instead of a silk or velvet mac, she is likely wearing something like the Blanford or Mattamac coat, in which case price is the garment's sole virtue. Like West's Margaret Grey before her, then, Kilman wears a coat that marks her as out of place in upper-class homes. When wealthy women criticize these characters' coats—Clarissa describes Kilman's appearance as inflicting "positive torture"[94]—such comments reveal as much about upper-class assumptions and values as they do about the women who wear the mackintosh.[95] Horrified reactions to the garment neatly emphasize divisions that neither class can bridge; if the war purportedly unified the nation, reactions to the mackintosh signal deep rifts in postwar unity. Moreover, while Margaret and Jenny kiss "not as women, but as lovers do,"[96] Kilman "genuinely loved" the "beautiful" Elizabeth Dalloway, wishing to "grasp her," "clasp her," and "make her hers absolutely and forever and then die."[97] The female body that is produced by the cheap mac can thus be regarded as queer; economic alterity necessitates the adoption of a garment that affords—or, rather, *produces*—a gender identity and sexuality at odds with the femininity and heterosexuality that Kilman finds out of her reach.

The qualities that Clarissa mentally attributes to the mackintosh indicate that it figures more than the garment's persistent class connotations. The coat makes Kilman appear clumsy and awkward in its expression of practicality. While a child might be expected to wear a mackintosh, an adult—particularly a woman—should have other values, whether they are "dress[ing] to please" or personal expression.[98] Although her pragmatic and authentic appearance no doubt contributes to the tutor's appeal to Elizabeth, Kilman herself "minded looking as she did,"[99] and her mackintosh is not so much an attempt to transcend fashion (or a bold assertion of a lesbian identity) as an admission of sartorial defeat.

The power of the negative qualities that Clarissa imagines "in a mackintosh coat" signals, furthermore, that the garment embodies the "cruel and unscrupulous" war that Virginia Woolf and the other writers discussed in this chapter, regarded as barbaric and wasteful. It is a reminder of the women and men, including Kilman's brother,[100] who died in their mackintoshes. As the sole character who wears such a coat—even the shell-shocked Septimus Warren Smith wears a "shabby overcoat" instead of a mac[101]—Kilman becomes a perambulating reminder of the war that most people wanted to forget.

No other garment could so succinctly mobilize the range of qualities that make Doris Kilman repulsive to Clarissa Dalloway. Kilman's child-like, unattractive appearance; anger and suppressed violence; and class status are all materialized in the mackintosh, which wears Kilman as much as she wears it. When Kilman stumbles into Westminster Abbey, which contains the "tomb of the Unknown Warrior,"[102] *Mrs. Dalloway* points toward the many traumatizing objects that continue to haunt postwar London. Kilman's coat suggests that the work of mourning continues, and is carried out, across time and space with the help of this one garment.[103]

Long-Lasting Legacies

Although the mackintosh would come to be associated with other qualities over time, it remained characterized, throughout the mid-twentieth century, by many of the traits I have discussed. What is, perhaps, most surprising about this persistence is that a range of texts aimed at quite different audiences deploy the mackintosh similarly. As I argued in chapter 1, there is continuity in representations of the evening gown across cultural strata, and yet feminist writers emphasized the potential pleasure that the garment offered in a manner that their contemporaries did not. The extent of agreement found in representations of the mackintosh is, therefore, striking, and it suggests a twofold rationale for British writers' figurations of the garment. World War I, as I have argued, helped to align the coat with battlefield experience and with the war more broadly; in the postwar period, representations of the mac point to a shared reaction against a thing that configured individuals as masses—a sartorial form reminiscent of a military effort that most Britons wanted to put behind them. Whether one regarded the war as a tragic waste or as a necessary endeavor, few were eager to return to the type of collective struggle in which the mac had emerged as a quasi-uniform.

Equally important, the early literary examples of mackintoshes were profoundly influential. Novels like *The Return of the Soldier* and *Ulysses* helped to configure the mac into a garment that uniquely complicated the relationship between person and thing. Such works are particularly good examples of Rita Felski's argument that "the significance of a text is not exhausted by what it reveals or conceals about the social conditions that surround it. Rather, it is also a matter of what it makes possible in the viewer or reader—what kind of emotions it elicits, what perceptual changes it triggers, what affective bonds it calls into being."[104] In highlighting the limited agency that characters in the coat can exercise, as well as their loss of identity, such representations provided later authors with a topos of the coat as diminishing singularity. In her popular novel *Rebecca*, for example, Daphne du Maurier deploys this model even as she extends the coat's de-individuation into the private home. The young second wife of Maxim de Winter suspects that the spirit of Maxim's first wife, the shadowy, glamorous Rebecca, "was in the house still . . . ; she was in that room in the west wing, she was in the library, in the morning-room, in the gallery above the hall. Even in the little flower-room, where her mackintosh still hung."[105] Rebecca's coat testifies to its former wearer's life and death, and the narrator observes that the mackintosh also opens a portal between the two women: "Perhaps I haunted her as she haunted me. . . . The mackintosh I wore, the handkerchief I used. They were hers. Perhaps she knew and had seen me take them."[106] The coat and handkerchief emerge as foci for a silent, mutual regard. Equally important, the mac suggests that it and other objects enable a succession of women whose personalities are poles apart. In a novel that focuses on the differences between the narrator and Rebecca, the mac serves to underscore parallels between the two characters. Although the wife of Maxim de Winter could easily afford to purchase a new mackintosh, du Maurier chooses the (used) item to communicate the novel's sense that humans are constituted by objects that render them not so much singular as sequential.

Graham Greene, in *The Third Man*, also represents the coat in a manner that underscores his dialogue with the mackintosh topos. The British military police officer Major Calloway appreciates the anonymity of his costume, which allows him to attend a funeral as "just a man in a mackintosh."[107] Like Joyce's M'Intosh, who receives his moniker in a report on Paddy Dignam's funeral, Greene's character wears the coat to witness a burial, but he strategically adopts the mac to blend into the group of mourners. Greene (and Calloway, who himself seems to have read *Ulysses*) inherits and deploys the tradition that the coat conferred anonymity and was associated with funerals, mystery, and violence.[108] Published after World War II, Greene's novel proposes that particular individuals might *embrace* the very qualities that seem troubling in *Ulysses*; Calloway is nothing more than a "man in a mackintosh" to facilitate an investigation, and while he does not become the thing, as M'Intosh does, it is perhaps because he understands the implications of his dress.

In these examples and others, the mackintosh rises above the inertia ascribed to the object world to suggest that, at a time of ongoing class differences punctuated by total war, characters find themselves at the mercy of their clothes. This quintessentially British garment emerges across a range of texts—including high modernism, "hard-boiled" crime fiction, middlebrow best sellers, and the condition-of-England novel—as a place to meditate on the collectivizing powers of particular garments. Representations of the mac highlight, and often intimate concern about, a person's inability to halt his or her own objectification: James Joyce's man in the mac becomes M'Intosh; Helen Zenna Smith's female noncombatant wearing a Burberry falls victim to the bombs dropped on male soldiers; Elizabeth Bowen's Irish rebels seem less men than animated coats. While the fashion press and advice columns of the period insisted that British citizens could choose from a range of fashionable macs—that men and women could look distinctive, stylish, and modern—fiction repeatedly took up the coat to reflect a lack of choice and even to suggest that the premise of human agency (on which the notion of choice rests) is mistaken.

As Alison Clarke and Daniel Miller have argued in their work on fashion and anxiety, dress transcends "the idiosyncrasies of individual agency, instead operating as manifestations of socialization and power relations."[109] Writers represented the mackintosh to manifest such relations, to articulate a time and place in which bodies were standardized and de-individuated. The coats were worn by some people who could transcend their social roles: when *Punch* ran a poem called "Happiness" in its June 18, 1924, issue, it depicted a little boy named John who had a "Great Big / Waterproof / Macintosh."[110] John would clearly grow up, and macs would stop being the very stuff of pleasure and fun. Most characters whom authors dress in the mac are, however, less able to move out of the places that fix them. Servants, the poor, soldiers, and officers had little opportunity to assert an individual agency. Such characters—in contrast to Charles Macintosh, who secured a type of fame and futurity through the coat that bears his name—become less persons than things in plots that emphasize inequality, straightened circumstances, and extreme physical vulnerability.

Only occasionally do characters get to decide whether they will wear such an overdetermined (and overdetermining) garment. This is the choice that Dorothy L. Sayers offers to her detective protagonist, Lord Peter Wimsey, in the mystery *Unnatural Death*. Like her contemporaries, Sayers was clearly willing to align characters in the coats with anonymity and violence: in both *Unnatural Death* and *Whose Body?* (1923), murderers wear the mackintosh to evade capture and to dispose of corpses, respectively. Given such examples, it is no wonder that Wimsey, a shell-shocked veteran of World War I, refuses to wait for his friend and brother-in-law, Chief Inspector Charles Parker, to don rain gear in the middle of an investigation, asserting, "No, Charles, I will *not* wait while you put on a Burberry."[111] Wimsey's dedication to solving crimes, and his desire to discover where the next clues will lead, renders him too impulsive and passionate to care about something so plebian as a little wetting. Sayers's character is particularly mindful that garments can transform the person wearing them. He is, moreover, all too aware of what can happen when wearing a Burberry. The mackintosh (and its upmarket translations) illumines the garment realm as remaking men and women into undifferentiated masses where they were dismissed, disparaged, and killed in numbers. Their coats sometimes survived to testify to the fragility of human bodies, which moved (and continue to move) through an object world seemingly only partially of their, and our, own making.

3   Aspiration to the Extraordinary

Materializing the Subject Through Fancy Dress

The evening gown and the mackintosh offered different lenses to writers seeking to explore the relationship between people and the things they wore. The evening gown provided a seemingly appealing sartorial form to middle- and upper-class women eager to enjoy the pleasure of individualizing, bespoke dress. Fiction and nonfiction of the period suggests, however, that the gown's articulation of a range of negative gender roles denied many wearers a sense of control and self-expression; whether the gowns invoked a "world of mourning" or a lost venue for aesthetic pleasure, writers position the garment as yoking women to a material array that assembled not confident, attractive subjects but things that were embarrassed, saddened, and viewed with cynicism.

The mackintosh seems worlds apart from the evening gown, which was exemplified by leisure and expense. A coat that was, for many years, associated with the poor and the dispossessed, it became a trope for the loss of individuality, for exposure to violence, and even for death. The mac came to serve as a reminder of the object world's surprising persistence and thus its contrast to the fragility of human bodies. If evening gowns assembled women in ways that turned them into abject things, mackintoshes *dis*assembled individuals: in the best cases, humans become masses; in the worst cases, they become corpses.

In this chapter, I take up the fancy-dress costume, which highlights the relationship between self and surface. Fancy dress holds out and withholds the promise that one can be what one wears. Like the evening gown, it proffers access to idealized subjectivities assembled through the cooperation of persons and things; like the mackintosh, it demeans because it refuses to cooperate—to work in harmonious assembly—with those who wear it. That only a very few literary characters can transcend their ordinary selves through fancy dress—indeed, that only *two* literary characters can abandon all pretense to an ordinary self—reveals a significant point of agreement across writers of modernist and popular fiction: only the very wealthy, extraordinary individual can manipulate a material world in which the self *is* the surface. While the repeated representations of fancy dress suggest that writers were intrigued by new models of the self that might be activated through clothing, such models seldom materialize. To be modern seemingly meant the desire for a flexible identity that remained out of reach for most Britons.

Fancy dress was a prevalent form of early-twentieth-century entertainment, a pervasive sartorial practice that made its way into cartoons, fiction, films, advice manuals, dancing guides, and other print media. The popularity and representation of fancy dress in the twentieth century has received little scholarly attention. Terry Castle, who writes about British masquerade practices in the eighteenth century, argues that masquerade had become marginalized in fiction by the turn of the twentieth century, when costume moved into "minor . . . subgenres such as the detective novel or the Harlequin romance type of pulp fiction."[1] While I will examine one text that fits this description (Dorothy L. Sayers's *Murder Must Advertise*, which Castle briefly mentions), I challenge her claim on two counts: by discussing a range of texts in which fancy dress features and by rejecting the assumption that the presence of fancy dress in popular work qualifies as marginalization.[2]

Before proceeding, however, a brief definition of what may seem a baggy term is in order. The *OED* defines "fancy dress" as "a costume arranged according to the wearer's fancy,"[3] which suggests that fancy dress is limited by only the wearer's imagination and originality. In the early twentieth century, fancy-dress balls and parties were largely invitation only and attended by social equals, whose costumes did not serve as genuine disguises. A costume did not leave the wearer's personality behind but temporarily infused his or her appearance with historical, artistic, or creative properties. In other words, fancy dress was intended to catch the eye and to encourage audiences to view the self *differently* without, generally, obscuring the identity. One late-nineteenth-century example, a costume worn by George J. Nicholls, is illustrative. Nicholls dressed as a side of bacon for the Covent Garden Fancy Dress Ball in April 1894, at which he won first prize for his costume (figure 3.1).[4]

FIGURE 3.1 George J. Nicholls dressed as a side of bacon, a costume that he designed, for the Covent Garden Fancy Dress Ball, April 1894.

The photograph makes plain that those who knew Nicholls would have been able to identify him; while his Dadaesque costume envelops his body, his face is uncovered. This image has appeared in many humorous posts on the Internet, but fancy dress allowed Nicholls—then a young man entering the grocery and provisions trade—to embody his love of bacon, a love so great that he would write the book *Bacon and Hams* in 1917. The costume thus emerges as a materialization of career aspirations, and Nicholl's choice to dress as a thing—indeed, as meat that used to be alive—also demonstrates the way that fancy dress enabled people to play with the idea of being something other than human. Nicholl's costume at once materializes his thoughts about his profession and covers an agential, thinking being in the guise of inert flesh.

Like the evening gown, fancy dress was normally worn by members of the upper and middle classes. Fancy dress could be rented, purchased at major retailers (such as Harrods), or bespoke, and men and women could adopt a popular type (such as Pierrot), a historical character, a place, an era, or an abstract idea. As articles and advertisements in fashion periodicals and newspapers suggest, fancy dress seemingly offered Britons a wide range of lenses to place over their normal identities— to enhance, but not disguise, their everyday appearance and persona. In the periodical press of the day, fancy-dress costumes emerged as the supreme sartorial form for projecting an idealized self, one that would be free from the quotidian demands of social norms and practicality that governed many garments.

While magazines and advice manuals celebrate the creative possibilities that fancy dress offered wearers, many novels and cartoons instead depict those in costumes as at the mercy of their clothes. Writers who aimed at a popular audience used fancy dress to reinforce the difference between subjects and objects—between persons and things. Current theoretical work complicates this binary; for example, anthropologist Daniel Miller argues that "there is no true inner self. We are not Emperors represented by clothes, because if we remove the clothes there isn't an inner core. The clothes [are] not superficial, they actually [are] what made us that we think we are."[5] Miller's work (and that of others) places an emphasis on the power of things, which work in harmony with persons to materialize a self. In this kind of argument, things play an active role; there is no opposition between subject and object but a profound synthesis between the two that we call the self. What we see in most early-twentieth-century work, however, is a *rejection* of this hypothesis; in the majority of the examples I discuss in this chapter, subject and object remain distinct and often at odds with each other.

The uneasy laughter and outright anxiety experienced by many British characters in fancy dress insist that people *are* more than what they wear. Most representations of fancy dress depict costumes as emphasizing (through correspondence or contrast) the existing qualities of the characters wearing them. Wealthy characters are what they wear, but this is less a sign that they have transcended their everyday identities than a materialization of upper-class vanity, perversity, and immodesty.[6] And middle-class characters fare no better; the aspirations captured in their fancy dress repeatedly fall short because they simply cannot become the costumes they adopt. After examining how popular forms maintain depth ontology—the belief that a self is located somewhere "inside" an individual—in the face of the potential challenge of fancy dress, I turn to two novels that celebrate the potential of persons to become things or, rather, to become *different* persons with the help of things. Virginia Woolf—herself immersed in a social circle where fancy dress was common—learned from fancy dress an appreciative and flexible understanding of the relationship between self and clothing that is reflected in *Orlando*. Woolf was not alone in creating a protagonist who can be what she wears. In *Murder Must Advertise*, Sayers similarly endows Lord Peter Wimsey with the uncanny ability to enjoy multiple selves through costume. In these two works, different in both cultural register and genre, fancy dress inspires ontological experiments that look ahead to postmodern models of identity. At the same time, the radical experiments are limited by a shared sense that aristocratic birth, wealth, education, and talent are necessary to evade depth ontology: fancy dress proffers a self that may be all surface, but only a limited number of characters get to enjoy the pleasures that such selfhood supplies.

If the 1920s and 1930s were the zenith of fancy dress, the 1940s and 1950s were its nadir. The few examples that emerged in this period are colored by nostalgia for prewar life. Doubtless, the wartime economy and postwar shortages made the idea that one could have clothing simply for "dressing up" a pleasurable fantasy. As with secondhand clothes, total war rendered the relationship between self and garment less troubling than it had been. Such historical shifts position the first half of the twentieth century as a particularly vivid moment during which writers, and their contemporaries, trained their eyes on the relationship between persons and garments.

An Epidemic of Fancy Dress

With the exception of the war years, the first four decades of the twentieth century witnessed a boom in the popularity and widespread use of fancy dress. This category of garb was not, of course, invented in the period; as Castle notes in her study of eighteenth-century masquerade, fancy dress first became popular in the 1720s. The masquerades that Castle writes about mixed social classes of participants who wore costumes that disguised their identities and features, but in the late eighteenth century, "these festivities were brought into the home and became part of the family's private life."[7] In part, the abandonment of public fancy-dress parties stemmed from the criminality and loose moral behavior that the disguises promoted. Costume balls again became socially respectable in the mid-nineteenth century only because of Queen Victoria's enthusiasm for historical costumes that did not conceal the wearers' faces.[8] Nanette Thrush argues that Victoria and her court used historical costumes "to differentiate their interest in 'fancy dress' from the licentious masques of the seventeenth and eighteenth centuries."[9] By flavoring fancy dress with educational and cultural virtues, upper-class Victorians were able to add costume parties and balls to a season's social events. As time went on, and as the middle class also warmed up to fancy dress, other types of costume became common, though historical fancy dress remained popular.

The nineteenth century witnessed the social redemption of fancy dress, but the twentieth century most widely embraced the costuming craze. Dress historians Anthea Jarvis and Patricia Raine observe that "in the years immediately preceding the First World War the wearing of fancy dress reached near epidemic proportions."[10] The outbreak of the war temporarily decreased the occasions for which fancy dress was thought to be appropriate—Jarvis and Raine note that "the anxieties and economies of wartime soon put a halt to its more frivolous aspects, although throughout the war pageants and *tableaux vivants* played an important part in raising funds for war charities"[11]—but what remains noteworthy from our historical vantage point is the presence of fancy dress in explicitly military venues. For example, some interned British *and* German soldiers were allowed to hold fancy-dress parties to help pass the time in captivity. The *Illustrated Sunday Herald* reported on a "Fancy Dress Ball for Germans" on April 11, 1915. According to a guard at one Irish prison, the German internees had "a fancy dress ball, at which they dressed up as Red Indians, clowns, Jack Johnsons, squaws, ballet girls, cowboys, etc."[12] Fancy dress was considered appropriate for soldiers no longer on active duty as well as their captors. In contrast, civilians were never able to enjoy fancy dress *unless* it were under the guise of war work. The *Illustrated Sunday Herald* column "Through the Eyes of a Woman" reported that "a dreadful rumour got about that the frivolous Lady X had given a masked ball, but she had only asked a few friends to bring their pet brands of respirators so that she could choose one for her husband's regiment."[13] The continued presence of fancy dress—and references to it—during the war years indicates how prevalent and widely embraced fancy dress had become by the second decade of the twentieth century. And after World War I, as Jarvis and Raine simply state, "there appeared to be no escape from fancy dress."[14]

In the 1920s, periodicals depicted fancy dress as pleasurable, fashionable play. As British *Vogue* reported on July 25, 1928,

> Never has London suffered such an attack of costumitis. Not content with the costume balls that crowd every night . . . addicts stray into other people's "plain clothes" dances. Thus, at Dorchester House (the Last Ball at), a highly decorous and distinguished company, trying to recover discarded pre-war grandeur, were startled by an invasion of wild monkeys from Lady Hillingdon and Mrs. Gerard Leigh's joint ball.[15]

Vogue elsewhere offered stylish fancy-dress suggestions so its readers would be inspired to range beyond "wild monkeys." For example, the article "By Their Fruits and Flowers Ye Shall Know Them," published in the Late January 1923 issue, suggests costumes such as "Citron" and "Pineapple."[16] These types of pieces underline the high premium placed on original fancy dress, and while *Vogue* aimed at an upper-class readership, other periodicals ensured that less-well-off Britons could make their own fancy dress. *Weldon's Patterns* was just one of several publications that provided designs for costumes, including one for "records" that was popular with young women in Blackpool in the 1930s.[17]

Fancy dress was, moreover, addressed by advice manuals, which guided readers in how to adopt an appropriate costume. In his book *How and What to Dance*, Geoffrey D'Egville urges "both sexes to take into consideration their personal characteristics, such as build, complexion, colour of hair, etc., before selecting their costumes. Incongruities such as a short stout man with glasses disguised as Mephistopheles, or a tall

Spanish-looking lady as Little Red Riding Hood are absurd."[18] Such books offered help but also highlighted the challenge of selecting an appropriate costume, a challenge that became the subject of many jokes in popular novels and cartoons. If D'Egville's suggestions did not provide enough guidance, Britons could seek out a copy of Ardern Holt's *Fancy Dresses Described: or, What to Wear at Fancy Balls*, first published in 1875 and reissued in six editions through 1900. The book's introduction (subtitled "But, What Are We to Wear?") informs readers that they could find "several hundred" suggestions in the volume, in addition to guidance on decoration, dances, hairdressing, and other topics. Holt offers ideas that range from "Alphabet" to "Charles I, Period" to "Zenobia." Those who desired historical accuracy and a British origin in their fancy dress could turn to Mrs. Charles H. Ashdown's *British Costume During XIX Centuries (Civil and Ecclesiastical)*, which drew on manuscripts, tomb effigies, and other sources to offer, for example, details about the appearance and construction of men's tabards during the reign of Edward II.[19] Holt urged her readers "to study what is individually becoming to themselves, and then to bring to bear some little care in the carrying out of the dresses they select, if they wish their costumes to be really a success."[20] Ashdown, for her part, regretted the "painful anachronisms" occasioned by historically incorrect costumes.[21] Such descriptions underline the work as well as the pleasure that went into selecting and wearing a fancy-dress costume.

Depending on a person's wherewithal, fancy dress could be made at home, rented, purchased off the rack, or bespoke. Companies like Clarkson's rented and styled costumes, and visits to the famous shop were chronicled in *Vogue*.[22] The department store Debenham and Freebody partnered with Holt and advertised that "any of the Dresses described in [her] book can be made to order."[23] Not to be outdone, Harrods offered its own selection of costumes, as evidenced by *Fancy Dresses at Harrods*, a catalog published in November 1927 that illustrates fancy dress for men, women, and children. The costumes, which could be purchased, ranged from the elaborate, such as the "Turkish Delight" guise shown on the cover, which cost 11 guineas, to the basic (figure 3.2).[24] All the costumes in this catalog were quite high end; the least expensive was a men's "Jazz Clown" outfit, which was an "economical" 18 shillings and 6 pence, still outside the budgets of most British consumers.

Such advertising materials provide evidence of the range of options in the period; other sources give a sense of what people actually wore. Some fancy-dress balls were amply documented, both by reporters and

FIGURE 3.2 The "Queen of Hearts," "Turkish Delight," and "Merry and Bright" on the cover of the catalog *Fancy Dresses at Harrods*, November 1927. (Courtesy of the Harrods Archive, London)

in photograph albums published to commemorate the events. Among the most lavish was undoubtedly the Devonshire House Ball, which was held in 1897 to celebrate Queen Victoria's Diamond Jubilee.[25] Fabulous costumes, such as Lady Arthur Paget's gem-encrusted rendition of Cleopatra's attire (made by the couturier Worth),[26] communicated the wearer's wealth and standing and support Thrush's point that fancy dress often "went far beyond modern conceptions of costume to a level of extravagance that is nothing less than stunning" (figure 3.3).[27] Paget's "oriental" costume, which gave her the chance to pile on the gems, demonstrates that fancy dress could serve as an occasion to display one's wealth beyond that offered by the ordinary evening gown.

The costumes of wealthy men and women were also documented in society columns and the fashion press, such as a photograph of Lady Abdy that was published in the August 22, 1928, issue of *Vogue* (figure 3.4).[28] Although this is but one example of a twentieth-century fancy-dress costume, its spectacular nature and its appearance in *Vogue* provide insight into the heights to which fancy-dress wearers might aspire. According to the caption, Abdy's costume represented "sea mist: large amber coloured balloons shrouded in a cloud of grey and green tulle rise from the waist and float about the silver cockleshell head-dress."[29] In large part, this specific spectacle warranted the attention of *Vogue* readers because Abdy had selected a creative and unique natural feature to portray; the bespoke origin of Abdy's costume—the originality of her dress—made it worthy of this profile. Abdy's fancy dress, moreover, employed a contemporary fashion vernacular: the *moyen âge* line of her costume was stylish for evening wear in the late 1920s and had been popularized by the French designers Jean Patou and Coco Chanel, among others. Abdy's gown and inspiration, therefore, suggest two important challenges to appearing in fancy dress: the selection of an appropriate, and appropriately unusual, idea for the costume, and the integration of contemporary styles into it. Discussion of Abdy's costume would not be complete without considering one of her most notable accessories: the cockleshell hat. This arresting headgear proclaims the wearer's mastery of modernity through its evocation of a shell as an architectural, not a realist, form. Abdy was crowned with a construction reminiscent of the Eiffel Tower and of the bones of skyscrapers going up in cities around the world; her costume thus referenced the natural world through ultra-modern styles and materials. This costume thus proclaimed the wearer's creativity, wealth, and aristocratic status while highlighting her personal beauty; from our historical vantage point,

FIGURE 3.3   Lady Arthur Paget dressed as Cleopatra for the Devonshire House Ball, 1897. (© Victoria and Albert Museum, London)

the photograph also demonstrates the high stakes involved in achieving a creative, flattering costume.

As this brief introduction to fancy dress has demonstrated, the wearing of costumes was widespread among the middle and upper classes, and the costumes could be spectacular. They offered an outlet for creativity and fun—as *Fancy Dresses at Harrods* enthuses, "Dressing up! . . .

FIGURE 3.4 Lady Abdy dressed as "sea mist," *Vogue*, August 22, 1928. (George Hoyningen-Huene / Vogue; © The Condé Nast Publications Ltd.)

What fun masquerades are!"[30]—but they also demanded a fair degree of money, taste, and time if they were to be a success. Writers in the early twentieth century repeatedly took up fancy dress, doubtless because it was such popular garb both before and after World War I. Their attitude toward such dress speaks, however, less to the pleasure that such garments offered wearers than to the genre's inability to make wearers anything other than what they were. While readers catch glimpses of fancy dress's aspirational qualities—of the hope that costumes may assist individuals in transcending their everyday selves—such yearning is more often punished than realized. Moreover, on the rare occasions when a transformation is effected through fancy dress, it is not the transformation that the characters desire. These types of representations emphasize the immobility of Britons in an interwar class society; whereas some characters gain access to garments and accessories formerly out of their reach, punishment for wearing aspirational fancy dress reminds readers that class was not only an economic but a social hierarchy that few could transcend.

Being "Natural Always": Middlebrow Representations of Fancy Dress

British authors who wrote for a popular audience deployed fancy dress to highlight the relationship between persons and the things they put on. Although I examine an exception at the end of this chapter, the majority of such works use costume to reinforce depth ontology—the idea that a self is located deep within a person's psyche or being. The class of the characters depicted in middlebrow works plays a significant role in how fancy dress is inflected: wealthy characters wear fancy dress that materializes their negative traits, while middle-class (and the very occasional working-class) characters are mocked for wearing costumes that cannot conceal who they "truly" are. The sheer number of characters who appear in fancy dress suggests that the practice of costuming raised profound questions about the potentialities of clothing: Can a person enhance or otherwise alter his or her identity through a "simple" change of attire? The answer, in texts that extend from cartoons in *Punch* to novels by E. M. Delafield, P. G. Wodehouse, and Evelyn Waugh, is a resounding no. While most of these authors treat fancy dress lightheartedly, their repeated rejection of the aspirations embodied in this form betrays a collective disquiet about the potency of things, which may work in assemblage with a person and, in so doing, change who that person "really" is. The rare works in which a character *is* changed through wearing a costume configure the experience as a cautionary tale: they suggest that such a transformation is not that to which the wearer aspired. Together, such examples demonstrate what Faye Hammill has called a key quality of the English middlebrow—its lack of pretension[31]—and suggest that fancy dress punished pretentious characters of all classes.

Middlebrow fiction of the period consistently mocks wealthy characters and "intellectuals" whose fancy dress serves to emphasize their negative traits. Delafield's *Diary of a Provincial Lady*, for example, concludes with a party at which some guests wear fancy dress. The host, snobbish Lady B., receives her guests "in magnificent Eastern costume, with pearls dripping all over her, and surrounded by equally bejewelled friends."[32] When she "smiles graciously and shakes hands without looking at any of us,"[33] readers can infer that Lady B.'s vanity and sense of social superiority are reflected in her costume. Delafield's social satire takes aim not only at the local aristocracy (who fancy themselves Eastern potentates) but also at self-professed intellectuals who similarly adopt costumes that materialize an inflated sense of self-worth. The narrator is "greeted by an unpleasant-looking Hamlet, who suddenly turns out to be Miss Pankerton."[34] Pankerton's highbrow pretensions and domineering personality are perfectly captured by her Hamlet costume, which offers not a gender-bending take on identity (à la *Orlando*) but a literalization of Pankerton's masculine style and sense of intellectual superiority. Delafield extends her satire when Pankerton "accusingly" asks why the protagonist is not wearing fancy dress and insists, "It would do me all the good in the world to give myself over to the Carnival spirit. It is what I *need*."[35] Readers are meant to regard the "Carnival spirit" as an affectation, as pride and self-satisfaction; wealthy "highbrow" characters embrace fancy dress that literalizes their everyday personae, and Delafield implies that her narrator has been wise to wear ordinary dress to the party. She does not appear spectacular, but she does look appropriate.

Like Delafield, Evelyn Waugh repeatedly deploys fancy dress in his satire, and such garments serve to magnify the character defects of the upper class. In Waugh's fiction, the shallow Bright Young Things materialize their pursuit of pleasure, superficiality, and shamelessness particularly clearly through costumes. From Waugh's perspective, fancy dress as a practice reveals the bankruptcy at the heart of the pleasure-bent, liquor-filled 1920s. The biblical allusion of the title of *Vile Bodies*,[36] for example, is profaned during a conversation between the protagonist, Adam, and his on-again, off-again fiancée, Nina, about all the parties they have attended, including "Masked parties, Savage parties, Victorian parties, Greek parties, Wild West parties, Russian parties, Circus parties, parties where one had to dress as somebody else." This reminiscence ends with the phrase "Those vile bodies,"[37] which at once reflects and judges the frenetic leisure and abject physicality of the Bright Young Things.

Their corruption and waste of time are encapsulated in the list of fancy-dress themes, a constantly changing array of garb that visually manifests their folly. Adam, Waugh's middle-class-author figure, hopes to escape the round of parties and is notably never depicted in fancy dress. As someone who is in, but not of, the orbit of the Bright Young Things, Adam focalizes Waugh's criticism of upper-class characters.

Waugh's satire, like Delafield's, takes particular aim at wealthy women in fancy dress; in Waugh's novel, such attire not only materializes character flaws but poses a threat to the respectable middle class. Miss Runcible, a feckless society beauty whose behavior offers staple material to the gossip columnists in *Vile Bodies*, wears fancy dress at the "Savage" party, a "Hawaiian costume" that makes her "the life and soul of the evening."[38] While Runcible's costume and behavior are accepted by her cohort—indeed, they are of so little note that neither the narrator nor the other partygoers describe them—Waugh's satire of his character becomes clear after she spends the night in the home of Jane Brown, daughter of the prime minister du jour. The Brown family enjoys (temporary) political power, but Waugh indicates that the Browns are not of Runcible's class and do not enjoy her celebrity status; the prime minister's son, for example, works "in a motor shop."[39] When Runcible comes downstairs the next morning still wearing her Hawaiian costume, the prime minister is shocked by their encounter: "Suddenly the door opened and in came a sort of dancing Hottentot woman half-naked."[40] Part of the joke here is about the prime minister's conventional and conservative response to Runcible, but the novel focuses more attention on Runcible's extreme exposure in her costume, which materializes her decadence and impropriety. Fancy dress may be amusing, *Vile Bodies* implies, but it also facilitates departures from conventional attire that push the boundaries of decency. Moreover, Runcible's fancy dress serves as a vector for her negative influence on the Brown family's fortunes. The character unwittingly brings down the government after she is photographed leaving No. 10 Downing Street "trailing garlands of equatorial flowers."[41] In Waugh's novel, Hawaiian fancy dress signals Runcible's lack of substance—like the costume, there is little to her—and the damage that extends outward from a few garlands. The mere suggestion that the prime minister tolerates Runcible's fancy dress suffices to ruin his political career, a turn of events that (however amusing) sounds Waugh's caution: the superficiality endemic to the upper classes and evident in their fancy dress can suck the life out of respectable homes and politicians.

In the 1930s, Waugh repeatedly turned to fancy dress as a sartorial form that neatly materializes the character flaws of wealthy Britons. In his hilarious short story "Cruise (Letters from a Young Lady of Leisure)," his shallow narrator gets her costume idea—to dress as a sailor—for an onboard fancy-dress ball from the ship's purser. Such balls were "a popular feature of holiday cruises, which enjoyed a boom in the 1920s."[42] Waugh's character is, however, disappointed by the reaction to her costume:

> Well the Ball we had to come in to dinner in our clothes and everyone clapped as we came downstairs. So I was pretty late on account of not being able to make up my mind whether to wear the hat and in the end did and looked a corker. Well it was rather a faint clap for me considering so when I looked about there were about twenty girls and some women all dressed like me so how cynical the purser turns out to be. Bertie looked horribly dull as an apache. Mum and Papa were sweet. Miss P. had a ballet dress from the Russian ballet which couldn't have been more unsuitable so we had champagne for dinner and were jolly and they threw paper streamers.[43]

Fancy dress makes visible the narrator's lack of creativity or originality; her appearance in the sailor costume underlines her status as a generalized "young lady of leisure," a type that Waugh represents as all of a (vacuous) piece. Notably, her wealthy companions are equally satirized through fancy dress that is conventional (her brother's "dull" Apache costume) or, if creative and modern, "unsuitable" (Miss P.'s Russian-ballet costume). In "Cruise," it seems that there are *no* costumes that are at once seemly and striking. Fancy dress serves to expose the correspondence between the appearance and the personae of the Bright Young Things in Waugh's fiction: they and their costumes are shameless (Miss Runcible in her Hawaiian garb) and substance-less (the narrator of "Cruise" in her sailor suit). Such representations of fancy dress suggest that there is nothing *more*—no hidden depths—to Waugh's characters.

Middlebrow works thus employ fancy dress to satirize wealthy and "intellectual" characters whose foolish costumes precisely reflect their pretension, immodesty, and lack of originality. Such examples suggest that these characters lack depth of any kind. There is almost no self to speak of in Lady B., Miss Runcible, and others like them, and they certainly do not know (what there is to know about) themselves. A related form of fancy-dress humor focuses on characters who attempt to but *cannot* take on new physical qualities or personal traits by donning costumes.[44] This type of humor particularly punishes characters who put on aspirational fancy dress: costumes that materialize more wealth, education, and breeding than the wearers are thought to possess ordinarily. Like the satires of upper-class characters, these works support depth ontology because the self cannot be refashioned by material objects, and characters are inconvenienced and shamed because they cannot achieve the heights to which their costumes aspire. If fancy dress purportedly offers the wearer the ability to alter her appearance and identity for an evening, middlebrow texts suggest that, instead, the garment reveals the folly of even trying to "better oneself" temporarily.

Punch, "that barometer of middle-class conservative opinion" in D. J. Taylor's words,[45] exemplifies the embrace of depth ontology. Its cartoons repeatedly mock middle- and working-class characters' desire to enhance their ordinary selves through fancy dress. In 1936, for example, the weekly depicted a couple wearing false noses and carrying balloons at a seaside "Carnival Week." The man queries his companion: "Ethel, why can't we be natural always?"[46] This cartoon mocks the notion that fancy dress can ever be "natural"—can ever express a person's genuine personality. This image, which may be described as gently mocking, has company in more pointedly negative representations of characters who want to transcend their class and condition through fancy dress. In 1938, the magazine ran a cartoon in which two working-class characters ask a costumer, "'Ave you any Elizabethan fancy gent's suitings?"[47] The incredulity on the costumer's face draws attention to the disjunction between his customers' working-class appearance and accents and their desired type of fancy dress. Such men, the cartoonist suggests, could never carry off the costume of an Elizabethan gentleman: their aspiration and naïve faith in the power of clothing to transform them are simply laughable.

These types of characters are the repeated targets of *Punch*'s cartoonists. There are, for example, several jokes about men dressed as Father Time not knowing the correct time (figure 3.5). Although the ways in which class works in such cartoons may not be immediately evident, the uncomfortable situations in which these characters find themselves—Father Time and his wife have missed the last subway train, a circumstance that would matter only to someone who cannot afford a private car or taxi—repeatedly point to the folly of men and women who attempt to better themselves in any way through fancy dress. Such betterment may

FIGURE 3.5 Arthur Watts, "After the Fancy-Dress Ball," *Punch*, February 15, 1922, 128.

be of small (knowing the correct time) or large degree, but it is seldom achieved. This type of joke was also prevalent in periodicals other than *Punch*; W. K. Haselden (cartoonist for the *Daily Mirror*) and Joseph Lee (*Evening News*) repeatedly depict people who cannot live up to the virtues of an idea or a character represented in their fancy dress.

Even characters *slightly* lower on the economic and social scale than middlebrow protagonists end up being punished for donning aspirational costumes. P. G. Wodehouse's *Right Ho, Jeeves!* chronicles the misadventures of yet another friend of Bertie Wooster who cannot manage to get engaged to the woman he loves. When Gussie Fink-Nottle appears in Wooster's sitting room dressed as Mephistopheles, the occasion allows Wooster to denigrate fancy-dress costumes and parties in general terms before taking aim at Fink-Nottle's unusual selection:

> The spectacle before me was enough to nonplus anyone. I mean to say, this Fink-Nottle, as I remembered him, was the sort of shy, shrinking goop who might have been expected to shake like an aspen if invited to so much as a social Saturday afternoon at the

vicarage. And yet here he was, if one could credit one's senses, about to take part in a fancy-dress ball, a form of entertainment notoriously a testing experience for the toughest.

And he was attending that fancy-dress ball, mark you—not, like every other well-bred Englishman, as a Pierrot, but as Mephistopheles—this involving, as I need scarcely stress, not only scarlet tights but a pretty frightful false beard.[48]

Wooster decries Fink-Nottle's specific costume because it will make him stand out, and for a moment, the joke seems to be about Wooster's excessive caution in the matter of fancy dress. As the scene develops, however, Fink-Nottle reveals that Jeeves—Wooster's omnicompetent valet—has recommended that particular fancy dress: "He said that the costume of Pierrot, while pleasing to the eye, lacked the authority of the Mephistopheles costume" and further explains, "Jeeves is a great believer in the moral effect of clothes. He thinks I might be emboldened in a striking costume like this."[49] Fink-Nottle then reports that while the costume has yet to embolden him, he still has faith that he will rise to the level of his garments:

I feel a most frightful chump now, yes, but who can say whether that will not pass off when I get into a mob of other people in fancy dress. I had the same experience as a child, one year during the Christmas festivities. They dressed me up as a rabbit, and the shame was indescribable. Yet when I got to the party and found myself surrounded by scores of other children, many in costumes even ghastlier than my own, I perked up amazingly, joined freely in the revels, and was able to eat so hearty a supper that I was sick twice in the cab coming home.[50]

Fink-Nottle's childhood memory of a costume's transformative power gives him hope that he "might quite easily pull off something pretty impressive."

His hopes are completely dashed when he takes a cab to the wrong address and cannot correct his mistake or pay the taxi driver, having left his ticket to the dance, his money, and his latchkey at home. Jeeves, seeking to explain why his normally good advice has failed in this instance, explains that "these aberrations of memory are not uncommon with those who, like Mr. Fink-Nottle, belong essentially to what one might call the dreamer-type," and Wodehouse's point is made: a good costume cannot bestow on Fink-Nottle qualities that he does not possess. Fink-Nottle might aspire to a commanding, powerful form of masculinity, but he cannot ultimately achieve his dreams by changing into fancy dress. Wodehouse's reader might suspect that only Jeeves— an aristocrat of taste, if not birth—could make such aspirational attire work for him.

Works such as *Right Ho, Jeeves!* depict characters who wish for fancy dress to overpower them, expressing the hope that, at times, working-, middle-, and even upper-class Britons could be borne along by things they had selected with a particular end in view. When such transformations actually occur in popular publications, however, a disquiet sets in as the characters in fancy dress lose control of themselves and end up punished for their pretensions. While characters fantasize about challenging depth ontology, those who find their fancy dress shaping their behavior and impact on others are inconvenienced and shamed. Costumes, such stories demonstrate, can alter their wearers, but not always for the better and seldom in the manner that they hoped.

The mildest examples of such transformations are featured in *Punch*. Arthur Moreland's "Simple Stories: The Fancy-Dress Dance" tells the tale of Mr. Boomer, who looks nothing like Henry VIII—he is described as "little" and "very small"—but who attends a dance dressed as the king because his domineering wife wants to go as Catherine of Aragon. The character thus contravenes the advice provided in such books as Geoffrey D'Egville's *How and What to Dance* and Ardern Holt's *Fancy Dresses Described*, but his folly initially bears fruit. When the Boomers arrive at the dance, "everybody started clapping and then laughing because they looked so silly," but "Mr. Boomer's silliness didn't last long because something had been coming over him ever since he had put on the costume. And directly he came into the hall and saw the Vicar dressed up as Cardinal Wolsey it came over him altogether that he was really Henry VIII."[51] What "came over" Boomer is less a vague "something" than the transformative power of his costume, which makes him feel and behave like the famous monarch. Boomer orders "Cardinal Wolsey" to procure a divorce for him, treats other partygoers as his wives, and responds with kingly anger to those who remonstrate with him. Boomer is finally persuaded to go home when his wife speaks to him in character ("my liege it is time we wended homewards"), and he recovers his normal self only when she tells him, "You looked very nice as Henry VIII considering you are almost a dwarf."[52] The short tale concludes with Boomer being told,

"Mind you lock up everything before you go to bed,"[53] a reminder that the character has returned to his old role as henpecked husband.

In this story, Boomer is temporarily transformed by aspirational fancy dress, or, rather, he is transformed through a costume based on his wife's aspirations. All his conversion requires is a good costume and the happenstance of context for it, which is provided by the vicar's appearance as Cardinal Wolsey. Identity, the sketch seems to suggest, is less inherent than contextual and sartorial. Despite the story's brief intimation that garments can transform people in the right circumstances, Moreland emphasizes the transient nature of such experiences when Boomer's transformation is reversed and hints that the character may later regret many of his actions as Henry VIII. Although his marriage remains unscathed, the story represents Boomer as offending numerous powerful people at the fancy-dress party, including the vicar, Mrs. Crow (who lives in the largest house in town), and her husband (who becomes "angry"). When Boomer leaves the party, the consensus of "everybody" is that "perhaps he has gone a little too far."[54] If fancy dress effects a transformation, the story suggests, then that change is not generally for a character's long-term good.

The dangerous transformative power of aspirational costume is rendered even more starkly in Daphne du Maurier's best-selling novel *Rebecca*. Unlike the popular texts I have discussed to this point, du Maurier writes in a tragic, not a comic, vein; as a result, her representation of fancy dress is the darkest of the lot. Despite this significant difference, however, du Maurier's text similarly punishes a character who seeks to better herself through fancy dress. As readers of the novel will remember, the narrator and protagonist of *Rebecca* is an impoverished (albeit genteel) young woman who suddenly finds herself elevated to upper-class status when she marries the wealthy Maxim de Winter. Despite her good fortune, the narrator never feels herself of the class into which she has married, and she provides an outsider's view of the elite to which she so desperately wishes to belong.[55] Because *Rebecca* was written and published during the lead up to World War II, scholars have read the novel as critical of the class that partied as Hitler rose to power.[56] What critics have not examined, however, are the class concerns embedded in du Maurier's depiction of fancy dress; while the narrator enthuses that the fancy-dress ball to be held at Manderley, Maxim's ancestral home, will be "mad ridiculous childish fun!"[57] it instead offers a sinister lesson in aspirations punished and the unpredictable changes that costumes can work.

With the encouragement of the baleful Mrs. Danvers, the housekeeper at Manderley, du Maurier's young protagonist decides to adopt the costume of Caroline de Winter, who is memorialized in a portrait by Sir Henry Raeburn that hangs in the house's gallery. The narrator knows that Caroline was a sister of Maxim's "great-great-grandfather. She married a great Whig politician, and was a famous London beauty for years."[58] These details, which are irrelevant to the precise garments in which Caroline was painted, suggest why the young woman so readily accepts Danvers's suggestion. While "I always loved the girl in white,"[59] in reproducing Caroline's appearance for the fancy-dress party, the narrator clearly hopes to approximate not only the sitter's wardrobe but also her class, confidence, and powers of attraction. To an insecure and decidedly unglamorous nobody, the fancy-dress costume of Caroline de Winter holds out the possibility of self-improvement, if for only a night. She might finally feel not only *in* but *of* Manderley.

When the costume arrives, it briefly works the wished-for magic. In her dress and wig, the narrator is "amazed at the transformation. I looked quite attractive, quite different all together. Not me at all. Someone much more interesting, more vivid and alive."[60] Here, du Maurier captures the possibility of being "quite different" in a costume. That the protagonist describes her appearance as "not me at all" but *better* than her everyday self seems to indicate that the costume will emerge as a rare example of aspirations achieved. Note, too, that in the costume the narrator looks "more . . . alive"; the novel hints at the liveliness that may be conferred by material objects, a liveliness that the human body and persona do not possess on their own. Under the fancy dress, "my own dull personality was submerged at last,"[61] and the protagonist "watched this self that was not me at all and then smiled; a new, slow smile."[62] Du Maurier's character could not be clearer: fancy dress has provided her with a new body and self, an experience that controverts models of identity premised on interiority. She even makes plain that her face, which is not covered by the costume, is different: "The eyes were larger surely, the mouth narrower, the skin white and clear."[63] No surgery or other type of self-care generates this change, which suggests that good fancy dress may enable physiological transformations. Finally, a reader may think, here is a literary character who *can* improve her lot through a costume.

Before proceeding with my analysis of this scene, it is instructive to pause and compare the young protagonist's experience to this point with mirror scenes discussed earlier, specifically in the works by Rebecca West and Virginia Woolf analyzed in chapter 1. In those novels, characters gaze into a mirror and see not themselves but things; reflections of women in evening gowns do not consolidate the characters' sense of self but profoundly alienate that self, making it seem less human. Evening gowns, which, like fancy dress can be aspirational attire, are repeatedly represented as *failing* to help their wearers achieve the status of the Ideal-I, Jacques Lacan's formulation of a coherent, self-sufficient body and psyche. Du Maurier, in contrast, suggests that fancy dress *may* provide access to something approaching that state, but what her protagonist sees in the mirror is not an Ideal-I but an Ideal-*other*: as the narrator "paraded up and down in front" of her reflection, she "did not recognize the face that stared at me in the glass."[64] For a moment, *Rebecca* suggests that fancy dress, more than any other type of attire, offers women and men the opportunity to assemble a new and improved self through the cooperation of wearer and garments.

It is, however, a brief moment. When the narrator reveals herself to her husband, her sister-in-law Beatrice, and her brother-in-law Giles, they respond with shock and anger. "What the hell do you think you are doing?" Maxim asks before ordering her to "go and change."[65] As the protagonist runs to her room, Danvers looks on in triumph. Beatrice later explains the narrator's "terrible mistake": "[T]he dress, you poor dear, the picture you copied of the girl in the gallery. It was what Rebecca did at the last fancy dress ball at Manderley. Identical. The same picture, the same dress. You stood there on the stairs, and for one ghastly moment I thought . . ."[66] The young protagonist has aspired to appear as Caroline de Winter and has instead appeared as a dead (and, as readers later learn, monstrously sexual) woman. Her night and her aspirations have been shattered.

Rebecca offers an admittedly extreme example of the critique of aspirational fancy dress. While the protagonist enjoys "becoming" Caroline de Winter in the privacy of her room and in the reflection in her mirror, she is shocked and horrified to become Rebecca-in-costume in the eyes of Maxim, Beatrice, and Giles. Significantly, becoming Rebecca (however momentarily) initiates a series of events that permanently alter the protagonist, who is unable to return to her old self even after she discards her fancy dress. Although she rejoins the party in an ordinary blue evening gown and thinks, "I might have been my old self again,"[67] she is emphatically *not* her old self. She suffers throughout the evening, enduring a party at which she had hoped to shine.

Post-costume, the narrator realizes that her time in fancy dress did transform her, albeit not in the ways she had hoped. She observes, "The girl who had dressed for the fancy dress ball . . . had been left behind,"[68] and she begins to see the ways that material objects—like the costume—merge her old self with Rebecca: "That mackintosh I wore, that handkerchief I used. They were hers. Perhaps she knew and had seen me take them. Jasper had been her dog, and he ran at my heels now. The roses were hers and I cut them."[69] The fancy-dress portrayal of Caroline de Winter literalizes the fact that the protagonist walks in her predecessor's shoes (literally, in her fancy dress). When Maxim later regretfully observes, "It's gone forever, that funny, young, lost look that I loved" and "you are so much older,"[70] readers see that the narrator has developed a new, hybrid identity. She is no longer the ingénue, nor is she the decadent, sexually wayward Rebecca: she has become something in between.

Rebecca thus implies that aspirational fancy dress can challenge depth ontology, as costume provides first a desired and then an undesirable transformation. In both cases, fancy dress has the power to change who the protagonist is, and her self is revealed to be partly *in* her and partly *on* her, an artifact of what she wears and the history of those garments. The changes that fancy dress effects are, however, uncontrollable, and as the novel continues, du Maurier repeatedly links fancy dress (and the parties at which it is worn) with negative, undesirable outcomes. Immediately after the costume ball, Rebecca's body is discovered in the cabin of her sunken boat, and the de Winters are immersed in the formalities of an inquest and consumed by fear that Maxim's role in the death of his first wife will come to light. The local newspaper seizes on the timing of the discovery of Rebecca's body; the protagonist reads "the little line about myself at the bottom, saying whom Maxim had married as his second wife, and how we had just given the fancy dress ball at Manderley. It sounded so crude and callous, in the dark print of the newspaper."[71] Two London papers follow suit, making "great play of the fact that Rebecca's body had been found the day after the fancy dress ball, as though there was something deliberate about it."[72] These reports represent the de Winters' exposure to public gossip and legal scrutiny, but they also underline du Maurier's own "deliberate" choice to juxtapose the fancy-dress ball with the discovery of Rebecca's corpse. This decision sharpens the novel's critique of Maxim's class and lifestyle—Gina Wisker observes that the de Winters' "fairytale lifestyles are exposed through the contradictions of the text as artifice, a dangerously decadent, culpably blinkered sham"[73]—but it more importantly highlights the binary between body and self, thing and person, complicated by the protagonist's fancy-dress costume. After the narrator has been taken for Rebecca, the corpse surfaces, seemingly of its own volition, no longer the husk of a personality but mere matter. All we are is stuff, the corpse seems to say; dead or alive, we are things known to ourselves and others through material objects. As Maxim notes, the identification of Rebecca's body will be possible even if it has decomposed beyond recognition: "[H]er things will be there still."[74] Such things—Rebecca's rings, the protagonist's costume—make du Maurier's characters who they are in life *and* death.

Rebecca offers an extreme version of the larger critique of fancy dress: when wealthy characters wear costumes, their personality flaws are materialized; when lower- and middle-class characters wear fancy dress, they are mocked and punished for aspiring to better their condition, even if for only a night. In fiction and cartoons, characters who hoped to be spectacular in their costumes become instead spectacles, and at their most extreme, costumes effect undesirable changes. If, as contemporary theorists like Daniel Miller argue, "stuff actually creates us in the first place,"[75] popular literature works to contravene this understanding of self and stuff. Identity is located in a self, not on a body, such texts repeatedly insist. Moreover, representations of fancy dress instruct readers that the material world does not behave according to our wishes. This resistance to the possibilities inherent in costume (and in other types of dress) is startling, but it suggests that most writers accepted a class system that might have been challenged by models of selfhood indebted to materiality (instead of interiority).[76] For two writers, however, the promise of a transformation through fancy dress would fuel radical experiments with character. Having learned about the potential of fancy dress from their own experiences of wearing or observing it, Virginia Woolf and Dorothy L. Sayers would not reinforce depth ontology but leave it behind.

"Abandonment at Not Being One's Usual Self": Bloomsbury, Fancy Dress, and *Orlando*

It is striking to note how many of the recollections of Bloomsbury parties focus on costumes. When asked about the parties held in the interwar years, George "Dadie" Rylands unequivocally asserted that "the parties were mostly fancy-dress parties."[77] He focused on "a marvelous party, called the Sailors' Party, in which we all had to go wearing naval costume. I went as a lower-deck type, and Lytton went as a full Admiral of the Fleet. As you can imagine, with his beard and his cocked hat and his sword he was impressive."[78] As this account suggests, fancy-dress parties complemented Bloomsbury's campy play with gender, frankness about sexuality, and pleasure in mocking authority; Lytton Strachey's guise as an admiral, for example, worked in ironic tension with his status during World War I as a conscientious objector and with his penchant for younger men. Fancy-dress parties such as the one Rylands remembered often served to mark birthdays but also were thought appropriate to celebrate artistic accomplishments, such as the opening of exhibitions. Bloomsbury's fancy dress, however, offered more than a brief opportunity for revelry and celebration. Virginia Woolf saw in costumes a chance to abandon her normal self for an evening, and she embraced fancy dress that did not flatter her normal traits and features but deviated quite far from them. This sartorial practice influenced one of Woolf's best-known novels, *Orlando*, which contains photographs of sitters clad in costumes and employs a model of character (and thus of self) based on principles that Woolf came to understand through wearing fancy dress.[79] Dorothy L. Sayers, like Woolf, celebrates the transformative power of costume but *only* when it is employed by aristocratic, extremely wealthy, and cultured individuals.

Virginia Woolf and her sister, Vanessa Bell, wore fancy dress on many documented occasions, and their choices suggest that they enjoyed the way in which costumes could contrast with, instead of enhance, their everyday selves. Ironically, the best documentation of their costumes comes from people who did not appreciate the sisters' decisions. The most detailed record of the Artists Revels of 1909, for example, comes from the pen of Ottoline Morrell, who was disappointed in their selections: "Vanessa's Madonna-like beauty surely could have found a happier alias than that of a Pierrot, and Virginia [Stephen] was hardly suited to pose as Cleopatra, whose qualities, as I had imagined them, were just those that Virginia did not possess."[80] Morrell's comments may seem merely frivolous, but they point to a fundamental disagreement about the proper relationship between costume and wearer: Should fancy dress *enhance* one's persona, thus rendering aspects of the self highly visible, or should it *contrast* with one's "self," thus complicating and perhaps transforming it in the process? Morrell clearly embraced the former view, while the sisters seemed to be leaning toward the latter. While Virginia

Stephen did not record her reasons for choosing to attend as Cleopatra, it is possible that she selected the costume precisely because it would materialize qualities she did not possess but could put on, albeit temporarily.

Other costumes worn by Woolf and Bell similarly suggest that the sisters reveled in the opportunity to transform (and not simply beautify) themselves through fancy dress. In "Old Bloomsbury" Woolf remembers her costume—and the reaction to it—for the ball to celebrate the end of the Second Post-Impressionist Exhibition in 1912. She and Bell "dressed ourselves up as Gauguin pictures and careered round Crosby Hall. Mrs. Whitehead was scandalized. She said that Vanessa and I were practically naked."[81] No pictures of these costumes survive, but the sisters' transformation was racial *and* sexual: if they were not in fact "practically naked," they must have displayed more flesh than was common in the period; and by disguising themselves as Tahitian women, they would have complicated their racial and national identities. It is instructive to compare the Gauguin-inspired costumes with those donned in the *Dreadnought* hoax of 1910, which similarly involved racial and sexual transgression, particularly for Virginia Stephen, the lone woman who participated.[82] While the *Dreadnought* costumes *concealed* the wearers' English identities—disguised them as someone else, however fictional—the Gauguin-themed costumes *complicated* the sisters' selves by, in Woolf's words, filtering them through the "variegated lights" of Postimpressionism.[83] Fancy dress allowed Virginia and Vanessa to materialize artistic commitments at odds with the status of respectable British middle-class virgin and wife, respectively.

There are intermittent references to additional fancy-dress parties in the sisters' diaries and letters throughout the 1920s and 1930s. Although their costumes are not always described, these documents recall the impact of wearing fancy dress in glowing terms. In January 1923, Woolf recalled a costume party as stimulating and transformational: "Suppose one's normal pulse to be 70; in five minutes it was 120: & the blood, not the sticky whitish fluid of daytime, but brilliant & prickling like champagne."[84] In her "mother's laces," Woolf thought of Shakespeare and concluded that he "would have liked us all tonight."[85] On this occasion and others, fancy dress created sparkling new selves for Woolf and Bell. In January 1930, for example, they wore costumes to an "Alice in Wonderland" party held to celebrate Angelica Bell's birthday. This is the only Bloomsbury fancy-dress event to have been photographed, though the image is, unfortunately, out of focus (figure 3.6). Virginia Woolf was

FIGURE 3.6 Celebrants at the "Alice in Wonderland" party, January 1930. It is possible that Virginia Woolf is standing next to Leonard at the left, but it is difficult to be certain. (Vanessa Bell [1879–1961], Bell Album 5, p. 24 A15. © Tate, London 2015)

disguised as "the March hare" and wore white as well as "a pair of hare's ears, and a pair of hare's paws."[86] Leonard Woolf dressed as the Carpenter; Bell's costume was not recorded.

Like her earlier costumes, which had allowed Woolf to put on a new role for a night, her fancy dress—"a hare . . . and mad at that"—left her "encouraged by the extravaganza."[87] As she wrote to Clive Bell, she "turned . . . and tapped Dotty on the nose" and complained that "she flared up like a costermonger; damned my eyes; . . . ; and swore that I had wiped all the powder from her face."[88] Dorothy Wellesley's costume is not identified in Woolf's letter, but it obviously did not cover her face, as she wore standard makeup with it. Her reaction to Woolf's gesture suggests that she shared Morrell's standards for fancy dress, which she regarded as enhancing, not mocking or ironizing, female beauty. March hares were not compatible with these criteria.

Throughout the 1930s, Woolf continued to enjoy the play with identity that fancy dress afforded.[89] As she would write of a costume party held in 1939, fancy dress offered "a kind of liberation . . . , tipsiness & abandonment at not being one's usual self."[90] This personal experience with fancy dress doubtless informed Woolf's increasingly radical approach to character, which surfaces in *Orlando*'s suggestion that there may not be a "self" under a costume—that costume and self are one. While scholars have noted that Woolf's fantastical "biography" provides a literary example of Judith Butler's theory of gender performance,[91] I argue that Woolf's novel depicts identity *itself* as a performance. By means of fancy dress, Woolf came to see selfhood as assembled by the cooperation of person and material objects: *Orlando* argues that selves are multiple and dependent on what one wears.

Of course, this isn't to say that Woolf regarded all fancy dress as liberatory. Her novel *Jacob's Room* uses costume to highlight the difference between the educational and economic status of men and women. As the impoverished and lovelorn Fanny Elmer struggles to make sense of *Tom Jones*, she muses, "There is something . . . about books which if I had been educated I could have liked—much better than ear-rings and flowers, she sighed, thinking of the corridors at the Slade and the fancy-dress dance next week. She had nothing to wear."[92] Elmer's inability to appreciate Henry Fielding's novel—or her inability to like it *better* than fancy dress—rests squarely on her inadequate learning, and Woolf aligns women with the pleasures of costumes and men with the benefits of higher learning throughout this section of the novel. Although Jacob Flanders, the novel's protagonist and Elmer's love interest, briefly goes along with plans for the fancy-dress ball, "and though he looked terrible and magnificent and would chuck the Forest, he said, and come to the Slade, and be a Turkish knight or a Roman emperor (and he let her blacken his lips and clenched his teeth and scowled in the glass), still—there lay *Tom Jones*."[93] *Jacob's Room* thus represents fancy dress as an example of the unsatisfying pleasures available to the uneducated Elmer, an artist's model for whom fancy dress serves as a transient—and ultimately disappointing—form of self-expression.

The contrast between *Jacob's Room* and *Orlando*, published a mere six years later, could not be starker. In Woolf's later work, she offers to a character the "liberation . . . , tipsiness & abandonment at not being one's usual self" that costume allows,[94] and Orlando's "selves" are achieved not only through the novel's famous sex change but through an attitude toward clothing that treats *all* garb as fancy dress. In other words, while *Orlando* contains no textual references to fancy dress per se, it displays what Woolf most valued in such costumes: the ability to be not disguised but *different* from what one had been before. *Orlando* all but dismantles depth ontology, as Woolf's main character is (almost entirely) what he or she wears. Things emerge not as more powerful than people but as mutually constitutive, and ontological distinctions between self and surface are largely abandoned.[95] This experiment offers a radical contrast to the texts discussed in the previous section; at the same time, it is important to remember that only *one* extraordinary character enjoys the power to make things do her bidding.

The illustrations that pepper *Orlando* underline the ways in which fancy dress shaped Woolf's attitude toward her character. These images, readers and scholars have long understood, include a range of media: reproductions of paintings from Vita Sackville-West's childhood home, Knole; society portraits and snapshots of Sackville-West; and photographs taken expressly for publication in *Orlando*. The last category includes images of Woolf's niece Angelica Bell and Sackville-West in fancy dress. Vanessa Bell, who took these photographs, and her sitters assembled the individual costumes; Sackville-West, for example, was instructed to bring "your curls and clothes" to one photo shoot.[96] As R. S. Koppen has noted, "What is striking is the degree of care taken in the assembling and production of these illustrations, and at the same time the fun that was obviously generated by the fancy dress and the staging involved."[97] The costumes depicted in these photographs are far from historically accurate—"Orlando about the year 1840" is represented by Sackville-West in a "checked wool skirt, an eastern shawl and a garden hat"[98]—but they point generally to the investment of Woolf (and the Bloomsbury circle) in fancy dress and specifically to the ways in which this sartorial form influenced the novel. In the pages of Woolf's mock biography, Angelica, for example, *is* "The Russian Princess as a Child"; while readers who were intimates with the Woolfs and Bells would have known that she was also a specific young girl, that knowledge would be filtered by the transformation effected by the costume. In other words, within the pages of the novel, this illustration works a kind of material magic, demonstrating the power of fancy dress to offer new forms of identity, if for only an evening or, in *Orlando*, the time it takes to turn a page.

The character of Orlando pays little attention to clothing until after the dramatic scene of transmogrification that turns him into a woman. The narrator's response to that metamorphosis initially suggests that Orlando has an essential self that is entirely independent of *all* material trappings, including her sexed body: "Orlando had become a woman—there is no denying it. But in every other respect, Orlando remained precisely as he had been. The change of sex, though it altered their future, did nothing whatever to alter their identity."[99] This description, which insists that Orlando's identity remains intact after the sex change, seems to affirm depth ontology, positing a self so deeply rooted that even becoming a woman cannot alter it. Orlando's face remains "practically the same," and "her memory . . . went back through all the events of her past life without encountering any obstacle."[100] As Orlando's life as a woman unfolds, however, the narrator suggests that it is less what is *in* the body than what is *on* it that makes Orlando who she is.

Although the narrator's struggle over the relationship between clothing and self will be familiar to many readers, revisiting that quandary through Woolf's experience of fancy dress and the novel's photographs of costumed figures sheds new light on the material constitution of Orlando's identity. When Orlando is in England and dressed as a woman, the narrator muses that the character's behavior had changed and that "the change of clothes had, some philosophers will say, much to do with it. Vain trifles as they seem, clothes have, they say, more important offices than merely to keep us warm. They change our view of the world and the world's view of us."[101] This line of reasoning suggests that the things on a body make a person who he or she is. It is precisely this aspect of fancy dress, a form of garment worn for events premised on changing "the world's view of us," that compelled Woolf and her contemporaries. The narrator continues, "There is much to support the view that it is clothes that wear us and not we them; we may make them take the mould of arm or breast, but they mould our hearts, our brains, our tongues to their liking."[102] This mutual constitution of object and person, and Woolf's personification of clothing, positions garments as more than inert matter: if they can change heart, brain, and tongue, they assemble personality, self, and identity rather than reflect an interior being.

After floating the theory that "clothes make the (wo)man" in a profound sense, Woolf's narrator abandons this line of reasoning. This retreat reminds the reader not only of the narrator's conservative bent—he or she is, after all, the persona who can scarcely behold the sex change—but also of the appeal of depth ontology, which rigidly separates person from object. The narrator notes, "That is the view of some philosophers and wise ones, but on the whole, we incline to another. The difference between the sexes is, happily, one of great profundity. Clothes are but a symbol of something hid deep beneath."[103] The desire that identity and personality be a stable entity "hid deep beneath" both garments and body points to the investment in depth ontology felt by Woolf's narrator and, as we have seen, many of her contemporaries. The popular examples examined earlier, which direct laughter or fear at costumes that aim to change their wearers, underline a collective unease with the idea that, in Miller's words, "clothing plays a considerable and active part in constituting the particular experience of the self, in determining what the self is."[104] Although "philosophers and wise ones" like Miller may think otherwise, Woolf's narrator and many of her contemporaries insist on locating the self inside rather than outside characters. The narrator thus defends against the creeping suspicion that identity is more changeable and random than purposeful.

Orlando's biographer soon realizes that this defense of depth ontology is impossibly flimsy. After positing clothes as symbol, the narrator confronts "a dilemma. Different though the sexes are, they intermix. In every human being a vacillation from one sex to the other takes places, and often it is only the clothes that keep the male or female likeness, while underneath the sex is the very opposite of what is above."[105] Here, Woolf's use of the word "sex" (which she does not distinguish from "gender") obfuscates the precise changes "underneath" clothing. In the world of *Orlando*, it seems perfectly possible that the narrator means that miraculous sex changes occur daily; less fantastically, the narrator may be speculating on gender identity or sexual orientation. Regardless of how the term "sex" is employed in this passage, what most matters is that "clothes . . . keep the male or female likeness"—clothes assemble the sex of the person who wears them. Because sex was such a central component of self in Woolf's day (as, indeed, in our own), the narrator concludes that the self may be so transitory—so vacillating—that humans *need* garments to materialize the appearance of a stable identity. According to this view, clothing provides a consistency that personality, identity, sex, and self lack.

As Woolf's mock biography continues, the fancy-dress principle—the concept that clothing confounds ontology by making persons through things—emerges in full flower as *all* of Orlando's clothing comes to seem costume. As the eighteenth century unfolds, the narrator finds it difficult to keep track of Orlando because "she found it convenient to change frequently from one set of clothes to another."[106] These continual changes of clothing go beyond the normal sartorial contortions that an eighteenth-century lady would have experienced; as the narrator observes, "She had, it seems, no difficulty in sustaining the different parts, for her sex changed far more frequently than those who have worn only one set of clothing can conceive."[107] Orlando's frequent transformations illuminate the difference between Woolf's character and historical figures in the eighteenth or even the twentieth century; instead of having everyday garments and special-occasion ensembles—instead of wearing a costume that filters and reconstructs the self for *only* evening parties and performances—*every* garment that Orlando dons constructs a different self. Woolf thus plays with the possibility that her character may not be her "usual self"[108]—may not *have* a "usual self"—because clothing lets her sustain a range of selves. These selves, and the costumes that construct them, are, moreover, explicitly queer: "From the probity of breeches she turned to the seductiveness of petticoats and enjoyed the love [emotional or physical, the narrator does not say] of both sexes equally."[109] Freed from a stable, singular identity, Orlando is also freed from a stable (that is, confining) sexuality—multiple selves increase "the pleasures of life,"[110] reports the narrator.

The narrator's description of some of those selves demonstrates that clothing constructs not only sex and sexual orientation (always important in *Orlando*) but distinct beings. I quote at length to give the flavor of the garments the character wears and the selves they enable:

> So then one may sketch her spending her morning in a China robe of ambiguous gender among her books; then receiving a client or two (for she had many scores of suppliants) in the same garment; then she would take a turn in the garden and clip the nut trees—for which knee breeches were convenient; then she would change into a flowered taffeta which best suited a drive to Richmond and a proposal of marriage from some great nobleman; and so back again into town, where she would don a snuff-coloured gown like a lawyer's and visit the courts to hear how her cases were doing . . . ; and so, finally, when night came, she would more often than not become a nobleman complete from head to toe and walk the streets in search of adventure.[111]

Thus a reader sees that Orlando wears clothing to assemble who she is at different times: a reader, a wealthy landowner, a gardener, a potential marital partner, a legal petitioner, and a nobleman. Some, but not all, of these selves are sexed and gendered; some, but not all, of Orlando's clothing is dictated by specific physical activities. The novel relishes the thought that *all clothing may be fancy dress*, that one can be coherent and yet have the qualities of one's being constantly change to suit the moment. Orlando's clothes, like fancy dress, do not disguise; they multiply possibilities and suggest that one *is* in part what one wears.

Orlando finds such quick changes difficult to sustain after the eighteenth century. The nineteenth century influences her to marry, and Orlando subsequently becomes a mother, but these life events are significantly motivated by the clothing she adopts. As she muses on the alterations the nineteenth century has wrought, the character thinks, "Tomorrow she would have to buy twenty yards or more of black bombazine, she supposed, to make a skirt. And then (here she blushed), she would have to buy a crinoline, and then (here she blushed) a bassinette."[112] Orlando's blushes reveal the character's (Victorian) modesty about the pregnancy that a crinoline may conceal, but the novel's description makes it appear that bombazine and crinoline are enough to impregnate the character: clothing implants the *idea* of motherhood and *facilitates entry* into that state. The biographer indeed notes that, in Orlando's case, "the crinoline [was] blushed for before the husband" and blames "the irregular life she had lived before."[113] Such attempts to rationalize Orlando's behavior do not conceal the fact that she, in the nineteenth century, as before, dresses for the person she wants to become—that she designs a costume that will mold her heart, brain, tongue, and even uterus as long as she wears it.[114] Although this dress will create an Orlando seemingly different from the eighteenth-century character—she becomes a wife and a mother—readers soon see how little these changes influence her. Her child, a boy, is twice mentioned by the narrator, and her husband remains with Orlando only briefly.

The conclusion of Woolf's novel most clearly depicts the model of identity that Orlando's many costume changes impart. This section posits each "human spirit" as a collection of selves that surface in different conditions.[115] Orlando "had a great variety of selves to call upon,"[116] and the narrator lists some of them, each of which requires a specific set of clothes to adopt and abandon. As the novel embraces a model of identity that is changeable, deliberate, and transitory, the narrator briefly alludes to a "Captain self, the Key self, which amalgamates and controls" all others.[117] Here, the novel appears to advance a version of depth ontology, but the Key self refuses to arrive for some time. As Orlando switches from self to self, from memory to memory, she may seem incoherent and (as some have argued) ill, but what Woolf instead depicts is the instability of self when it is not dressed for a particular part.[118]

Orlando finally settles—for the space of the book's final pages, if not for all time—on a particular self only through the memory of another character, who is identified by his clothes. She recalls a figure who may have been Shakespeare: "'[H]e sat at Twitchett's table,' she mused, 'with a dirty ruff on.'"[119] This memory, constructed as it is through place and dress, launches Orlando into a recollection of her lifelong work as an author, and the narrator describes the impact as "the addition of this Orlando, what is called, rightly or wrongly, a single self, a real self."[120] In this passage, Orlando's biographer once more refuses to specify what he or she believes—the passive voice and "rightly or wrongly" identifies only possibilities—but the actions of the character demonstrate that this self, too, needs a costume to remain "single" and "real." At this moment, Orlando again changes her clothes, this time adopting "a pair of whipcord breeches, and leather jacket."[121] The breeches are, perhaps, incidental to the character's identity as author, but the jacket importantly features a pocket large enough to contain a bound copy of *The Oak Tree*, Orlando's prize-winning verse.[122] In these garments, the author tours her house, walks to (and sits underneath) the tree that inspired her verses, and muses about her long history. In the novel's final moments, even the character's accessories inflect a particular self: Orlando helps her husband return to her by bearing her necklace "so that her pearls glowed" and "burnt like a phosphorescent flare in the darkness."[123] Through her breeches, jacket, and finally pearls, Orlando is able to put together the specific self that the reader encounters in the novel's present day; as the narrative concludes, one can only wonder what dress, what self, Orlando will adopt in the speculative life that continues beyond the final page of the book.

In *Orlando*, Woolf provides a literary character with the type of freedom that she experienced only while wearing fancy dress. The "kind of liberation . . . , tipsiness & abandonment at not being one's usual self"[124] that she relished when dressed as Cleopatra, a Tahitian woman, the March Hare, Sappho, and Queen Victoria was, obviously, limited to the social occasions for which fancy dress was appropriate, but these fleeting events clearly inspired her to think about the ways in which identity can be mobilized (instead of stabilized) through deliberate changes of clothing. This model of the self, a model that counters depth ontology, is one that the author offered to Orlando—a character whose long life, aristocratic status, artistic talents, education, and sex change place in the category of the extraordinary—and her life becomes one extended series of events for which she dresses different selves. Woolf's novel celebrates the idea that one's persona is constructed from moment to moment, largely through the garments and accessories one puts on.

Orlando's challenge to depth ontology indicates that one of the most popular fictional works of high modernism shares its sensibility with a sartorial form we have all but forgotten, even as the novel's illustrations remind us of the interwar popularity, and the author's love, of fancy dress. This example is rare, doubtless because much canonical high-modernist fiction is invested in depicting psychological processes that depend on depth ontology.[125] Moreover, only *exceptional* characters are able to martial the resources, select the right items, and sustain the effort required for ongoing changes of clothing and self. Fancy dress demanded a fair degree of work to wear successfully, and it seems that only a singular being like Orlando can take advantage of the opportunities that costumes impart. Maintaining a single identity, such examples imply, may be easier than constructing a self from moment to moment. One final example—Dorothy L. Sayers's mystery *Murder Must Advertise*—underlines this point.

The Extraordinary Lord Peter

Sayers, like Woolf, came of age in a milieu where fancy dress was popular. During her first week at Somerville College, Oxford, in 1912, she attended a "Fancy Dress affair" and informed her parents that her costume "was much admired."[126] This party, her biographer Barbara Reynolds writes, began her social life "with a swing."[127] Throughout her time at Oxford, Sayers repeatedly found herself in fancy dress, and she clearly prided herself on witty costumes, including one modeled on Dr. Hugh Percy Allen, the organist at New College and conductor of the Oxford Bach Choir.[128] On another occasion, she dressed as Tristram, a "most successful" costume that led Sayers to confess that "it surprises everyone that I make up so well as a man. It surprises me rather."[129] In fancy dress, Sayers discovered that she could astonish not only others but *herself* through the transformative (and transvestive) power of garments. Like Woolf, Sayers would pass on this talent to one of her protagonists.

Like most literary detectives, Lord Peter Wimsey is master of a range of skills, among them the wearing of disguises *and* fancy dress. In *Murder Must Advertise*, Sayers's character emerges as not one but three personae: Wimsey; the successful advertising copywriter Death Bredon (a "disguise"); and Harlequin, a mysterious figure in fancy dress. While Wimsey manages to juggle these three roles throughout the novel, they bleed into one another toward the end, suggesting that dressing means becoming a part. Wimsey's costume changes are much less frequent than Orlando's, but Sayers's popular work is parallel to Woolf's modernist experiment in allowing an extraordinary figure to abandon a usual self not for the rare occasion but repeatedly. Ironically, this aspect of Sayers's character has been criticized by a range of scholars, who prefer later incarnations of Wimsey.[130] Read in light of the way that *Orlando* employs costumes, however, *Murder Must Advertise* reveals not inadequate characterization but an attitude to self informed by fancy dress. Wimsey can become two other selves because he, like Orlando, is an exceptional individual, and Sayers's protagonist highlights the limitations of a fixed subjectivity.

Wimsey's disguise as Death Bredon is remarkable for being no disguise at all. As Bredon, the character wears spectacles and a side part,[131] but he otherwise maintains the same wardrobe as Wimsey, which causes some comment at Pym's, the advertising agency where Bredon works. Despite the small differences between Wimsey's and Bredon's appearance, Sayers's narrator suggests that a few accessories are enough to transform one self into the other: "[I]n a taxi rolling south-west, Mr. Bredon removed his spectacles, combed out his side-parting, stuck a monocle in his eye, and by the time he reached Piccadilly Circus was again Lord Peter Wimsey."[132] Throughout the novel, Sayers identifies her protagonist as Mr. Bredon or Lord Peter, depending on which self he adopts. This narrative choice means that readers can easily keep track of the character's many changes, but it also positions him as not in the disguise of but *as* Bredon. Sayers's character is thus a master of using a (very) few material objects to become someone else in a manner that persuades not only Pym's employees but also the reader.

As the novel develops, Sayers's protagonist continues to display a mastery of costuming that underlines both his extraordinary abilities and the way that fancy dress proper creates a new self. When Bredon attends a fancy-dress party in pursuit of clues, Sayers draws a sharp contrast between the skills of the protagonist and the failures of other, ordinary characters. Mr. Willis, a Pym's employee who sets out to follow Bredon, adopts the costume "of a member of the Vehmgericht, with its black Cossack and black, eyeleted hood covering the whole head and shoulders."[133] Willis is middle class and does not approach the main character's degree of wealth, breeding, and taste. Small details establish his lack of elite experience and savoir faire: at the famous Simpson's—a restaurant in the Savoy Buildings in the Strand—he picks "with nauseated reluctance at the finest roast saddle in London,"[134] and he takes a taxi, not his own car, to the fancy-dress ball. Like the works discussed earlier, *Murder Must Advertise* criticizes an ordinary person who aspires to be someone else in fancy dress. At the wild party the characters attend, "his costume was hot and heavy, and the sweat poured down his face beneath the stifling black folds of his hood."[135] This discomfort turns out to be entirely pointless as Bredon knows that Willis is following him; Sayers's protagonist later observes, "It was frightfully comic to see old Willis sneaking in after us in a sort of Ku Klux Klan outfit—incredibly stealthy, and wearing the same shoes he wears in the office and a seal-ring on his little finger that one could identify from here to the Monument."[136] Willis's inability to transform himself through fancy dress serves to emphasize Wimsey/Bredon's success, particularly as Willis's identity is revealed through his footwear. Small changes are enough to make Wimsey into Bredon and vice versa, but major changes cannot transform other characters' identities.

At the same party, Bredon adopts a "harlequin black and white,"[137] fancy dress that was ubiquitous in the period.[138] While this costume may not be creative, it facilitates extraordinary physical feats: Harlequin (who is not identified as Bredon after he enters the party) climbs a statue in the center of a shallow pool, "dripping and glittering like a fantastic water-creature."[139] Incited by a crowd to dive, "the slim body shot down through the spray, struck the surface with scarcely a splash and slid through the water like a fish. Willis caught his breath. It was perfectly done. It was magnificent."[140] The success of this difficult feat—before the dive, one partygoer states that the pool is too shallow for diving—implies that the costume of Harlequin confers unusual physical prowess, and the daring plunge impresses witnesses so much that Dian de Momerie, a decadent society beauty, kisses and then runs off with Harlequin. For the rest of the novel, Dian knows the protagonist only as Harlequin, a figure who occasionally materializes to engage in similar physical feats and to ask her questions about Victor Dean, the victim around whose murder the novel revolves. When she later cries because Harlequin does not love her, he responds, "Who would believe that Dian de Momerie could fall for a fancy-dress and a penny whistle?"[141] This slightly disingenuous question belies the fact that the main character has been transformed into someone exceptional and unusual by his costume; in putting on the "fancy dress" of Harlequin, he also puts on an air of mystery and incredible physical ability to become someone new.

Toward the middle of *Murder Must Advertise*, readers begin to see that while Wimsey may be a master of disguises and fancy dress, the costumes he adopts are not distinct roles he plays so much as new selves that alternate with his original identity. The weeks during which he works at Pym's take on "an odd dreamlike quality" because of his labors as "the shadowy simulacrum of himself that signed itself every morning in the name of Death Bredon."[142] The word "simulacrum" seems to underline the falsity of Bredon—that Bredon is less a self than a disguise—but Sayers's novel suggests that her character lacks "any world of reality to which to return; for then the illusionary Mr. Bredon dislimned and became the still more illusionary Harlequin."[143] The protagonist is cast as entirely cut off from "reality" because he is caught up in selves that vanish with a change of clothes. When Wimsey later claims that Bredon has been investigated for impersonating him,[144] and the different identities that the character puts on and takes off are criminalized within the world of the novel, his ability to use fancy dress to become someone else takes on a sinister aspect. A drug dealer dreams that "Death Bredon, in his harlequin dress, was hanging him for the murder of Lord Peter Wimsey,"[145] a nightmare that seems both impossible and true: the reader knows that Bredon, Wimsey, and Harlequin are the "same" character, and yet they are so fully realized as to seem independent of one another.

As the novel draws to a conclusion, neither Sayers's protagonist nor other characters can tell which man he "really" is. He is "so intimately in the skin of Mr. Death Bredon" that he swears in a matter uncharacteristic of Wimsey;[146] the man who hired the detective to investigate Dean's murder remarks that Bredon has been such a successful copywriter that "I'd almost forgotten what you were really here for";[147] and Chief Inspector Charles Parker, Wimsey's friend and brother-in-law, encounters Wimsey and is "not quite certain whether he was being hailed by Lord Peter Wimsey or by Mr. Death Bredon."[148] When a fellow employee finally consults *Who's Who* and discovers an entry for "Wimsey, Peter Death Bredon (Lord),"[149] she has less solved the mystery of the character's identity than revealed the interpenetration of his various selves: Death Bredon is part of Wimsey's name, a component of his identity, and emerges as at once an alias *and* who Wimsey "really is." When the murderer finally confronts Sayers's protagonist and asks, "Which are you?" the response is "Both." The detective then proves that "I really was Bredon" by discussing advertising strategies.[150] This use of the past tense suggests that he is no longer Bredon, but given Wimsey's full name, he always will be.[151]

Murder Must Advertise thus employs costumes—a disguise and fancy dress—to help Lord Peter Wimsey solve a curious case. As I have argued, the protagonist's many changes of costume not only help him investigate a murder but also reveal the way in which clothing makes three different selves that the character moves among. In one of the novel's final chapters, the protagonist is depicted in the newspapers as Bredon ("in a dark lounge suit and soft hat") and Wimsey ("in neat breeches and boots and a bowler"). The narrator observes, "There was, needless to say, no photograph of the metamorphosis of the one gentleman into another,"[152] a metaphor that nicely captures the role of clothes as chrysalis, less disguise than locus of transformation. His many metamorphoses are certainly strategic, but they are no less substantive than Wimsey "himself"; indeed, Sayers will later suggest that *everything* her character wears is fancy dress. In *Gaudy Night*, American visitors to Oxford ask, "Does he need that glass in his eye or is it just part of the costume?"[153] As both a joke about American tourists and a comment on Wimsey's choice of accessories, this line points to the role of material objects in constructing Sayers's protagonist throughout her oeuvre.

It is the character's extraordinary set of gifts and talents—his wealth, creativity, intelligence, extensive social connections, education, and physical fitness—that make him a brilliant detective *and* that enable him to change his selves with his clothes. Like those of Orlando, Wimsey's many changes challenge depth ontology; read together, *Orlando* and *Murder Must Advertise* reveal surprising parallels between high modernism and detective fiction, both of which experiment with identity as a fusion of subject with objects. As Matthew Levay has argued in his analysis of Gertrude Stein's interest in detective fiction, such comparisons suggest that our understanding of period literary culture "might be enriched by a more nuanced approach to the connections between highbrow and lowbrow forms."[154] Sayers, who worked in a comparatively restrictive genre, experiments with character construction in a manner parallel to that of Woolf's modernist "biography."

Sayers, like Woolf, offers this challenge with a caveat. Only her heroic protagonist, Wimsey, can become Bredon and then Harlequin; other characters, as I have shown, cannot transform themselves through fancy dress. In this respect, Woolf and Sayers (while writing for different audiences)[155] offer a qualified model of the modern self, one that may be regarded as a riff on T. S. Eliot's famous comment in "Tradition and the Individual Talent" that "only those who have personality and emotions know what it means to want to escape from these things."[156] Orlando and Lord Peter Wimsey do not seek to escape from emotions, but they filter and reformulate their personalities and personae by means of canny and ongoing changes of attire. Sayers and Woolf offer models of identity premised on the attitude to self that is embodied in fancy dress, but they limit the number of characters who can enjoy—and present to others—"a great variety of selves."[157] Only those who need not aspire to any class or condition superior to their own, only those with talents and qualities beyond the ken of mere mortals, know what it means to put on a different self with a China robe, a pair of spectacles, or a Harlequin "black and white."

"The Sense of Anachronism": Fancy Dress After 1939

As the British nation went to war, fancy dress quietly left the sartorial scene. As I have noted, costumes were occasionally donned during World War I, but as Jarvis and Raine write, "There was not much interest, understandably, in fancy dress during the Second World War. With shortages of practically everything and strict rationing, most people were obliged to use all their ingenuity, and create miracles of 'make due and mend' in order to have clothes for everyday life."[158] Such austerity continued after the war, and while there was a spate of fancy-dress parties for the coronation of Queen Elizabeth II in 1953, they quickly dropped out of favor. Even the Chelsea Arts Ball, the most famous fancy-dress party, "held annually since 1909, ceased after 1958."[159] Perhaps the long years of material shortages had left Britons without memories of the pleasures of fancy dress, or perhaps those memories were too closely associated with prewar days to inspire a revival. As Jarvis and Raine speculate, "Modern society seemed too inhibited, or too self-conscious, to enjoy fancy dress any more."[160] In any case, without the experience of fancy dress, the British lost the experience of transformation that costumes offered—the chance to experiment with other selves that fancy dress could provide.

As the frequency of fancy-dress parties dwindled, references to costumes in postwar fiction similarly diminished. Castle argues that in "late appearances of the masquerade topos, one has the sense of anachronism. These are miniatures and ornaments, and though they may be delightful, they hardly have great importance."[161] While this description scarcely fits the many examples discussed earlier, it is an apt characterization of the role of fancy dress in British fiction after World War II. P. G. Wodehouse's novel *Joy in the Morning*, for example, depicts Bertie Wooster—formerly a critic of fancy dress for men—as a lover of flashy costumes. He claims that "fancy-dress binges have always been my dish" and procures Sinbad the Sailor garb to wear to a party near his aunt's estate.[162] He later tells a friend, "You know me when I hear rumours of these entertainments. The war horse and the bugle."[163] Wooster's enthusiasm carries him through a series of fancy-dress high jinks—an ill-fitting costume, a business deal, and a drunken uncle among them—but the party, while hilarious, serves as a reminder of prewar entertainment rather than a reflection on the relationship between person and fancy dress. As we have seen, Wodehouse's novel *Right Ho, Jeeves!* uses fancy dress to highlight the aspirations behind particular types of costumes and to insinuate that such aspirations cannot be achieved. *Joy in the Morning*, published twelve years later, in contrast, deploys the form solely as an opportunity to depict amusing shenanigans. This difference suggests that the challenge to depth ontology that fancy dress mounted in British texts earlier in the century no longer seemed interesting or important after the war.

* * *

Fancy dress provided Britons with a sartorial window through which they could consider a mutually constitutive relationship between persons and things. Many people enjoyed the experience of wearing costumes: the diaries of Virginia Woolf, the biography of Dorothy L. Sayers, and the many reports on fancy-dress parties in the periodical press indicate that this sartorial genre was valued as a means of getting away from, and occasionally rising above, one's normal self. Given the pleasure that fancy dress provided, it is striking that so few period texts celebrate the form. Most writers suggest that a costume can only magnify who a person wearing it really is: wealthy figures manifest their vanity, immodesty, and empty-headedness through fancy dress, while middle- and working-class characters are inconvenienced and shamed when they adopt costumes that aspire to a higher class, condition, or quality than they normally possess. The few characters in popular works who are transformed by fancy dress are not altered in ways that they desired or anticipated: in dressing as Henry VIII, Mr. Boomer in Arthur Moreland's "Simple Stories: The Fancy-Dress Dance" becomes not a respected monarch but a cad who offends his neighbors and friends; in dressing as Caroline de Winter, the protagonist of Daphne du Maurier's *Rebecca* becomes not a confident beauty but a haunted, harassed mature woman. Such representations suggest that most writers (and, one suspects, readers) did not value the capacity of the thing to alter the individual who wears it; instead, as with the mackintosh, there is a fear of the power of the object world *over* people, of being at the mercy of one's clothes. We cannot know the precise impact of the garments we put on, such texts suggest, but we can assume that the impact will be negative.

The *desire* that the relationship between person and thing might be different—that fancy dress might collaborate with its wearer to differently and positively inflect a self—is achieved by a few rare characters. The awe-inspiring protagonists of *Orlando* and *Murder Must Advertise* offer visions of a world in which humans can select and manipulate objects to materialize whatever identity they want at a given moment. This model of the self is heroic; it is not offered to characters who are ordinary in any respect, and it provides little hope that a reader may achieve the same success. In these two novels, fancy dress does not so much have a life of its own—in this respect, it is quite different from the evening gown and the mackintosh—as display the capacity to work *with* the individual who dons it. As we have seen in the previous two chapters, garments are often represented as having *separate* lives, *separate* desires, from those of their wearers; in *Orlando* and *Murder Must Advertise*, objects instead offer liberatory opportunities to take on a new life with a change of clothes. Such a representation of fancy dress, it seems, offered a safe space to celebrate a relationship between person and thing that was wielded by a select few. For Virginia Woolf and Dorothy L. Sayers, it provided a perfect glimpse of the extraordinary lives a person might lead if willing to abandon a constrained model of the self: fancy dress modeled an approach to clothing in which all garments could be costume, providing the self with new options with a simple change of attire.

Of course, not everyone could enjoy or would welcome this possibility. As the nameless narrator of *Rebecca* discovers, clothes that remake the self—or, rather, clothes that *are* the self—can serve as a vector for an alien personality to impose itself on a wearer. Representations of secondhand clothes echo this concern: clothes threaten the self by absorbing the personality of the original owner, who is thereby diminished as a garment takes some of the self away. And the wearer of used clothing can find him- or herself taking on the self of the person who previously wore a hat, a coat, or a pair of shoes.

4 Serialized Selves

Style, Identity, and the Problem of the Used Garment

On the face of it, fancy dress has little in common with secondhand attire. Fancy dress is elective, worn by individuals who can afford to purchase or make an outfit for one occasion; secondhand clothing is the lot of those who cannot buy new garments even if they might be worn every day. Fancy dress is aspirational and often quite spectacular; secondhand garments save face and generally try to avoid notice. In moving from fancy dress to secondhand attire, we track down the social and economic scale.

When placed side by side, however, fancy dress and secondhand clothing collectively highlight the complex relationship between self and surface; they point to how persons understand who they are in relation to the things they wear. If representations of fancy dress interrogate the idea that costumes can transform the self—that one can aspire to, and occasionally reach, new heights through the cooperation of wearer and costume—representations of secondhand clothing highlight an inverse process. Used clothes challenge depth ontology by suggesting that self and surface are so connected that garments can detach from and mobilize aspects of the initial wearer's identity. This relationship to materiality is troubling for characters who sell or donate their old clothes, but it poses the most significant problem for those who must accept or purchase castoffs.

Consider, for example, Rachel Ferguson's middlebrow novel *Alas, Poor Lady*, which chronicles the diverging fortunes of five originally upper-middle-class sisters. The three who marry live out their days in relative comfort, but the two who do not drift into increasing poverty. Ferguson uses the arrival of the well-off sisters' castoffs to reflect on the role of secondhand attire in Mary and Grace Scrimgeour's social lives and sense of self. The two sisters discover that "the passed-on gown can influence social opportunity. It wasn't *likely*, Mary pondered, that people would invariably recognize it in drawing-rooms of friends known also to the relations, but it was at least possible."[1] The verb "recognize" points to the close relationship between clothing and the initial owner; Ferguson identifies a dress not as a freestanding object but as belonging to the first person who wore it, even when on the body of another woman. The narrator suggests, moreover, that this realization only skims the surface of what secondhand attire does to Grace and Mary:

> [N]either of the sisters got as far as the discovery that the wearing of other people's frocks and coats also robs of personality: that with the putting of them on an actual dimming of individuality can set in.
>
> The governess. The spinster. The Aunt Sallies of life and stand-bys of British serialized humour. Submerged in other people's garments.[2]

Alas, Poor Lady here suggests that secondhand attire, no matter how finely constructed, flattering, or well preserved, diminishes the personality and individuality of those who wear it. Moreover, a used coat or dress remains *someone else's* garment; it "submerges" subsequent owners under the original owner's impress. The two Scrimgeour sisters can neither lay claim to a culturally valued subjectivity—they are, as the narrator notes, "the governess" (Grace), "the spinster" (both sisters), and "Aunt Sallies"—nor even hold onto disparaged identities as they drown under their well-meaning sisters' clothes. Fortunately, Mary and Grace remain largely unaware of what the castoffs they wear do to them.

Ferguson's assessment of secondhand clothing was not idiosyncratic or unusual in the literature published between the wars. Drawing from a range of popular and experimental fiction, I argue that representations of secondhand clothing highlight an economy of subjectivity mediated through used garments. Secondhand attire provides the most direct example of human subjects reduced and diminished through garment actants—of those at the mercy of their clothes. Characters who donate or sell their clothing part with more than mere material; their things take part of the donors with them. And those who buy castoffs discover that they become auxiliary to the original owner of the attire as garments serialize characters. Representations of used garments figure a limited economy; the hierarchy between subject and object—the wearers of garments and the garments themselves—is leveled or at least realigned as humans become absorbed and influenced by their dress. Equally important, the secondhand garment troubles the boundaries between different owners and characters, presenting a dividual model of the person. Representations of castoffs point to a shared experience of the world, a shared interaction between people and objects, that works to unravel individualism.[3]

Examining the limited economy of secondhand clothing provides both a historical and a critical payoff. The trade in used clothes offers a window onto economic changes that threatened British social class between the wars; this optic sheds light on the profound role of things in constituting identity in the early twentieth century. As historian Ross McKibbin has documented, the British middle class generally spent double what the working class devoted to clothing, not only because the middle class had more disposable income but also because clothing represented a "different order of urgency," since garments *constructed* class identity: "Suitable clothing was necessary both for the job and for social status: it was one of the last things that could be sacrificed."[4] Middle-class men and women who struggled in the difficult economic climate between the wars were driven to the used-clothing market to appear suitable. Dress historians have long asserted that Great Britain experienced a "democratization of dress" in the early twentieth century, but this argument ignores the booming trade in secondhand clothing. The "new poor"—a class of people economically disadvantaged after World War I—found themselves, often for the first time, having to resort to used clothes in order to maintain a respectable appearance. There were almost as many forms of and prices in the secondhand-clothing trade as there were in the sale of new garments; used garments could be worn and appreciated, but they had to be fully distanced from their original owners and in "like-new" condition to avoid the "submersion" that Ferguson's novel outlines.

Representations of secondhand clothing also offer insight into stylistic and affective differences between middlebrow and modernist texts, which approach used garments with quite different emphases. Secondhand attire repeatedly receives comic treatment in cartoons in *Punch* and in fiction aimed at a middlebrow audience.[5] Examples point to the difficulty of maintaining one's identity when discarding used clothes: whether they are driven to raise money by finding a market for old garments or are encouraged to engage in acts of charity by donating castoffs, characters demonstrate that to give away clothing is to give away oneself (figuratively or literally). Readers and viewers are encouraged to laugh at characters in these texts, which use the comic mode to dispel the anxiety that the "new poor" felt about their sudden dependence on the secondhand-clothing trade. While middlebrow fiction suggests that used clothing was a component of many people's wardrobes, it highlights the fact that the self is not self-contained but dependent on material and experiences that assemble it; identity, such texts demonstrate, can thus be partitioned and mobilized through material items that take unpredictable journeys away from the self.

In contrast to this comedic treatment, high-modernist representations of secondhand garments generally take on a tragic or militant cast. James Joyce, Jean Rhys, and Virginia Woolf figure selling, buying, and wearing used clothing as endangering individuality. Although they depict specific, narrow circumstances under which characters may purchase secondhand clothing without damage to their sense of self, they more often imply that the relational pressures of used garments cause the very borders of a character to break down. A dress one sells may take something of the original owner with it; a coat one buys may defamiliarize one's own arms and torso. In these examples, it becomes unclear who or what is wearing whom. Characters feel that they cannot become or be themselves but are the auxiliaries of another self, a self distributed by a used garment.

Examined together, texts aimed at different reading publics express a shared sense of how secondhand clothing affects those who wear it *and* opposing attitudes about that impact. If everyone agreed that clothing can extract, circulate, and impose the initial wearer's personality and identity on another, then they disagreed about how to regard that economy. Middlebrow characters—perhaps reflecting the tastes of their writers and readers—choose not to dwell on such assumptions. The comic representation of secondhand attire reflects a comparative degree of comfort with looking—and reading and writing—like others. Modernist characters and narrators, in contrast, regard the sharing of clothes as an unbearable imposition, one that particularly forces artist-figures to be less true to themselves and their art. The alignment of attitudes between reading publics and sartorial style—an alignment that, as I will demonstrate, does not apply to other secondhand objects—suggests that used attire, however prosaic, became a site of conflict between persons and (some of) the things they wore.

The New Poor and Old Clothes: Modern Experiences of the Secondhand

Advertisements for secondhand-clothing dealers haunt the margins of fashion periodicals of the 1920s and 1930s. Issues of *Vogue* and *Eve* reported on the latest Paris models, but small notices reminded readers that many women came into contact with designers like Coco Chanel and Paul Poiret—as well as less august names—only after other women had worn the garments and decided to sell them. Scholarship on fashion in modernity generally focuses on the rise of industrialization and mass-production and the emergence of designer brands; Beverly Lemire speaks for many scholars when she asserts that secondhand apparel was socially acceptable and widely worn only *before* industrialization made cheaper, ready-made garments available.[6] Stanley Chapman, for his part, asserts that by 1860, 80 percent of the population of Britain purchased ready-made clothing.[7] Such arguments, which focus on the nineteenth century, occlude the ongoing demand for secondhand merchandise that persisted well into the twentieth century, when preindustrial forms of the clothing trade quietly persevered at the edges of modernization.

Although middle-and upper-class individuals wore secondhand clothes less frequently after nineteenth-century advances in mass-production lowered the cost of textiles and ready-to-wear clothing, secondhand-garment stores remained a fixture of many cities and neighborhoods (figure 4.1). They functioned not only as a source of inexpensive clothing but also as an opportunity for moralizing. For example, in his essay "The Londoner Out and at Home," George R. Sims observes that "second-hand clothes shops abound all over the Metropolis, and they are usually stocked to the full limit of their space. If the faded finery of a second-hand clothes shop could speak, it could tell many a tale of the great human comedy, and alas! Of the great human tragedy also."[8] As Sims's comments make plain, individual garments and the volume in each shop were thought to bear witness to the lives of people who had long abandoned their clothing. Such figuration seems the privilege of a writer who does not himself

FIGURE 4.1 Secondhand-clothing shop in London (Hackney), 1905. (Source of Image: London Borough of Hackney Archives)

patronize this type of establishment, but the educated classes could treat the "faded finery" in used-clothing shops only with philosophical distance before 1914.

The secondhand-clothing trade resurged during World War I. Between 1914 and 1918, a popular means of raising money for charity involved holding fairs or bazaars where working-class individuals could purchase designer clothing donated by aristocrats and even royalty.[9] As the war lingered on, the National War Savings Committee urged British citizens to limit their clothing budgets and to donate what they might have spent on new clothes to war bonds and loans (figure 4.2).

Cartoons in *Punch* suggest that complying with such directives led individuals to wear outmoded, and perhaps secondhand, clothing; it was "rotten bad form" to wear "quite new" garments, although one suspects that few people sported visible patches or crushed top hats (figure 4.3). This image reflects, perhaps, hyperbole on behalf of the cartoonist and magazine, but other periodicals quoted society women who claimed to have turned their back on fashion for the duration of the conflict.[10]

FIGURE 4.2 Poster issued by the National War Savings Committee, 1916. (Courtesy of the Imperial War Museum, London)

FIGURE 4.3 A. Wallis Mills, "War Economy," *Punch*, November 24, 1915, 425.

During a national crisis, wearing used clothing could be made palatable because it was patriotic.

While consumers hoped for a return to normal patterns of consumption after the war, a class self-identified as the "new poor" found that it could no longer afford a prewar standard of living. According to Simon Gunn and Rachel Bell, postwar "newspapers were full of stories of the 'new poor,' of well-to-do families who had fallen on hard times caused by inflation and the effects of post-war economic dislocation."[11] In January 1920, the *Queen*, a women's periodical aimed at the upper class, described this category as "those classes of education and refinement who have to meet the enormous increases in the cost of the barest necessities with steadily decreasing incomes, often enough on incomes reduced to the vanishing point by the loss of husband and father, or heavily encumbered, having the erstwhile breadwinner ill or disabled by wounds."[12] The *Lady*, for its part, exhorted its readers to adjust to the new economic situation with good grace: "In these days of increasing expenditure and diminishing income it behooves us—the New Poor—to adapt ourselves to altered circumstances."[13] Such adaptation included purchasing secondhand clothing, as a cartoon titled "The New Poor" makes clear (figure 4.4). The man at the door has come to purchase castoff clothing from the type of household that would have sold such garments in the past. The woman responds, however, with an undisguised eagerness: "Oh, how lucky! Do you think you have anything that would suit my husband?" Although the dealer's face registers some surprise, the cartoon suggests that the declassing of many people had shifted previous patterns of consumption and that readers of *Punch* would recognize the situation it depicts.

Advertisements in British periodicals indicate the extent of demand for secondhand clothing in the 1920s and 1930s as well as the lines along which such businesses were run. The sheer number of notices for individual dealers shows either that there were more people getting into the trade or that there was more demand for their goods (or both); while the Late May 1924 issue of *Vogue* has thirteen ads for used-clothing dealers,[14] the October 31, 1928, issue contains twenty-six.[15] The doubling in number of these advertisements was accompanied by an increasing variety of secondhand-clothes dealers. Some firms worked entirely by post and offered to send "all correspondence under plain envelope" so that a client's neighbors would not discover the sources of his or her "new" attire.[16] Other dealers operated "dress agencies," consignment or secondhand shops that were directed at declassed consumers; they included Patricia

THE NEW POOR.
"Good morning, Madam. I deal in cast-off clothing."
"Oh, how lucky! Do you think you have anything that would suit my husband?"

FIGURE 4.4 Bert Thomas, "The New Poor," *Punch*, January 21, 1920, 45.

Carr, who promoted "a new Dress Agency run on original lines for the 'new poor,'"[17] and "The New Poor and Molly Strong Dress Agency, run by gentlewomen in the interests of gentlewomen."[18] *Vogue* itself, while continuing to feature new clothing and designs in its articles and illustrations, appears to have acknowledged the need for such businesses, touting "The Shoppers' and Buyers' Guide" as a place to find buyers for (if not sellers of) castoff clothing: "Here, when you are tired of your clothes and yet can't afford to give them away, is the name of a discreet firm who will buy them from you."[19] Whether a reader chose to patronize a trader who did business by mail order or a dealer who owned a physical shop, *Vogue* promised discretion and anonymity, qualities that underline the potentially shaming nature of the transaction. The "new poor," such advertising suggests, were not habituated to buying secondhand garments, and if necessity compelled them to do so, they would seek to put distance between themselves, the previous owners of the clothing they purchased, and even the traders who dealt in castoff clothing.[20]

While little information about secondhand-clothing dealers has survived—as Lemire writes, the secondhand trade was "largely invisible" and left "few records"[21]—the archives of Robina Wallis, who ran such a business by post between 1926 and 1959, indicate how British consumers felt about buying used clothing.[22] Wallis inherited the business from her mother and moved it from Devon to Cornwall. After building her clientele through advertisements in the *Lady*, a weekly women's magazine, she sent and received garments from as far north as Scotland to the southern coast of England. Wallis acquired clothing from society women, including the Duchess of Roxburghe and Lady Victor Paget, as well as from women in more modest circumstances. Some of Wallis's clients bought *and* sold apparel, which suggests that certain garments made their way through multiple owners over time.

Many letters from Wallis's customers demonstrate that women who patronized secondhand-clothing dealers expected and received garments that were modish, in good condition, and, to all outward appearance "new." For example, Barbara Armstrong wrote to request a "smart black evening frock in either lace or georgette" and asserted, "I want a really good model."[23] Armstrong evidently got precisely what she wanted, later writing that the black lace evening dress "was most successful."[24] In addition to satisfying specific requests, Wallis received correspondence that praised her merchandise in general terms. Mrs. Alderson Archer, who was evidently recovering from an illness, confessed that "I feel clothes are a bit of a nuisance when one isn't feeling well, but, if one gets just what one wants, it certainly does cheer one up."[25] Although Archer's praise is conditional—"*if* one gets just what one wants"—her letter suggests that she thought it possible to acquire such garments on the secondhand market. These letters, and others like them in the archive, demonstrate that many customers were open to and satisfied with the clothes they bought secondhand. If such purchases were necessitated by economic circumstances and thus not a purely free choice (as they can be in today's vintage-clothing market), the writers frame their purchases as flattering and emotionally fulfilling.

At other times, however, Wallis's clientele wrote to express their frustration with secondhand garments that she had sent on approval. Their complaints indicate that used clothes were often unappealing or in poor condition, bearing traces of the first owner's inadequate taste or insufficient care. A. Bailey, writing from lower Hampshire, thanked Wallis for a parcel but rejected some of the items it contained: "The jumper [sweater] is not as smart as I wanted. I wonder if you have another one. I am sorry to give you so much trouble but I wanted a very nice one."[26] Bailey's desire for something *more* fashionable—by "smart," she meant highly stylish—points to an obvious condition of purchasing secondhand garments: because the original owners had generally worn them for at least one season, castoffs were unlikely to be in the latest styles and served as a reminder that someone else had enjoyed them first. Other women did not want the most eye-catching modes available—G. Birch returned a sequined coat in 1935, as it was "a little too striking for me"[27]—because such styles were suitable for only the kind of woman who owned a lot of clothes and could wear each piece infrequently. Thus whether a used garment was unfashionable or too stylish, it reminded clients like Bailey and Birch that another woman had worn it earlier, and often in very different financial circumstances.

The letters in the Wallis archive also make it plain that many secondhand garments bore traces of the original owner.[28] Lesley Paul wrote to return an ensemble because of its condition: "[T]he coat and skirt is just rather well worn for what I want as I am invited to a very smart 'house party' in August. It includes some of my relations who would know at once that it was not new as they see me every day!"[29] Paul, who wanted to keep her purchase of secondhand garments secret from even close "relations," could wear only clothing that looked unworn. Other buyers could not afford to be so choosy. A. Linton, who wrote from Edinburgh, used condition to negotiate more favorable terms from Wallis. In an undated letter, she noted that "the tweed suit fits well, but it has several large stains on the front of the skirt—perhaps you didn't notice them—I would give £3 for it."[30] These letters delineate the range of clients who purchased secondhand clothes. Some buyers insisted on "like-new" items, while others were willing to take flawed merchandise, provided that it was inexpensive. Perhaps Linton thought that she could remove the stains from the skirt, but it is also possible that she needed the suit so much that she would live with its imperfections. If so, the "large stains" would become an ongoing sign of the bodily experiences of another woman and would visually fix Linton in the class system.

Buying used clothing was thus a strategy that a range of people used to supplement or fill a wardrobe. It allowed comparatively well-off women to purchase designer garments for a fraction of the items' original cost; it also enabled poor women to dress themselves appropriately on a small budget.[31] And yet, the secondhand-garment market was replete with frustrations. An undated letter from M. A. Smith lamented, "The suit fits nicely but the color is too light and makes me look so big. I was very disappointed."[32] Smith's letter implies that the suit's original owner lacked taste, since the color was inappropriate for women of their size; her complaint bespeaks the frustration that Smith experienced at having to work within the parameters of another woman's history and choices. Although many women were satisfied with their purchases—the letters from Armstrong and Archer are not isolated—the secondhand market required patience, flexibility, and negotiation in order to achieve that satisfaction. And it was replete with reminders that other consumers were more fortunate.

The Wallis archive, and the many advertisements for secondhand-clothing shops and dealers published in periodicals between the wars, thus serves to complicate the impression of commentators in the period (and later dress historians) that dress was democratized in the first half of the twentieth century. In 1929, the *Encyclopaedia Britannica*, for example, confidently opined:

> Class distinctions, in so far as they are indicated by dress, have disappeared. It is not easy to detect differences of degree among the great bulk of the people. Partly this is due to the spread of democratic ideas and institutions. Cheap means of transport, for example, bring all classes together. The intermixing produces similarity in style of attire. Partly, also, the cause is economic. There are more wage-earners, at better rates of pay. There has been a tremendous increase in the number of women wage-earners. Every one has more money available to spend on dress.[33]

This assessment that "every one" could afford to spend money on clothing was widespread. Twenty-three years later, C. Willett Cunnington similarly opined that "fashion has now become a democratic expression instead of being, as it once was, the exclusive symbol of the upper class outlook."[34] These kinds of assertions are celebratory, and they offer an appealing account of period fashion (and material culture more generally) as free from the taint of class, which characterized dress in earlier eras.

The problem, however, is that such accounts are wrong. While it is true that, as Gilles Lipovetsky argues, Chanel and other designers popularized styles that made it "no longer obligatory for the upper classes to dress with ostentatious luxury," such "dressing down" did little to help those on the other end of the economic scale "dress up."[35] As Christopher Breward observes, "Few even in the 1930s could afford the new clothes in the shops."[36] Secondhand dealers provided options to buyers for whom new clothing was out of reach, but the very need for such businesses—and the very fact that they had to operate discreetly—reinforced class distinctions. Purchasing items from Wallis was not "a democratic expression" but a reminder that the buyer's social and sartorial aspirations were at odds with her economic class. Wearing a skirt with stains, returning a suit because it was well worn or in an unflattering shade, and rejecting a sweater that was "not as smart as [the purchaser] wanted" are all experiences that confronted the new (and old) poor, with their limited access to appropriate and attractive dress. A woman might hope for a garment that was clean and new, but she might be able to buy only an item marked by the initial owner. Even if observers thought that Wallis's clients were well turned out, the individuals wearing secondhand attire knew that their appearance was achieved by dint of a discreet dealer, a modicum of luck, and hard bargaining. The secondhand-clothing market thus serves to trouble narratives about the triumph of mass-production in the twentieth century.[37]

The range of real-life experiences with secondhand attire that I have detailed is replicated in period cartoons, fiction, and nonfiction. Occasionally, the acquisition of used clothing proceeds smoothly, particularly if characters are able to purchase such garments through the distancing medium of secondhand shops. Notably, however, British literature emphasizes the proximity inculcated through castoffs and the concern that secondhand clothes enchain wearers: garments take something away from those who discard them and impinge on the selfhood of subsequent wearers. Writers align feelings of self-deprecation, shame, and even anger with a category of clothing that has, seemingly, a life of its own—or, rather, a life siphoned off that of the first purchaser. They suggest that castoffs acquire something of the original owners' personality and *distribute* that personhood, a function that limits subsequent wearers' ability to own them fully. Secondhand garments thus render class materially as well as trouble the boundaries of the body and the individual, locating characters in hierarchical relationship with one another and radically expanding the notion of embodiment. By enchaining wearers to initial owners—individuals who cannot control the movement of their distributed selves—secondhand garments imply that buyers and sellers are diminished by contact with garments that appropriate power from the human in a zero-sum game.

Popular Culture's Comedies

At the turn of the twentieth century, secondhand clothes made an occasional appearance in the fiction published in middlebrow magazines. Elizabeth C. Pilkington's story "Milly's Old Lavender Gown" serves as an early exemplar of a subject that would become increasingly common after World War I when, as I have documented, many people were driven to purchase secondhand garments for the first time. The short piece begins with the title character's lament that her family must sell their old clothes because "we can't afford to give them."[38] Milly's sister exhorts the family members to discard everything they can, so Milly reluctantly goes to her wardrobe to retrieve a cotton dress that "seemed to shrink into the background."[39] Pilkington here animates the frock, which appears to "shrink" and thus reflects Milly's sentimental attachment to a dress that she had worn during a brief flirtation abroad. Divesting herself of the dress, in Milly's view, means putting aside pleasurable memories as well as her desire for the future; her clothes take with them "my treasured hopes—they and my old lavender gown find a grave in Mrs. Briggs's big black bag!"[40]

Readers of the *Windsor*, in which this story was published, could rest assured, however, that the "grave" would not entirely consume Milly's dress or dreams. Like many publications of its type, the magazine offered fiction with happy endings, and the plot of Pilkington's tale turns when the gown is purchased by a servant in the household of Milly's former beau:

> [W]ho was this coming down the plantation towards him but the veritable "Sweet Lavender" herself!—lissom figure, golden-brown hair, deep blue eyes, and even the same lavender gown, butterflies and all.
>
> He stood as one petrified: but as the figure drew nearer the golden hair assumed a carroty hue . . . and there stood before him a respectful-looking woman-servant from the house.[41]

The dress has the power to deceive the eyes, if only at a distance; although the story painstakingly explains that the servant does not look like Milly, the frock can evoke her appearance even when worn by another. As a result of this apparition, Rupert Courtenay-Leigh locates Milly and proposes marriage. In the final paragraph, the protagonist plans similar unions for her sisters, and her fiancé predicts, "No doubt my wife will prove a wonderful maker of marriages when even her old gown turned matchmaker."[42] "Milly's Old Lavender Gown" thus redeems the title character's inadequate means, loneliness, and unwilling sale of her dress through the conceit that the garment distributes her identity—her persona—and bears witness to her existence in a remote location.[43] The gown thus emerges as *the* most important "character" in the story; it becomes a shadow self that advances the character's hopes and the story's narrative. Pilkington's gentle animation of the dress serves to palliate Milly's involvement in an economic exchange that she would prefer to avoid; participation in the secondhand-clothing trade could be redeemed through the conventions of coincidence and the romance plot.

This comedic understanding of used garments is echoed in many other works read by middlebrow publics between the wars. These texts not only reflect an era when an increasing number of British citizens bought and sold castoffs but also, more importantly, shape that experience through a positive tone that emerges in sharp contrast to that of contemporary modernist fiction. Middlebrow novels and cartoons depict the need to sell (and, occasionally, buy) castoff clothing as humorous, an example of the shared predicament in which the "new poor" found themselves. While the taint of the secondhand market threatens characters' social status and self-worth, and garments are occasionally animated, optimism colors representations of used garb. In part, readers are encouraged to position themselves with the creators of such portrayals, who can clearly see what their characters do wrong. The repeated humor directed at secondhand-clothing exchange, however, reveals a strategy to defuse the anxiety and shame of buying old garments at a time when the new was at a premium. I trace representations of secondhand clothing in popular texts from the most intimate, casual exchanges (such as purchasing or receiving an item from a friend) through sellers and buyers of castoffs in professional markets. While sellers come in for a greater degree of ribbing than buyers—middlebrow texts were more willing to mock the upper and middle classes than those on the bottom rung of the economic ladder—these accounts depict the secondhand garment's power to tarnish the subject who exchanges it, to enchain individuals in a relationship through the agency of an object. The one exception is historical fiction, which illuminates why the modern castoff was so troubling.

Writers direct some of the most cutting humor at middle-class characters who procure used clothes from friends, the most intimate form of acquisition. In Molly Keane's *Devoted Ladies*, a middlebrow novel devoted to romantic intrigues in an Anglo-Irish hunting set, a character ignominiously nicknamed "Piggy" bewails the fate of a "black *Patou* dress Joan gave me, *rather* lovely, cut with a *terrible* deep V at the back and that marvelous swathed line."[44] The name Jean Patou, a French designer popular in both Great Britain and the United States in the 1920s and 1930s, was associated with elegance, expense, and high style. But Piggy's dressmaker, whom she charged with remaking the three-year-old gown so that it would fit her, had unwittingly destroyed it. Piggy and the seamstress "sought to recapture the infernal subtleties of Mr. Patou's three-year-old inspiration. Their minds in a fog, their hands cold, their mouths full of pins, to what strange shapes had they tortured this hellish garment before despair had settled in on them and they sought to put it back as it was before and could not."[45] Instead of remaking the dress into an innovative new garment or adapting Patou's dated vision, the dressmaker and Piggy find their time, emotional energy, and labor wasted by the "hellish garment" they mangle through their efforts. This dress remains "the black dress she [Joan] wore at hunt balls three years ago" and cannot be made to fit Piggy.[46] In fact, this may have been Joan's intention, as the character is repeatedly represented as using her "friends": the Patou dress thus works on behalf of Joan in remaining stubbornly resistant to Piggy's appropriation.

Keane's characters are largely deaf to the unflattering ways in which trade in secondhand garments positions them, but cartoons published in *Punch* in the 1920s depict characters as shamefully exposed by their attempts to sell or donate their clothes. In part, the humor hinges on the original owner's overvaluation of his or her used clothing, as in an August 19, 1925, cartoon in which a "lady" tries to sell a "real golf-coat." The old-clothes man responds, "Is it a nine or eighteen moth-'ole, or 'aven't yer counted 'em?"[47] The dumbfounded look on the lady's face expresses her shock and surprise at this assessment, and readers are expected to chuckle not only at the buyer's clever wordplay but at the would-be seller's conviction that *her* castoff is particularly valuable.

Although this assumption is never articulated, this cartoon relies on the seller's presence in the garment—the fact that the coat works as a component of the owner's identity.[48] In offering a "real golf-coat" to the wardrobe dealer without acknowledging its condition, this seller has opened herself to mockery and laughter. Such a cartoon would be funny, one suspects, only to readers who would pride themselves on never making a similar mistake.

Other *Punch* cartoons similarly suggest that owners are often unpleasantly surprised by the value of their castoffs—or by precisely *why* they are valued. A cartoon from 1924 depicts a "Grateful recipient" in the act of taking used boots from the "Vicar's wife," a scenario that presents a seemingly ordinary charitable act. In this cartoon, however, the donor receives not only thanks but a shaming reference to her size as the recipient states, "My missus 'as such long feet, an' yours are the only boots I can get to fit 'er with any comfort."[49] The surprise on the lady's face indicates that she has opened herself to an indirect insult—a comment on her large feet—through her act of charity. Here, donating a castoff serves to broadcast an unflattering aspect of the donor's physique that she would doubtless prefer to keep private; once the boots are in the hands of the recipient, they distribute biological facts about the donor's body. This cartoon suggests that one peril of engaging in the secondhand market is that the donor gives *herself*, as well as an object, away. Proximity of donor and recipient, or of buyer and seller, generates *Punch*'s humor, which repeatedly depicts the secondhand garment as tarnishing the first owner with unintended consequences as it changes hands.

These examples, albeit humorous, point to one of the reasons that the "new poor" may have preferred to deal with the secondhand market through the post. Traders like Robina Wallis are never the subject of *Punch*'s brand of comedy, in large part because the distance between buyer and seller provided a cushion of privacy that protected the original owner of garments. Distribute your garments over enough distance, Wallis's clients may have assumed, and they will never come back to haunt you. But middlebrow fiction still directs humor at protagonists' transactions with professional secondhand-clothing traders, which open characters to judgment and embarrassment. E. M. Delafield's *Diary of a Provincial Lady*, for example, represents the title character's attempts to rectify a negative bank balance by selling her old clothes: "Financial situation very low indeed, and must positively take steps to send assortment of old clothes to second-hand dealer for disposal." She later collect[s] major portion of my wardrobe and dispatch to address mentioned in advertisement pages of *Time and Tide* as prepared to pay Highest Prices for Outworn Garments, cheque by return. Have gloomy foreboding that six penny stamps will more adequately represent value of my contribution, and am thereby impelled to add Robert's old shooting-coat, mackintosh dating from 1907, and least reputable woolen sweater.[50]

The lady raids not only her own closet but also that of her husband in an attempt to raise money. Unlike the donors in the *Punch* cartoons, Delafield's protagonist is well aware of the probable low value of her castoffs. Such savvy does not, however, prevent disappointment: "Rather inadequate Postal Order arrives, together with white tennis coat trimmed with rabbit, which—says accompanying letter—is returned as unsalable. Should like to know *why*."[51] Selling her clothes to a professional trader cannot help the lady realize the sums she wants, and even distance cannot prevent a mild form of insult. Her family's castoffs—reflections, at a remove, of her family's choices and taste—are remunerated inadequately, making the lady *feel* more than usually inadequate as well. The dealer's rejection also helps to underline the lady's folly in purchasing a sport jacket—a tennis coat—trimmed with an impractical material. The judgment that this item is "unsalable" reflects badly on the lady's discernment, and it positions her as less a "fashion victim"—a phrase that suggests that a wearer is at the mercy of bad design—than a victim of her earlier decision. The jacket will linger in her closet, an unworn reminder of this embarrassing episode.

Delafield's novel reveals and reinforces a set of middlebrow assumptions about the "new poor" and the secondhand trade: this class may look fashionable even as individuals struggle to make ends meet; secondhand dealers never pay sellers what they believe their garments are worth; and to sell one's clothes is to open oneself to insult, though working with a professional trader at a distance serves to mitigate the sting. The lady learns that discarding garments is a complicated act, serving as it does to circulate the original owner's economic struggles, physical shortcomings, or fashion sense around the country through the mobility of attire. Discarding clothing puts characters' identities, as well as their castoffs, on the market; in choosing to sell items with which they have had intimate contact, characters in middlebrow fiction distribute aspects of themselves beyond the body boundary.

In contrast to the fancy-dress costume, which offers a few fictional characters in the period the opportunity to enjoy additional selves, the secondhand garment *diminishes* the individual who originally owned it by absorbing the self and traveling uncontrollable paths. Sellers may be slightly richer for having sold old clothes, but they pay for their small profits—or acts of charity—through a reduced sense of confidence, control, and self.

Representations of working-class recipients of secondhand clothing are relatively rare in popular fiction, doubtless because the demand for castoffs reminded readers of economic disparities that were difficult to treat lightly. Flora Thompson's *Lark Rise* (1939), the first book in her immensely popular *Lark Rise to Candleford* trilogy, serves as an exception. The setting for Thompson's novel—Oxfordshire in the 1880s and 1890s—helped to assuage the difficulties of this subject; her book offers a nostalgic treatment of rural working-class life, which had vanished by the time *Lark Rise* was published.[52] Because of this historical distance, and because her characters are members of a respectable, rural working class, Thompson could treat the castoff's power to enchain wearers positively; in contrast to others writing in the 1920s and 1930s, she constructs secondhand clothing as distributing original owners and thus *helping* families and communities to cohere.

Thompson's characters rely on secondhand garments, which they receive from "daughters, sisters, and aunts away in service, who all sent parcels, not only of their own clothes, but also of those they could beg from their mistresses."[53] Like the two sisters in Rachel Ferguson's *Alas, Poor Lady*, which was published just two years before *Lark Rise*, Thompson's characters receive castoffs from family members, garments that come from intimate contacts and are identified with the donors. The correspondence between the two novels ends there, however: unlike Ferguson's protagonists, Thompson's characters desire and even *prefer* familial hand-me-downs to clothes that come from elsewhere:

> The daughter's or other kinswoman's clothes were sure to be appreciated, for they had usually already been seen and admired when the girl was at home for her holiday, and had indeed helped to set the standard of what was worn. The garments bestowed by the mistress were unfamiliar and often somewhat in advance of the hamlet vogue, and so were often rejected for personal wear as "a bit queer" and cut down for the children.[54]

This passage identifies two factors that shape the hamlet's opinion of what used clothing is wearable. It demonstrates, as *Lark Rise* notes elsewhere, that the rural community "had a fashion of its own, a year or two behind outside standards."[55] This "lag" partially accounts for the difference between *Lark Rise* and *Alas, Poor Lady*, in which the sisters receive hand-me-downs in 1920s London. If one operates outside or slightly behind the fashion system, Thompson's novel suggests, secondhand attire is acceptable and even welcome. More important, however, is the novel's assertion that the association of a dress or skirt with a specific kinswoman makes that item of clothing most desirable. The relative's contact with the garment, and her contact with her family while wearing that garment, makes it doubly familiar: it is intimately associated with a family member and previously known. In wearing a sister's, a daughter's, or another relative's clothes, the characters in *Lark Rise* link themselves to a relation working in service (generally in a larger town or city); if others in the hamlet recognize a dress as secondhand, it serves as a sign of enchainment with a *successful* family member—someone who is employed, helping to support the family back home, and a tastemaker for the community.

Such garments remained familiar—associated with the initial wearer—throughout their useful lives. In *Candleford Green* (1943), Laura dresses "for the Church Social in the cream nun's veiling frock in which she had been confirmed and in which her cousins Molly and Nellie had been confirmed before her."[56] The character is untroubled by the dress's rich history, by the manner in which it links her with her cousins, because she has no other means to acquire clothing. Her family, which is among "those too poor to buy at all at first-hand,"[57] must accept what they receive. Because Thompson sets her fiction in the late nineteenth century, and because all her characters come from the rural working class, she can depict secondhand clothing in a manner quite different from that of her contemporaries. Indeed, *Lark Rise* throws into relief some reasons that castoffs are so much more troubling for characters in other middlebrow novels. Ferguson's protagonists, who resent having to wear their sisters' old clothing, "had been used to [their] own original garments and the privacy and self-respect of that which is made for [their] own body and no one else's."[58] Thompson's characters have not had that experience—they can never regard clothing as the possession of the individual and not the family. As a result, the fictional inhabitants of Lark Rise welcome clothing that was made for and worn by other bodies.

Thompson's work focuses on—indeed, celebrates—a historical moment when fashion was the province of cities and when the rural poor could not expect to own many new garments. Her novels do not always depict secondhand clothing in a positive light, however; they suggest that purchasing used garments from a shop—clothes that have no familiar associations—sets up characters for humiliation. Laura and her mother watch as one young woman leaves the hamlet to go into service, wearing

> a bright blue, poplin frock which had been bought at the second-hand clothes shop in the town—a frock made in the extreme fashion of three years before, but by that time ridiculously obsolete. Laura's mother, foreseeing the impression it would make at the journey's end, shook her head and clicked her tongue and said, "Why ever couldn't they spend the money on a bit of good navy serge!" But they, poor innocents, were delighted with it.[59]

Thompson does not depict the young woman's shaming when she arrives at her destination, and the narrator's voice offers sympathy to the "innocent" character who purchased a completely outmoded and loud secondhand garment. While this young woman would likely be perceived as poor and rustic no matter what she wore, a castoff from a family member in service would not have been made in "the extreme fashion," nor would it be quite so outmoded. Thompson's novel thus represents secondhand clothes from family members as *safer*, more appropriate attire than used clothes from a shop; if the former distribute the personae of relations and link each person who wears them to the donor, the latter are alien and isolating.

Thompson's treatment of secondhand clothing thus serves to sharpen the precise anxieties expressed in other middlebrow works. If novels by Ferguson, Keane, and Delafield; cartoons published in *Punch*; and other texts depict sellers and buyers of used garments as embarrassed by items that absorb and distribute personhood, such an experience is produced through historical, geographical, and class conditions that do not pertain to Thompson's characters. By setting *Lark Rise* at the end of the nineteenth century, and by focusing on a way of life long gone at the time she was writing, Thompson could figure secondhand clothing as one of the forms of intimate exchange that supported and bettered life in England's rural villages.[60] In the 1920s and 1930s, however, middle- and upper-class British citizens in towns and cities had come to *expect* to wear new clothing; the ideal had become, in Ferguson's words, clothing purchased or "made for [one's] own body and no one else's."[61] Individuals who found this ideal impossible to attain and resorted to the secondhand market were repeatedly reminded that their financial and social position *ought to be* better than it was. In the historical window between the wars, secondhand clothes emerged as a material resister of the gap between expectations and economic reality: no wonder sellers saw the need to profit from their old clothes as giving themselves away; and no wonder buyers regarded themselves as imprinted by garments made for, and shaped by, the bodies of others comparatively more privileged.

Varied as they are, popular representations of the secondhand-clothing trade share one important quality: although the type and texture of their treatment varies, they regard the exchange of castoffs lightly. Characters may be surprised or briefly discomfited to discover that they have "given themselves away" in selling or donating used clothing, but the garments' ability to absorb aspects of the original owners—and to distribute their identities in ways that elude prediction or control—does not do extensive damage. Work written for a highbrow audience, in contrast, casts the used garment as far more sinister. These texts suggest that in wearing secondhand clothing, the human can be serialized—that castoffs create asymmetrical relationships as people are diluted by garments that either take something of the self with them *or* muddle the boundaries between different individuals. Secondhand clothing can render individuals secondary and subordinate to the clothes they once wore or that necessity requires them to put on.

High Modernism and the Problem of Proximity

At the same time the middlebrow work I have discussed was published, high modernists offered quite different visions of what it meant to buy and sell used clothing. Their texts, which often focus on protagonists struggling to establish a unique identity in a resistant social sphere, occasionally represent used apparel as acceptable, particularly when it can be purchased through the distancing medium of a shop. More often, however, they treat secondhand garments as imperiling individualism. They repeatedly suggest that characters cannot maintain their selves under the pressure of clothes that belong to known others; they also express the suspicion that the human might be auxiliary to the object world, worn and manipulated by purportedly inert material.[62] Used clothing emerges as so imbued with the bodies and selves with which it has contact that secondhand boots, pants, and dresses create a dividual human, one characterized by a compromised—because communal—self. If Flora Thompson's late Victorian English laborers take a communal and familial identification as primary, her modernist contemporaries wrote characters who fervently desire an individual relationship to clothing—indeed, who want to exempt themselves from all manner of serial relationships.

This is not to say that modernist texts never see the humor in the necessity to wear used clothing. *Ulysses*, for example, deploys secondhand garb to have great fun at a minor character's expense. In "Sirens," Father Cowley and Ben Dollard remember that Molly Bloom used to run a secondhand-clothing business.[63] They call it "the other business," which Don Gifford glosses as "Molly and Bloom collected and sold secondhand clothes and theatrical costumes."[64] The fact that Cowley and Dollard do not explicitly identify the trade suggests that there is something disreputable in selling secondhand clothes. Such disrespect could stem from the fact that Molly works in a culture that naturalizes women's domestic, but not commercial, labor or from the long historical association between Jewish men and women and the old-clothes trade.[65] The novel thus briefly references the Blooms' former business as a sign of ethnic difference and the gender distortions created by colonial poverty.

Instead of focusing on the business, however, characters in *Ulysses* are much more preoccupied with one specific occasion related to the Blooms' secondhand stock. Dollard says he "remember[s] those tight trousers,"[66] a memory that Bloom later fills out: "Ben Dollard's famous. Night he ran round to us to borrow a dress suit for that concert. Trousers tight as a drum on him. Musical porkers. Molly did laugh when he went out. Threw herself back across the bed, screaming, kicking. With all his belongings on show. O, saints above, I'm drenched! O, the women in the front row! O, I never laughed so many!"[67] In "Penelope," Molly too recalls "Ben Dollard . . . the night he borrowed the swallowtail to sing out of in Holles street squeezed and squashed into them and grinning all over his big Dolly face like a wellwhipped childs botty didn't he look a balmy bullocks sure enough that must have been a spectacle on the stage."[68] All three characters recollect Dollard's bodily exposure in a pair of tight secondhand pants. Bloom and Molly remember that the trousers emphasized Dollard's genitals as well as his girth; the poor fit resulted in an unwitting and comic sexual display, and the high-cultural spectacle of musical performance was transformed into an obscene exhibition facilitated by secondhand trousers. Although none of the characters identifies the original owner of the suit, and Dollard does not experience it as a vector for the distributed persona of someone else, the trousers draw attention to the role of clothing, which constitutes individuals as artists, in performance. Dollard's pants do not fail in the spectacular ways that other manmade objects do, but they become resistant things through a poor fit that denaturalizes his identity as a purveyor of high-cultural entertainment. Since the pants, in Molly's view, will be the most obvious and entertaining aspect of "Dollard's" performance, he becomes subordinate to the dress suit he borrows.

While Joyce deploys secondhand trousers to generate humor at the expense of a minor character in *Ulysses*, used clothing represents a significant (and decidedly uncomic) threat to Stephen Dedalus. He wears used clothes in both *A Portrait of the Artist as a Young Man* and *Ulysses*, and differences among the examples from these texts clarify the precise manner in which particular castoffs impinge on the self. In *Portrait of the Artist*, secondhand clothing is intimately tied to Stephen's escape from Ireland. The end of the novel documents his acquisition of "new secondhand clothes" as part of his preparation for life in Paris: "April 26. Mother is putting my new secondhand clothes in order. She prays now, she says, that I may learn in my own life and away from home and friends what the heart is and what it feels. Amen. So be it. Welcome O life! I go to encounter for the millionth time the reality of experience and to forge in the smithy of my soul the uncreated conscience of my race."[69] Although Stephen, who has by this point assumed his position as the novel's first-person narrator, uses the adjective "new" to identify the clothes that will help his body fly by the nets of family, nation, and Church, a reader quickly detects the oxymoron in the phrase "new secondhand," which gestures toward Stephen's poverty and qualifies the preparations for his escape.[70] *Portrait of the Artist* uses his secondhand attire to code an economic problem, but it is important to note that only the reader, and not Joyce's character, regards the garb in this light. Stephen records the acquisition of the garments in a neutral manner, and this detail is placed in close proximity to his highly emotional final declarations, including "Welcome O life!"[71] and "Old Father, old artificer, stand me now and ever in good stead."[72] Stephen's "new secondhand clothes" are thus not separate from, but associated with, his artistic ambitions and pursuit of exile.

Portrait of the Artist provides no other details about the secondhand garments that Stephen takes on his journey, but *Ulysses* opens with the journey ended ignominiously and Stephen, once again, in secondhand togs. In his conversation with Buck Mulligan on the roof of the Martello tower, Buck asks Stephen, "How are the secondhand breeks [trousers]?" to which Stephen simply responds, "They fit well enough."[73] Buck then continues:

> —The mockery of it, he said contentedly, secondleg they should be. God knows what poxy blowsy left them off. I have a lovely pair with a hair stripe, grey. You'll look spiffing in them. I'm not joking, Kinch. You look damn well when you're dressed.
> —Thanks, Stephen said. I can't wear them if they are grey.
> —He can't wear them, Buck Mulligan told his face in the mirror. Etiquette is etiquette. He kills his mother but he can't wear grey trousers.[74]

This passage signals Stephen's poverty and respect for the mourning rituals of the period; as I discussed in chapter 1, mourning dress was pervasive in Britain in the early twentieth century, and while gray garments were appropriate for half-mourning, only black could be worn in the period immediately following a close relative's death. The exchange is also significant because Buck draws attention to the original owner of Stephen's trousers and thus to the fact that they are secondhand. Stephen's trousers (unlike Dollard's borrowed pants) fit, but Buck emphasizes their cast-off status and specifically their anonymous origins ("God knows [who] left them off"). He speculates that their original owner must have been both diseased ("poxy") and unattractive ("blowsy"). He thus positions the secondhand trousers not as inert material but as linked to the body and persona of the man who sold them.

Read in this light, Stephen's "secondleg" pants might imperil his health—they could literally carry infection—and they enchain him with another man whose qualities may influence Stephen. Perhaps for these reasons, Buck offers Stephen a pair of his own pants, which he represents as flattering and implicitly free from the taint of the other pair. If Stephen is going to face the world in clothes that distribute another person, then Buck's offer conveys an opportunity to put on the known, the healthy, and the familiar. In his refusal to wear Buck's pants, Stephen cites mourning conventions, but his reflections later in the novel suggest that he resents wearing Buck's clothing.

In "Proteus," readers learn that Stephen concurs that clothing distributes the person who originally wore it. As Stephen reclines on the rocks and contemplates his footwear, *Ulysses* points out that he wears Buck's shoes: "His gaze brooded upon his broadtoed boots, a buck's castoffs *nebeneinander* [juxtaposed or next to each other]. He counted the creases of rucked leather wherein another's foot had nestled warm. The foot that beat the ground in tripudium, foot I dislove."[75] The passage renders Stephen's body strange to him as it first identifies the boots as his, and then recalls Buck's feet in the same boots. The next sentence identifies the feet in the boots as having "beat the ground in tripudium," a "solemn, religious three-beat dance" that Stephen will perform in "Circe."[76] In this sentence, Stephen either is once again seeing the feet in the boots as his, perhaps in a future time, or is recalling a dance performed by Buck that is not recorded in *Ulysses*. As a result, the final phrase—"foot I dislove"—is *either* Stephen's or Buck's foot, an irresolvable identification generated and maintained by the secondhand boots. The German word *nebeneinander* nicely captures Stephen's problem: in putting on Buck's castoffs, he juxtaposes himself with the friend from whom he wants to be distinguished.

This passage provides an acute example of Garry Leonard's observation that "Joyce shows us self-awareness is the result of an unanticipated gap in the narrative of the self, a gap that briefly exposes selfhood as a fiction."[77] Secondhand attire, I am arguing, has the power to *produce* such gaps; because Stephen cannot view the boots as a neutral commodity, they disrupt the fiction of his independence and self-authoring.[78] His musings also highlight the problem of possession acutely raised by the castoff: Does Stephen own these boots, or does Buck? Or, to put it differently, might the used boots take possession of Stephen himself?

As Stephen takes on Buck's distributed persona through used clothing, *Ulysses* points to the problem of wearing garments whose histories are all too familiar. Joyce's character can never lace up "his broadtoed boots" without recalling the man who first wore them; the boots thus conjure up the "brother soul" who, Stephen speculates, "will now leave me."[79] The boots have a history with a specific body, and while that body may not have marked the clothing in a manner perceivable by the senses, Stephen *constructs* such a mark. Although he insists on being accepted "as I am. All or not at all,"[80] the boots have the power to qualify or taint who he is. They refuse the inert role of the commodity and position Stephen and Buck in a serial relationship—one in which Buck comes *first*.[81]

Joyce's representations of secondhand garments thus mirror the accounts of other writers in the period who depict used clothing as constructing associations between people through material goods that extract and impose aspects of the original owner's being. For a character who wants to exempt himself from *all* reciprocal obligations, hand-me-downs from a friend signal a sartorial colonization, a material form of association that reminds the would-be artist of his dependence on and enchainment with others.[82] While Stephen might pride himself on self-fashioning, he is instead partially fashioned by others through the medium of used clothing. What serves as a form of mild embarrassment or an occasion for self-deprecating humor in middlebrow texts becomes an experience that rankles: Joyce's nascent modernist artist resists secondhand clothes that render him *nebeneinander,* and he resents the limited economy in which castoffs force him to participate.

Joyce's texts imply that if one has to wear used clothing, it does the least damage to one's integrity if it comes through a shop or another venue that obscures the garment's origins. Jean Rhys's characters similarly emphasize the import of distancing secondhand garments from the bodies who first wore them. They routinely purchase used clothing, including Julia Martin in *After Leaving Mr. Mackenzie,* who procures a few items in preparation for a trip from Paris to London. The narrator reports, "The idea of buying new clothes comforted her, and she got out of bed and dressed. At three o'clock she was back at her hotel, carrying the clothes she had bought at a secondhand shop in the Rue Rocher—a dark grey coat and hat, and a very cheap dress, too short for the prevailing fashion." Although the dress she purchases is not fashionable, and when she "dressed herself in the new clothes, . . . the effect was not so pleasing as she had hoped,"[83] her disappointment with the coat, hat, and dress appears to stem from a general problem of fashionability, not from the garments' status as someone else's castoffs. Like the Stephen Dedalus of *Portrait of the Artist,* Julia can regard her acquisitions as "new" and "secondhand" at once, and she uses the adjective "new" two times in describing the used garments. Because Julia buys these garments at a shop, her experience of consumption is almost identical to the purchase of genuinely new clothing; by decisively separating a garment's first and second owners, the store on the Rue Rocher provides the distance that obscures a given item's history and renders it acceptable.

Contrast this experience with that of Rhys's protagonist Teresa in "A Solid House," a short story set during an air raid.[84] She is forced to buy unattractive secondhand clothing from her landlady, Miss Spearman, but Teresa is most upset when she observes her own castoff languishing in Spearman's stock: "[S]he recognized her own black dress in the cupboard. It was next to a shapeless purple coat. A cast-off self, it stared back so forlornly, so threateningly that she turned her eyes away."[85] Rhys's story presents the inverse of Buck and Stephen's boots. While Stephen experiences frustration and alienation because he wears boots that mobilize their original owner, Teresa finds herself unsettled by the proximity of the unsold castoff, which her imagination animates. In her view, the dress can see—it stares—and *feel*: it regards its owner with sadness and anger. As in "Illusion," the short story by Rhys discussed in chapter 1, in "A Solid House," Rhys figures the garment as a quasi-subject; while the emphasis falls differently in the stories, in both the unworn garment emerges as malign. In "A Solid House," the dress's purported malevolence stems from its status as not just a castoff but a "cast-off *self*," a thing that has captured something of Teresa's history and identity—of who she was while wearing it. The garment-self is not valued by the marketplace, as Spearman identifies it as "well cut" but also "depressing" and not worth very much,[86] a comment that sheds light on Teresa's own figurative worth. In this example, the secondhand dress confronts its original owner because it is not (yet) distributed. Moreover, "A Solid House" suggests that if the dress is sold for the cheaper price that Spearman recommends, it will move downward in the marketplace, devaluing Teresa's selfhood and history with it.

This movement is cast as sorrowful and threatening in Rhys's story, and it is useful to remember that similar experiences were treated lightheartedly in texts aimed at popular audiences of the same period. The narrator of Delafield's *Diary of a Provincial Lady*, for example, is shocked to discover that a "grey georgette [dress] only sacrificed reluctantly at eleventh hour from my wardrobe" for a local rummage sale has been priced at a mere "three-and sixpence."[87] The dress's value to the narrator, who regards parting with it as a sacrifice, is challenged by its low worth in the estimation of the community, but she does not dwell on this discovery, nor does she anthropomorphize the frock. In a less kindly version of this situation, the "fussy little man" in a cartoon published in *Punch* on September 22, 1926, attempts to retrieve some of his garments, which his wife donated to a charity rummage sale, only to be scathingly informed that he might find them "at the fourpenny stall."[88] In these texts, readers are encouraged to laugh with or at characters who overestimate the value of their old clothes. The comedy takes some of the sting out of the discovery; if buying and selling used garments disappoints fictional characters across cultural strata, only modernist novels figure the castoff as a painful threat to individuality and selfhood.

One final example illustrates British modernism's charged response to secondhand clothing, which it collectively depicts as a form of material interdependence that thwarts independent action and development. In chapter 2 of her polemic *Three Guineas*, Virginia Woolf responds to a "letter" that requests, in part, donations of used clothing to be sold at "bargain prices" to "women whose professions require that they should have presentable day and evening dresses which they can ill afford to buy."[89] Woolf asks why the representative of professional women is so poor "that she must beg for cast-off clothing for a bazaar,"[90] a query that launches the author into an exploration of the continued economic disparities between professional men and women and of the difficulty that women faced in entering the professions. While the need for secondhand clothing recedes into the background of her analysis, it seems clear that Woolf (like Joyce and Rhys) regarded the consumption of genuinely *new* clothing as a norm for all but the working class; her selection of the castoff as a telling detail locates *Three Guineas* at a particular historical moment when Woolf (and many others) assumed that most people ought to be able to purchase new garments. If, as she reflects elsewhere, "a cast-off dress here and there are the perquisites of the private servant,"[91] the castoff is emphatically *not* desirable for the daughters of educated men, representing as it does a form of material dependence that compromises the "weapon of independent opinion"[92] that, Woolf argues, women must wield if their social and political activities are to work for peace. *Three Guineas* positions women's poverty—encapsulated in the fact that they can "ill afford to buy" new clothes—as a threat to independent thinking and action; like the castoff in the fiction of Joyce and Rhys, used clothing in Woolf's polemic figures an interrelationship that compromises those who must put on the dresses—and even stockings—that have been molded to another body.

In her influential study *Adorned in Dreams*, Elizabeth Wilson has argued that the modern consumer was "fearful of not sustaining the autonomy of the self. . . . The way in which [he or she] dress[ed] may [have] assuage[d] that fear by stabilizing . . . individual identity."[93] But if and when characters in and subjects of modernist fiction and nonfiction are forced to dress in the clothing of people they know, or if they cannot sell their old clothes, Wilson's formulation is reversed. Instead of "stabilizing . . . individual identity," secondhand garments compromise it: they trouble boundaries between self and other at the material and psychological levels. The proximity of used garments to multiple owners complicates the status of the individual in such works, insinuating that humans are dividual creatures constituted by objects that have histories that precede and survive them. Although the characters and authors I have discussed do not welcome this knowledge, readers are reminded that the self is not autonomous or stable: it is instead, sometimes literally, walking in another man's shoes.

The Threat of Secondhand Style

As I have argued, secondhand garments rendered people at the mercy of their clothes in the early twentieth century due to a specific historical circumstance: a number of consumers were obliged to purchase the castoffs of others *after* becoming used to genuinely new clothing. While the economic problems faced by the new and old poor undoubtedly meant that individuals and families bought other material goods on the secondhand market, such purchases are represented as unproblematic. Consider, for example, Stephen Dedalus in *Portrait of the Artist*, who owns a copy of Horace and regards the pages as "human" because they were turned by two brothers whose names are inscribed on the flyleaf.[94] Previous ownership infuses the book with warmth and human interest, perhaps because Joyce's character wants to make a distinction between market (clothing) and symbolic (written word) economies.[95] But this difference also inheres in the fact that clothing admits of a more intimate relationship to the original owner than do other objects; secondhand clothes are most comfortable, and least alienating, when the original owner *cannot* be identified. As noted in the introduction, Jacques Lacan's model of the mirror stage and Charles Cooley's "looking-glass self" theorize that garments and accessories become one with the human body at the crucial moment when an infant first apprehends her reflection or when an adult attempts to imagine his identity in the eyes of others. The process of self-awareness can proceed smoothly if the objects that help to assemble identity cooperate—if they do not communicate histories separate from that of the human subject working to consolidate a self-owning, self-determining individuality. The fictional treatment of secondhand attire illustrates the obverse of this process and the temptation to animate matter in a way that complicates modern identity. A character finds it difficult to extract a castoff item from the first owner's selfhood; if the owner and the garment remain close to each other, the process is all but impossible.

Between the wars, a range of writers depicted used clothing as particularly able to compromise individuality. Whether in cartoons, short fiction, or novels, they suggest that part of the original owner stays with a garment that he or she wore. This association works at several levels. Most basically, a castoff conveys information about the person who first wore it, such as the size of his feet, the extent of his or her parsimony, or the shape of her body. More significantly, secondhand clothes can carry memories and identity, such as the way Buck Mulligan's boots convey his personality whenever Stephen Dedalus looks at them on his own feet.

Texts across a range of cultural registers trace the activity of the used garment as thing, but there is a marked difference in tone. In part, the comedy with which most popular works take up the subject stems from the general style that writers employ; as Faye Hammill has noted, middlebrow prose is often characterized by "witty, polished surfaces" that, as in the examples discussed, minimize the difficulties that characters encounter.[96] Modernist writers seldom minimize difficulties; moreover, they are invested in models of the artist—specifically in an iconoclastic individualism—that colors their protagonists.[97] As Fredric Jameson argues, literary modernism was

> predicated on the invention of a personal, private style, as unmistakable as your fingerprint, as incomparable as your own body. But this means that the modernist aesthetic is in some way organically linked to the conception of a unique self and private identity, a unique personality and individuality, which can be expected to generate its own unique vision of the world and to forge its own unique, unmistakable style.[98]

This investment in the unique, the personal, and the private was shared by artists who worked in other media: witness the words of architect Le Corbusier, who in 1919 opined (in a reference to music and architecture) that "to rise above oneself is a profoundly individual act. One doesn't do so with second-hand clothing."[99] Anne Anlin Cheng, who reads this passage, observes, "Art, it would appear, cannot be born from secondhand clothing."[100] This is indeed modernism's claim. Castoffs functioned as tropes as well as material goods in the interwar years; Le Corbusier used secondhand attire as the figurative opposite of the original, the independent, and the transformative. Characters like Stephen Dedalus appear to have been schooled at Le Corbusier's knee; when *literally* wearing secondhand attire whose initial owner he knows, Stephen frets about his relationship to the donor and about his ability to live autonomously and to create in a "unique, unmistakable style."

Such investment in newness—in garments that few consumers could afford—is also espoused by popular writers when they construct characters who self-identify as highbrow artists. For example, Sax Rohmer's *The Orchard of Tears*—the one "serious" work by the author of the popular Fu Manchu novels—depicts an illustrator who reacts with anger after being dubbed "the Dana Gibson of the trenches":

> "There is a certain type of critic," he said, "who properly ought to have been a wardrobe dealer: he is eternally reaching down the 'mantle' of somebody or other and assuring the victim of his kindness that it fits him like a glove. Now no man can make a show in a second-hand outfit, and an artist is lost when folks begin to talk about the 'mantle' of somebody or other having 'fallen upon him.' "[101]

Rohmer's character adopts modernism's attitude toward secondhand clothing and, in so doing, baldly explicates why writers like Joyce, Rhys, and Woolf were so suspicious of the castoff: no "man [sic] can make a show" in either a used suit or secondhand style, he claims, eliding material that one might wear with art that one might create. Like Le Corbusier's contemporary remark, Rohmer aligns self with surface; both artists aver that subject and garment-object are so aligned that one can *be* no more than what one *wears*. These comments illustrate the obverse of fancy dress, which promised that one might be transformed—indeed, bettered—through a new garment that conferred qualities and talents that one did not possess in ordinary clothes. For modernist writers, secondhand clothes had the opposite quality: they degrade, they muddle, and they qualify the person who wears them. By blurring borders between characters—by placing them in a serial relationship that compromises the ability to "rise above," to "make a show," or to exercise independent opinion in life or art—such works both suggest that the bourgeois individualist subject is a myth *and* mourn their characters' inability to inhabit that subjectivity.

Le Corbusier, Sax Rohmer, James Joyce, Jean Rhys, and Virginia Woolf saw in the sartorial world a correlative for artistic forms. They and their characters idealize modern commerce—the trade in the new—in a manner that few of their contemporaries could afford to emulate. If texts aimed at a middlebrow readership recognized the sartorial circumstances that many British citizens had to negotiate between the wars, modernist writers resisted the "foul rag and bone shop" that Yeats would so memorably invoke in "The Circus Animals' Desertion."[102] Yeats's speaker might resolve to "lie down" in the mire for poetic inspiration,[103] but he (like many modernist characters) emphasizes the abjection of the "old rags" on offer. Secondhand clothes offered an opportunity to think through the way the material world mediates human relationship and identity; the used dress, shoes, or trousers exemplifies the profound interconnection between persons and suggests that garments, more than other objects, highlight the serialization of people who would prefer to see themselves as unique individuals. While a range of writers recognize this fact, the realization was almost unbearable to those authors who aimed to break with tradition and who constructed characters who would resist a range of norms. Those who view clothing as an intimate part of the self—who see garments as part of their owner—refuse the shared narrative that might be inscribed through the castoff; or, if forced to wear it, they feel a profound dispossession and loss of selfhood.

Coda

Precious Clothing

The advent of World War II put an end to a period when garments—at once newly plentiful and thus purportedly reflective of individual choice—rendered wearers at the mercy of their clothes in British fiction and nonfiction. As rationing (instituted on June 1, 1941) restricted access to new clothing, garments came to seem increasingly precious. The war changed all: official rhetoric suggested that funding weapons was far more important than purchasing clothing. Oliver Lyttleton, president of the British Board of Trade, advised his compatriots that "when you feel tired of your old clothes, remember that by making them do you are contributing some part of an aeroplane or a gun or a tank,"[1] and most British citizens came to agree. The sartorial genres of the evening gown and fancy dress all but ceased to exist. As during World War I, these types of attire were framed as inappropriate in light of the suffering of both soldiers and civilians. In the words of Geraldine Howell, author of *Wartime Fashion*, "In practical as much as ideological terms the exuberance of evening dress [became] démodé."[2] Howell notes that the *Vogue Pattern Book* of January 1940 figured evening dress as the "first 'casualty of war'"[3]; other period observers recalled that "it was bad form to wear evening clothes" as the war went on.[4] Howell's study contains no mention whatsoever of fancy dress, which became an artifact of prewar life.

British identity embraced uniforms and informal, practical styles; evening dress and, to an even greater extent, the fancy-dress costume were out of place at nightclubs and restaurants.

The mackintosh, in contrast, became a part of wartime clothing vernacular. As during World War I, soldiers and civilians adopted a coat that was practical and serializing, a quality that seemed less problematic in a country at war. Whether in cities or in rural areas—to which, for example, evacuated children were encouraged to bring a mac[5]—the coat's essential qualities were protection, durability, and practicality. Doris Kilman in her mackintosh would have excited no notice on a London street. Because group identity was rendered acceptable, if not unproblematic, the mac could once again assemble a visual impression of a cohesive British nation. Moreover, under the rationing scheme, purchasing a high-quality mackintosh required more coupons than did buying most other garments. Because the mac required a good deal of fabric as well as chemicals for waterproofing, it demanded a considerable percentage of a buyer's clothing ration and thus was not "cheap" in the same way it had been before the war.[6]

As the evening gown and fancy dress slipped from the sartorial scene, and as the mac became ever more difficult to purchase, secondhand clothing was transformed from an abject to a prized commodity. The "Make-Do-and-Mend" campaign encouraged British women to preserve or make over their family members' garments: *How to "Make-Do-and-Mend,"* a short film in the archives of the Imperial War Museum, suggests that castoffs largely remained within individual households during the war. A "fashion show" at Harrods featured pajamas made from "great-grandmama's bed valance" and a dress fashioned from a "husband's old plus-four trousers."[7] The film's narrator closed by advising men to "lock up your favorite old clothes before you leave home in the morning," lest the women of the house appropriate them.

Such rhetoric echoed Flora Thompson's representation of welcome familial castoffs in *Lark Rise* (1939). If Thompson's vision of late-nineteenth-century rural Oxfordshire and 1940s Britain had little else in common, the practice of adapting and wearing family hand-me-downs emerged as acceptable in both fiction and real life because it was widely practiced *and* because there were few better options. In 1943, the Ministry of Information went so far as to animate a family's old garments in a short film: after knocking at the door and suggesting "Perhaps we can help," the clothes jauntily move about and vocalize possible ways in which they might be remade.[8] The contrast between this personification of garments and those published in literature before the war is startling. Secondhand clothes, the film suggests, are helpful, kindly things that aim only to assist those who may transform and wear them.

The trade in castoff clothing thus dwindled. In May 1945, E. Baxter promised the secondhand-clothing dealer Robina Wallis to "send you any clothes which come my way, only people are hanging on to them so,"[9] a lament that points to the continued wearing (and reuse of) garments by those who had initially purchased them. What good-quality used clothes came to market were, like new clothing, subject to rationing.[10] Thus the need to devote not only money but rationing coupons toward the purchase of clothes rendered the difference between new and secondhand almost negligible.

World War II and the clothing shortages that came with it made secondhand items at once harder to come by and more desirable. Castoffs emerge as valuable in wartime fiction such as Angela Thirkell's *Marling Hall*, a novel about the "descendants" of Anthony Trollope's characters. The Marlings need clothing for their only servant, Ed Pollett, but Mrs. Marling asserts, "I should think there isn't a secondhand pair of chauffer's breeches left in England."[11] Although this remark sounds like hyperbole, none of the characters involved in the discussion can suggest how to locate such pants; Howell confirms that secondhand trousers were particularly scarce during the war.[12] The severe material restrictions of wartime made castoffs the stuff of dinner conversations and decreased the power of secondhand items to distribute identity, a power that had disturbed artists ranging from Le Corbusier to Jean Rhys. If one had to search all of England to locate a specific castoff, it was unlikely that successive owners would know one another—and, if they did, the mere fact of clothing's scarcity made it easier to overlook an item's origins.

This book has argued that the early twentieth century provided a temporal window through which writers came to consider, through clothing, the relationship between persons and things. At the onset of the new century, British citizens had unprecedented choices in what to wear as a result of the rise in wages,[13] the advent of mass-production and thus the availability of ready-to-wear clothing, and the increasing independence of women, young people of both sexes, and others. Although individual options may have been limited, the ideology of democracy of dress made clothing less an unquestioned necessity than a reflection of class, gender, identity, and immediate community. The myth of *unlimited* sartorial choice made what people—and literary characters—wore compelling for a time; the selection of a dress, a coat, or a costume could figure both an individual's sense of self *and* his or her sometimes unwitting relationship to larger ontological and epistemological structures. When that choice was radically restricted with the outbreak (yet again) of total war, this interest waned. Novels written and set during the war generally treat garments abstractly; in Thirkell's *Northbridge Rectory*, for example, characters make comments such as "we must be very careful and make our clothes last for a long time"[14] and "one couldn't get any decent clothes now."[15] Rationing receives extended attention, but narrators and characters seldom mention specific attire.

There were, of course, differences between what people wore on the street and how such clothing was transformed by literary representations. As dress historians have long noted, clothing in literature "can take us towards ... our emotional responses to clothes, how fabrics move, sound, smell, how clothes feel on the body and their impact on the way their wearers move in them, for example."[16] The affective experience of dress captivated British writers, who transformed this experience to meditate on what particular sartorial choices might mean for their characters and, sometimes, for themselves. There are often surprising parallels between the accounts aimed at different readerships; while the details of each work are unique to it, middlebrow and modernist representations of evening dresses, mackintoshes, and fancy-dress costumes are similar in terms of affective impact and ontological complication.

The discomfort that women felt about evening attire was expressed across a spectrum, for example, and the "frock consciousness" that Virginia Woolf (to take just one example) suffered emerges as less unique to her than symptomatic of an experience that ranged across classes and became part of middle- and high-brow fiction as well as of an emerging mass culture. Representations of the mackintosh reveal parallels between novels as widely divergent as Rebecca West's *The Return of the Soldier* (1918), James Joyce's *Ulysses* (1922), and Helen Zenna Smith's *Not So Quiet . . . Stepdaughters of War* (1930). Texts that employ literary styles that are poles apart, and authors with completely different reputations, emerge in quiet conversation about the impact of one specific garment on their characters. Together, they express a profound anxiety about the elision of subjects and objects—the ability of particular things to transform humans into passive matter.

This book's garment-centered approach also helps to delineate and parse differences between middlebrow and modernist works, as, for example, when representations of secondhand clothing correspond to different attitudes about artistic style. At the same time, it is clear that the "brows" understood each other's positions; when in *The Orchard of Tears* (1918), Sax Rohmer, the creator of the popular Fu Manchu franchise, pens a character who mouths the modernist distain for secondhand attire, it becomes obvious that authors knew and strategically deployed the positions of their contemporaries. My goal throughout this study has been to suggest that we achieve more accurate understandings of the literature of the early twentieth century when we examine work aimed at middlebrow and modernist readerships together instead of in isolation. Social issues such as class, war, gender, and identity—issues that writers examined through garments—come into sharper focus through a wide archive and a different angle.

Garments offered writers a way to think and write concretely about abstract social issues. While these authors represented inequities and cultural change through plot development and interpersonal communication—one thinks of Leonard Bast crushed beneath the weight of falling books in E. M. Forster's *Howards End* (1910) or the silent struggle between Mr. and Mrs. Ramsay in Virginia Woolf's *To the Lighthouse* (1927)—they also used objects, specifically clothing, to query the limits of individual human action and to highlight the agency of the object world. That agency could be used to human benefit; there are occasional moments when, as in *Orlando* (1928) and Dorothy L. Sayers's *Murder Must Advertise* (1927), things assemble with human bodies to allow unprecedented freedom and even physical power. In such texts, writers celebrate the promise of the array of clothing, and thus options, available to modern people. Characters can achieve their goals, such texts imply, through judicious and careful selection of the right garments; if the individuals who enjoy the collaboration of the object world are only upper-class aristocrats, then less privileged readers can enjoy this experience vicariously and hope to achieve it themselves in some unspecified future, if not at the present moment.

More often, however, garments in British literature turn against humans. The evening gown reveals that the woman wearing it is also a thing; the mackintosh serializes individuals into slaughtered masses; the fancy-dress costume fails to transform the wearer; and secondhand attire becomes the initial owner's shadow self, imprinting successive owners with an alien persona. In some cases, negative outcomes stem from objects figured to possess their own purposive will; writers personify and anthropomorphize clothing, in part to signify the power that garments exercise. These examples partially accord with Jane Bennett's observation that "a touch of anthropomorphism . . . can catalyze a sensibility that finds a world filled not with ontologically distinct categories of beings (subjects and objects) but with variously composed materialities that form confederations."[17] Modern British literature catalyzes such sensibilities, but the assemblages that emerge work less as confederations (voluntary collectives unified for a greater purpose) than as *misalliances*. The representation of such unhappy groupings—one thinks of the many comic, fictional versions of Ottoline Morrell's evening dress published in interwar novels—draws attention to an affective experience of a life so out of individual control that purportedly inert objects exercise more agency, more power, than the person who nominally owns and wears them. Clothes appear to think for, and even about, those who don them.[18]

At other times, British literature figures garments as less self-willed than carrying and distributing the will of specific characters or groups. The mackintosh, for example, came to serialize British citizens during World War I as the result of the armed forces' code of uniform, a code that reflected the will of military and political leaders who wanted to forge a unified fighting force and a supportive civilian population. Just as often, however, things *extract* and *deform* the will of humans with whom they come in contact; representations of secondhand attire in middlebrow works (just one example of the many this book has discussed) demonstrate that donors and sellers can find aspects of their private lives circulated by means of the garments they attempt to discard. Their will—an act of charity or an attempt to raise funds—is not embodied but rather subsumed by things that behave unpredictably. Such literature sends a cautionary message: at a historical moment when persons appeared to exercise increasing control over the material world, even highly civilized objects like garments remained fundamentally unpredictable. And individual activity is felt at a further remove than characters expect as information about them circulates with the things they once used and wore.

Modern British literature presents an array of authors and characters who are, like Jan Struther's popular Mrs. Miniver, "fool[s] about inanimate objects."[19] Miniver later qualifies this ontological category, musing that objects "become, in time, so much a part of one that they can scarcely be classed as inanimate. Insensitive, certainly—but so are one's nails and hair."[20] Although Miniver does not think about clothes in this manner—she focuses on cars, pens, toothbrushes, and other small items—her alignment of materiality with human "nails and hair" complicates long-standing binaries such as subject/object and person/thing. With the outbreak of World War II, the question became how to care for *all* British beings, be they human or nonhuman. The title of a paper by a Board of Trade officer captures the urgency: "Extension of the Life of Clothing—A Preliminary Investigation into Possibilities."[21] In contrast to an earlier period, when the "lives" of garments seemed to threaten individuation and human agency, the war recast clothes as precious things. Only by looking earlier in the twentieth century can we see a historical moment when the relationship between British citizens and what they wore seemed less friendly and less certain.

Notes

Introduction

1. Virginia Woolf, *Mrs. Dalloway* (1925; New York: Harcourt Brace Jovanovich, 1981), 12.
2. Ibid., 123.
3. The mackintoshes by Schiaparelli and La Tour were depicted in "For a Rainy Day in or out of Town" [advertisement], *Vogue* (Britain), May 11, 1932, 42; Harrods, Elevry, and others had advertised much less expensive but stylish macs in the previous decade.
4. James Joyce, *Ulysses* (1922; New York: Vintage, 1990), 49.
5. Daphne du Maurier, *Rebecca* (1938; London: Virago, 2003), 239–40.
6. In this regard, this book is part of the material turn in modernist studies. As critics like Judith Brown have demonstrated, to read substances like cellophane through contemporary eyes is to misread: materials that now seem ordinary, cheap, or unremarkable were regarded as modern and glamorous a century ago. Brown's readings of Chanel No. 5, plastics, and other materials are models in this regard. While I have been inspired by her example, we part ways in that Brown sees the "object recede" behind its effects (*Glamour in Six Dimensions: Modernism and the Radiance of Form* [Ithaca, N.Y.: Cornell University Press, 2009], 9). In contrast, the garments I discuss seldom recede; they remain palpable and in the foreground.
7. Jürgen Habermas, *The Philosophical Discourse of Modernity: Twelve Lectures*, trans. Frederick Lawrence (Cambridge, Mass.: MIT Press, 1987), 17.

8. As Faye Hammill notes, middlebrow writers often "responded to modernist innovation in serious ways, and some of their texts have affinities with experimental narrative projects." She therefore concludes, "It is possible to read them as participants, however tentatively, in modernist experiment" (*Women, Celebrity, and Literary Culture Between the Wars* [Austin: University of Texas Press, 2007], 9). See also Nicola Humble, who writes, "'Middlebrow' and 'highbrow' are far from impermeable categories, and many texts shifted their status from one to the other or were uneasily trapped in the no-man's land in-between" (*The Feminine Middlebrow Novel, 1920s to 1950s: Class, Domesticity, and Bohemianism* [New York: Oxford University Press, 2001], 26).

9. In Genevieve Abravanel's words, "There was no full-fledged *material* divide between modernism and mass culture, [but] the early twentieth century saw the development of *ideologies of division*, as embodied, for instance, in the use of the terms highbrow and lowbrow" (*Americanizing Britain: The Rise of Modernism in the Age of the Entertainment Empire* [New York: Oxford University Press, 2012], 17).

10. As Hammill writes, middlebrow authors were not cynical about this goal but regarded wide audiences and fame as "reward[s] for genuine achievement" (*Women, Celebrity, and Literary Culture*, 15).

11. I am in sympathy with Rita Felski's complaint that "context is often wielded in punitive fashion to deprive the artwork of agency, to evacuate it of influence or impact, rendering it a puny, enfeebled, impoverished thing. We inflate context, in short, in order to deflate text" ("Context Stinks!," *New Literary History* 42, no. 4 [2011]: 582). My aim throughout this book is not to use "context" to explain or pin down literary texts but to demonstrate the way fiction participates in a conversation about the affective and even physical power of garments.

12. Around the turn of the twentieth century, Britain was increasingly sidelined by the sartorial interchange between France and America, countries that Caroline Evans notes were "respectively, the most important exporter and the most important importer in the international fashion trade" (*The Mechanical Smile: Modernism and the First Fashion Shows in France and America, 1900–1929* [New Haven, Conn.: Yale University Press, 2013], 2).

13. "Dressing on a Post-War Income," *Vogue* (Britain), September 1923, 64.

14. Christopher Breward, *The Culture of Fashion: A New History of Fashionable Dress* (Manchester: Manchester University Press, 1995), 187.

15. Georg Simmel, "Adornment" (1908), in *The Rise of Fashion: A Reader*, ed. Daniel Leonhard Purdy (Minneapolis: University of Minnesota Press, 2004), 79–86; Thorstein Veblen, *The Theory of the Leisure Class* (1899); J. C. Flügel, *The Psychology of Clothes* (London: Hogarth Press, 1930); Walter Benjamin, "The Paris of the Second Empire in Baudelaire" (1937), in *The Writer of Modern Life: Essays on Charles Baudelaire*, ed. Michael W. Jennings (Cambridge, Mass.: Belknap Press of Harvard University Press, 2006), 46–133.

16. Woolf, *Mrs. Dalloway*, 126.

17. Barbara Johnson, *Persons and Things* (Cambridge, Mass.: Harvard University Press, 2008), 6.

18. Evans demonstrates that women who worked as mannequins (models in couture houses and department stores) occupied an ambiguous position between subject and object. Such women performed objecthood, so female spectators could imagine themselves in the clothes they modeled; their job was to "animate the dress" and to efface their particular identities (*Mechanical Smile*, 197, chap. 9 passim). My study complements her work by examining parallel ontological issues in British literature of the period; together, these books suggest that the boundaries between persons and things were uniquely troubled in the early twentieth century.

19. My project is in sympathy with Jessica Burstein's formulation of cold modernism, in which "the status of the human has no especial purchase, and thus the human form is on par with seemingly dissimilar entities in the world: clothing, cars, and curtains, for example" (*Cold Modernism: Literature, Fashion, Art* [University Park: Pennsylvania State University Press, 2012], 13).

20. Elaine Freedgood, *The Ideas in Things: Fugitive Meaning in the Victorian Novel* (Chicago: University of Chicago Press, 2006), 12.

21. Ibid., 156.

22. I am wary of drawing a sharp divide between Victorians and moderns, but there is something to Johnson's suggestion that "what defines such [literary] movements may well be the way they see the relationships between persons and things" (*Persons and Things*, 3).

23. Herbert Spencer, *The Principles of Sociology* (New York: Appleton, 1897), 1:311.

24. Ibid.

25. Bill Brown, "The Secret Life of Things (Virginia Woolf and the Matter of Modernism)," *Modernism/modernity* 6, no. 2 (1999): 3.

26. Johnson, *Persons and Things*, 142.

27. As Bill Brown succinctly states in a summary of Bruno Latour's *We Have Never Been Modern*, "The history of modernity, propelled both by capital and by instrumental reason, is the history of proscribing objects from attaining the status of things, proscribing any value but that of use or exchange, secularizing the object's animation by restricting it to *commodity* fetishism alone" (*A Sense of Things: The Object Matter of American Literature* [Chicago: University of Chicago Press, 2003], 185).

28. Johnson, *Persons and Things*, 232.

29. Bruno Latour, *Reassembling the Social: An Introduction to Actor-Network Theory* (Oxford: Oxford University Press, 2005), 72.

30. Ibid., 39. Latour calls the former an "intermediary" and the latter a "mediator." In what follows, I prefer Brown's less clunky "objects" and "things." Brown, who takes the fundamental distinction between these ontological categories from Latour, designates "objects" as those items that are inert and do not particularly influence the outcome of plots and "things" as those items that rise above the inert status of the mere object. See Bill Brown, "Thing Theory," in "Things," ed. Bill Brown, special issue, *Critical Inquiry* 28, no. 1 (2001): 1–22.

31. Latour, *Reassembling the Social*, 39.

32. Ibid., 148. The phrase belongs to Rem Koolhas, but Latour has popularized it.

33. Alfred Gell, *Art and Agency: An Anthropological Theory* (Oxford: Clarendon Press, 1998), 123.

34. Ibid., 21.

35. Ibid., 103.

36. Ibid.

37. For an economical account of modernity's ever increasing "scopic technologies," see Liz Conor, *The Spectacular Modern Woman: Feminine Visibility in the 1920s* (Bloomington: Indiana University Press, 2004), 23. Morrell, who sat for several unflattering portraits that were widely reproduced and discussed in periodicals, would realize how quickly the combination of new and old technologies could make an individual vulnerable (chap. 1).

38. Brown, *Sense of Things*, 18. Bill Brown, like Judith Brown, sets up his work as not always keeping a focus on things. In his words, the experiment his book represents "has been recast into essays that do not always maintain a focus on things, but that nonetheless show how the question of things has been integral to what the text at hand is trying to get said" (ibid.). My own study is a bit more literal minded in keeping the focus on garments, a strategy that results in brief readings of a variety of literary and cultural texts instead of the extended readings of single literary works that Brown offers.

39. Ibid., 187.

40. Flügel, *Psychology of Clothes*, 37.

41. I use "haunted" in the sense that Avery E. Gordon employs it: "In haunting, organized forces and systemic structures that appear removed from us make their impact felt in everyday life in a way that confounds our analytic separations and confounds the social separations themselves" (*Ghostly Matters: Haunting and the Sociological Imagination* [Minneapolis: University of Minnesota Press, 1997], 19). Haunting is thus less spectral than agency that appears out of place—when it is exercised by purportedly inanimate material.

42. Latour, *Reassembling the Social*, 79–81.

43. Ibid., 81; Gell, *Art and Agency*, 18.

44. For example, Peter Stallybrass and Ann Rosalind Jones have published on the glove in Renaissance portraiture ("Fetishizing the Glove in Renaissance Europe," in "Things," ed. Bill Brown, special issue, *Critical Inquiry* 28, no. 1 [2001]: 114–32); Stallybrass has worked on Karl Marx's coat ("Marx's Coat," in *Border Fetishisms: Material Objects in Unstable Places*, ed. Patricia Spyer [London: Routledge, 1998], 183–207); and Sophie Woodward has employed Gell's theory of the distributed person to interpret case studies of contemporary women in which "clothing opens up the person to wider layers of externalized, potentially distributed, mind" ("Looking Good, Feeling Right: Aesthetics of the Self," in *Clothing as Material Culture*, ed. Susanne Küchler and Daniel Miller [Oxford: Berg, 2005], 37). One exception that focuses on the early twentieth century is Christina Kiaer's work on the Constructivist flapper dress, which designers hoped might effect a transformation in Russian women's relationship to clothing ("The Russian Constructivist Flapper Dress," in "Things," ed. Bill Brown, special issue, *Critical Inquiry* 28, no. 1 [2001]: 185–243).

45. Brown, *Sense of Things*, 188.

46. George Orwell, *Down and Out in Paris and London* (1933; New York: Harcourt, Brace, 1961), 129.

47. Ibid..

48. Orwell's experience may seem a twentieth-century reflection of Swiss writer Gottfried Keller's short story "Clothes Make the Man" (1874). In this tale, an impoverished tailor is mistaken for an aristocrat, and the character eventually marries a society beauty whose dowry enables him to elevate his class status. Despite its title, Keller's story suggests that clothing alone cannot "make" a man: the tailor passes as a count not only because he is well dressed but also because he arrives in town in an expensive coach, displays fastidious table manners, and is a talented horseman. Keller's title has become an idiom, but his original story indicates (in contrast to Orwell) that it takes much more than clothes to make a man.

49. Anthony Giddens, *Modernity and Self-Identity: Self and Society in the Late Modern Age* (Stanford, Calif.: Stanford University Press, 1991), 99–100.

50. Ibid., 99.

51. Alan Sheridan, "Translator's Note," in Jacques Lacan, *Écrits: A Selection* (New York: Norton, 1982), xiii.

52. Jacques Lacan, "The Mirror Stage as Formative of the Function of the *I* as Revealed in Psychoanalytic Experience," in *Écrits*, 2 (emphasis in original).

53. My reading of Lacan builds on Johnson's argument that the reflection in the mirror is fundamentally an object (*Persons and Things*, 57), "the statue in which man projects himself," in Lacan's words ("Mirror Stage," 2). As Johnson writes, "For Jacques Lacan, the possibility of becoming a statue is not something that may or may not happen to a subject. It *must* happen if the little man is to become human" (*Persons and Things*, 57).

54. Mikkel Borch-Jacobsen, *Lacan: The Absolute Master* (Stanford, Calif.: Stanford University Press, 1991), 49.

55. I am indebted to LacanOnline.com for offering a compendium of "Lacan's antecedents in the mirror stage theory" (http://www.lacanonline.com/index/2010/09/what-does-lacan-say-about-the-mirror-stage-part-i/). Borch-Jacobsen notes that Lacan's claim to have "invented" the mirror stage is challenged by the work of several earlier thinkers who described and drew similar conclusions that "the body proper . . . is first of all an *image* of the body—that is, a *visual* image" (*Lacan*, 47). Darian Leader points to Charles Darwin, James Baldwin, Charles Horton Cooley, René Spitz, Henri Wallon, and Roger Caillois as forming the "backdrop" for Lacan's work, in *Freud's Footnotes* (London: Faber and Faber, 2000), 196–97.

56. Leader, *Freud's Footnotes*, 197.

57. Charles Horton Cooley, *Human Nature and the Social Order* (New York: Scribner, 1902), 151.

58. Ibid., 151–52.

59. Lacan, "Mirror Stage," 1.

60. Elizabeth Wilson, *Adorned in Dreams: Fashion and Modernity* (1985; New Brunswick, N.J.: Rutgers University Press, 2003), 58–60.

61. Burstein, *Cold Modernism*, 218.

62. Paul Poiret, advertisement, *Vogue* (Britain), May 16, 1928, 28.

63. Selfridges, advertisement, *Daily Telegraph*, May 3, 1920, 12. Elizabeth Outka has explained how Selfridges could reconcile such claims with the mass production of its wares. Her formulation "the commodified authentic" captures "both a dream of exclusivity and a select audience and at the same time a desire for ready accessibility and a wide market" (*Consuming Traditions: Modernity, Modernism, and the Commodified Authentic* [New York: Oxford University Press, 2008], 13).

64. *Oxford English Dictionary Online*, s.v. "fancy dress," http://www.oed.com/search?searchType=dictionary&q=fancy+dress&_searchBtn=Search.

65. Herbert Marcuse identifies such ontologies as those in which the "noncorporeal being of man is asserted as the real substance of the individual" ("Philosophy and Critical Theory," in *Negations: Essays in Critical Theory*, trans. Jeremy J. Shapiro [Boston: Beacon Press, 1968], 104).

1. What Do Women Want?

1. Elizabeth Grosz, "The Thing," in *The Object Reader*, ed. Fiona Candlin and Raiford Guins (New York: Routledge, 2009), 125.

2. My analysis of Jean Rhys alongside Virginia Woolf and Rebecca West is less natural than it seems, as Rhys articulated explicitly anti-feminist views throughout her life. She was, however, a sharp critic of cultural institutions and behaviors that worked to oppress women; she was, in the words of Rishona Zimring, "a dissonant female voice" ("The Make-up of Jean Rhys's Fiction," *Novel* 33, no. 2 [2000]: 226). Her works can therefore be placed in productive dialogue with those of her more clearly feminist contemporaries.

3. Jane E. Heglund, "Evening Dress," in *Encyclopedia of Clothing and Fashion*, ed. Valerie Steele (Farmington Mills, Mich.: Scribner, 2005), 1:428–30.

4. Ibid., 428.

5. "Every Evening Occasion Has Its Appropriate Style of Dress," *Vanity Fair*, March 1923, 8.

6. Quentin Bell, *On Human Finery* (1976; New York: Schocken, 1978), 166. In Bell's case, the "futility" of day wear inheres in "sporting wear" worn for everyday activities; the "futility" of evening gowns suggests, in contrast, the waste of time and money in conspicuous leisure.

7. Quoted in C. Willett Cunnington, *English Women's Clothing in the Present Century* (London: Faber and Faber, 1952), 211.

8. Ibid., 110–11, 171. While it was no doubt possible to find less expensive garments in each year, evening dress was consistently more expensive that other garments of the same quality due to materials and construction.

9. Georg Simmel, "Adornment" (1908), in *The Rise of Fashion: A Reader*, ed. Daniel Leonhard Purdy (Minneapolis: University of Minnesota Press, 2004), 81.

10. In Jane Bennett's words, "Bodies enhance their power *in* or *as a heterogeneous assemblage*. What this suggests for the concept of *agency* is that the efficacy or effectivity to which that term has traditionally referred becomes distributed

across an ontologically heterogeneous field, rather than being a capacity localized in a human body" (*Vibrant Matter: A Political Ecology of Things* [Durham, N.C.: Duke University Press, 2010], 23 [emphasis in original]). Although the language is different, Simmel's attribution of agency to evening dress when *on* a human body is in harmony with Bennett's concept of the heterogeneous assemblage.

11. C. Willett Cunnington, *Why Women Wear Clothes* (London: Faber and Faber, 1941), 19.

12. Ibid., 226.

13. *Encyclopaedia Britannica*, 14th ed., s.v. "dress."

14. Gilles Lipovetsky, *The Empire of Fashion: Dressing Modern Democracy*, trans. Catherine Porter (Princeton, N.J.: Princeton University Press, 1994), 61.

15. Heglund, "Evening Dress," 428.

16. Ibid., 430.

17. Elizabeth Wilson, *Adorned in Dreams: Fashion and Modernity* (1985; New Brunswick, N.J.: Rutgers University Press, 2003), 123.

18. Lady Duff ("Lucile") Gordon, *Discretions and Indiscretions* (New York: Stokes, 1932), 66–67.

19. Cunnington, *Why Women Wear Clothes*, 105.

20. Ibid., 207.

21. Fashion journals repeatedly noted that twentieth-century gowns, unlike those of the past, revealed as much as they concealed, including a woman's body type. An article on evening gowns, for example, observed that "we have outline— our own, whether we like it or not, for styles are statuesquely straight and clinging" ("The Evening Gown," *Women's Supplement*, October 1920, 50). For a detailed account of the new fashions that emphasized slimness and the role of mannequins in popularizing a "slender, active body," see Caroline Evans, *The Mechanical Smile: Modernism and the First Fashion Shows in France and America, 1900–1929* (New Haven, Conn.: Yale University Press, 2013), 211–15, chap. 10 passim.

22. The couturier Worth decided to close its London showroom for the duration of the war, as reported in *Sunday Pictorial*, August 15, 1915, 17. Standard or National Dress was proposed as an economizing measure toward the end of the war and relied on a simple design that conserved fabric and labor. While this style of dress never ousted individual styles and trimmings, it was somewhat popular in 1918. See "Page Mainly for and About Women," *Sunday Pictorial*, February 3, 1918, 10.

23. Cunnington, *English Women's Clothing*, 137.

24. Cunnington, *Why Women Wear Clothes*, 220.

25. *Encyclopaedia Britannica*, s.v. "dress."

26. Ibid.

27. Katherine Mullin, *James Joyce, Sexuality and Social Purity* (Cambridge: Cambridge University Press, 2003), 147.

28. *A Ballroom Tragedy* (New York: American Mutoscope and Biograph Company, 1905), 35-mm film, 1:10 min., YouTube, http://www.youtube.com/watch?v=iGuTer7iOy8. The American Mutoscope and Biograph Company distributed films to Great Britain.

29. Terry Castle, *The Apparitional Lesbian: Female Homosexuality and Modern Culture* (New York: Columbia University Press, 1995).

30. The male characters thus provide examples of what J. C. Flügel called "the great masculine renunciation." Briefly put, Flügel argues that men gave up "sartorial decorativeness" for political and social reasons and thus freed up for other purposes energy "that formerly expressed itself in clothes" (*The Psychology of Clothes* [London: Hogarth Press, 1930], 103, 107). Men's evening dress is undifferentiating in *A Ballroom Tragedy*, although Brent Shannon has called the renunciation of "decorativeness" into question in *The Cut of His Coat: Men, Dress, and Consumer Culture in Britain, 1860–1914* (Athens: Ohio University Press, 2006).

31. Kathlyn Rhodes, "The Harvest of Folly," *Sunday Graphic*, March 4, 1928, 16.

32. "Eve in Paradise," *Eve*, April 15, 1920, 198.

33. "Fashions at the Riviera," *Gentlewoman*, January 7, 1922, 12–13.

34. Jean Patou, advertisement, *Vogue* (Britain), October 17, 1928, 44.

35. Juliet Nicolson, *The Perfect Summer: England 1911, Just Before the Storm* (New York: Grove Press, 2006), 19.

36. Lou Taylor, *Mourning Dress: A Costume and Social History* (London: Allen & Unwin, 1983), 124.

37. Paquin, advertisement, *Times* (London), May 9, 1910, 9.

38. Frances Spalding, *Vanessa Bell* (New Haven, Conn.: Ticknor & Fields, 1983), 26.

39. Quoted in Taylor, *Mourning Dress*, 146.

40. Ibid., 277.

41. Although the voice comes from an earlier period, it is useful to listen to Charles Baudelaire, who wrote about men's formal wear, explicate the affective resonance of black evening dress:

> Is this not an attire that is needed by our age, which is suffering, and dressed up to its thin black narrow shoulders in the symbol of constant mourning? The black suit and the frock coat not only have their political beauty as an expression of general equality, but also their poetic beauty as an expression of the public mentality: an immense cortège of undertakers. . . . We are all attendants at some kind of funeral. (Quoted in Walter Benjamin, "The Paris of the Second Empire in Baudelaire" [1937], in *The Writer of Modern Life: Essays on Charles Baudelaire*, ed. Michael W. Jennings [Cambridge, Mass.: Belknap Press of Harvard University Press, 2006], 105–6)

42. Margaret Haig, *This Was My World* (London: Macmillan, 1933), 240.

43. Ibid.

44. Grosz, "Thing," 132.

45. Diana Crane, *Fashion and Its Social Agendas: Class, Gender, and Identity in Clothing* (Chicago: University of Chicago Press, 2000), 241.

46. Virginia Stephen to Emma Vaughn, April 23, 1901, in *The Letters of Virginia Woolf*, ed. Nigel Nicolson and Joanne Trautmann, vol. 1, *1888–1912* (New York: Harcourt Brace Jovanovich, 1975), 43.

47. Virginia Woolf, "Am I a Snob?" in *Moments of Being*, ed. Jeanne Schulkind, 2nd ed. (San Diego, Calif.: Harcourt Brace Jovanovich, 1985), 210–11.

48. Virginia Stephen to Emma Vaughn, August 8, 1901, in *Letters of Virginia Woolf*, 1:42. Although Stephen's dressmaker has not been previously identified, the woman she called "Sally Young" was Sarah Fullerton Monteith Young. Spalding gives the location of Young's premises as South Audley Street, in *Vanessa Bell*, 26–27; this was her address from 1895 to 1907, according to Amy de la Haye, Lou Taylor, and Eleanor Thompson, *A Family of Fashion: The Messels: Six Generations of Dress* (London: Wilson, 2005). Young's "hey-day" ran from 1890 to 1907 when she was a "fashionable court dressmaker" (ibid., 9, 37). Although Stephen's evening gowns do not survive, examples of Young's work are preserved in the Messel Collection, Brighton Museum & Art Gallery.

49. Virginia Woolf, "A Sketch of the Past," in *Moments of Being*, 150.

50. Ibid., 154.

51. Ibid., 150.

52. Ibid., 156.

53. Virginia Stephen to Violet Dickinson, September 1902, in *Letters of Virginia Woolf*, 1:55.

54. Woolf, "Sketch of the Past," 150–51.

55. Ibid., 151.

56. Ibid. In a discussion of this passage, R. S. Koppen describes the green dress as "Woolf's . . . attempted sartorial insubordination." Although she dismisses the dress itself as a "rather banal experiment," Koppen argues that the act of wearing it takes "on the force of conscious threats to cultural practice and to the norms and assumptions it embodies" (*Virginia Woolf, Fashion and Literary Modernity* [Edinburgh: Edinburgh University Press, 2009], 11).

57. Woolf, "Sketch of the Past," 152.

58. Ibid., 155.

59. Virginia Stephen to Violet Dickinson, December 27?, 1902, in *Letters of Virginia Woolf*, 1:63.

60. Virginia Woolf, *A Passionate Apprentice: The Early Journals, 1897–1909*, ed. Mitchell A. Leaska (San Diego, Calif.: Harcourt Brace Jovanovich, 1990), 168.

61. Kathryn S. Laing has compared the two writers to argue that "the metaphor of the feminine contributes to their evolving creation of new identities and spaces for themselves as women writers" ("Addressing Femininity in the Twenties: Virginia Woolf and Rebecca West on Money, Mirrors and Masquerade," in *Virginia Woolf and the Arts: Selected Papers from the Sixth Annual Conference on Virginia Woolf*, ed. Diane F. Gillespie and Leslie K. Hankins [New York: Pace University Press, 1997], 67). Although I am, like Laing, interested in parallels between Woolf's and West's figurations of clothes, I do not read the dresses they record as metaphors as she does.

62. Rebecca West, "The World's Worst Failure" (1916), in *The Gender of Modernism: A Critical Anthology*, ed. Bonnie Kime Scott (Bloomington: Indiana University Press, 1990), 580 (emphasis added).

63. Feminist psychoanalytic critics have framed discussions of the femme fatale in terms that are similar to West's. Jessica Benjamin, for example, argues that "the 'sexy' woman—an image that intimidates women whether or not they

strive to conform to it—is sexy, but as object, not as subject. She expresses not so much *her* desire as her pleasure in being desired; what she enjoys is her capacity to evoke desire in the other, to attract" (*The Bonds of Love: Psychoanalysis, Feminism, and the Problem of Domination* [New York: Pantheon, 1988], 89). While this formulation parallels West's view of the Frenchwoman, the subject/object binary on which Benjamin's claim rests is complicated by the narrator's experience of fashion in West's essay.

64. West, "World's Worst Failure," 581.

65. Ibid.

66. Ibid., 583.

67. For a discussion of the role of clothing in the formation of an ego ideal, see the introduction. West's experience approximates Charles Horton Cooley's "looking-glass self" and serves to contest Wilson's optimistic theory that fashionable dress consolidates "the shaky boundaries of the psychological self" (*Adorned in Dreams*, 60).

68. Laing, "Addressing Femininity in the Twenties," 69.

69. West, "World's Worst Failure," 583.

70. In another essay, West describes herself as "insane on the subject of clothes": "I may have half a dozen evening dresses hanging in my wardrobe; but if the fit comes on me I will sit blankly in my bedroom . . . because I am in the grip of the conviction that I have nothing to wear. I finally have to pull myself together and force myself to put on some dress, which then seems to me, though I know perfectly well that it is a worthy product of Nicole Groult [Parisian designer], a worthless rag" ("I Regard Marriage with Fear and Horror," *Hearst's International Cosmopolitan Magazine*, November 1925, 209). In this essay, the evening dress comes to be a locus of sorrow because it can be enjoyed only if it does not, through its highlighting of the wearer's femininity and body, lead West into marriage—in other words, if it fails in the traditional purpose of the dress.

71. Jean Rhys, "Illusion," in *The Collected Short Stories* (New York: Norton, 1987), 1.

72. Ibid., 2.

73. Ibid.

74. Ibid. As Laura Doan has demonstrated, during the 1920s "the sartorial distinction between the mannish woman and the lesbian was by no means 'clear.'" Nevertheless, Doan acknowledges that "*within* a discrete, perhaps miniscule, subculture, lesbians passed as stylishly recognizable lesbians as well as women of fashion" (*Fashioning Sapphism: The Origins of a Modern English Lesbian Culture* [New York: Columbia University Press, 2001], 112, 120).

75. Rhys, "Illusion," 3.

76. Ibid.

77. Ibid., 3–4.

78. Ibid., 4.

79. Ibid.

80. I am here in agreement with Zimring, who, in her brief analysis of the story's representation of cosmetics, calls "Illusion" "a tale of the closet" ("Make-up of Jean Rhys's Fiction," 217).

81. Rhys, "Illusion," 5.
82. Ibid.
83. Ibid., 4.
84. Ibid.
85. Ibid.
86. Ibid., 5. Zimring notes that Rhys's characters listen to commodities, in "Make-up of Jean Rhys's Fiction," 218. While such listening may seem an acute form of commodity fetishism, Bennett views anthropomorphism generally as a type of ontological experiment that "can catalyze a sensibility that finds a world filled not with ontologically distinct categories of beings (subjects and objects) but with variously composed materialities that form confederations" (*Vibrant Matter*, 99). Rhys's narrator in "Illusion" is aware of the vital potential of so-called mere objects.
87. Rhys, "Illusion," 5.
88. West, "World's Worst Failure," 581.
89. Descriptions of "Ott's" outrageous costumes pepper accounts of weekends at her home, Garsington Manor, and parties in London. Her sartorial performances led Vanessa Bell, Lytton Strachey, and Duncan Grant to debate whether she was an artist in her own right, but the Bloomsbury circle was largely unanimous in its critique of her appearance as, in Leonard Woolf's words, a "fantastic hotchpotch" (*Beginning Again: An Autobiography of the Years 1911 to 1918* [New York: Harcourt Brace Jovanovich, 1972], 198).
90. Janet Lyon includes Morrell in her study of the bohemian salon and notes that outlandish garb was common in such settings: "[C]ostumes, many of them referencing a kind of premodern, or perhaps countermodern, habitus, helped to link bohemian subculture to a whole set of anti-bourgeois postures, including, most obviously, the postures of unassimilated artistic and social freedom" ("Sociability in the Metropole: Modernism's Bohemian Salons," *ELH* 76, no. 3 [2009]: 694). Morrell was, however, mocked for adopting this posture.
91. Alfred Gell, *Art and Agency: An Anthropological Theory* (Oxford: Clarendon Press, 1998), 103.
92. Morrell Dress, Archive, BATMC 2000.191, Fashion Museum, Bath.
93. Miranda Seymour, *Ottoline Morrell: Life on the Grand Scale* (London: Hodder & Stoughton, 1992), 70.
94. Morrell Dress, Archive, BATMC 2000.299.
95. Seymour, *Ottoline Morrell*, 70.
96. Morrell's dresses may be understood as performative in a Butlerian manner, but as the rest of this chapter suggests, neither speech-act theory nor gender performance account for the relationship between a human subject and garment actants. As Judith Butler writes, "Within speech act theory, a performative is that discursive practice that enacts or produces that which it names" (*Bodies That Matter: On the Discursive Limits of "Sex"* [New York: Routledge, 1993], 13). Butler complicates the origin of discursive authority by critiquing naïve formulations of the voluntary subject/individual, but her argument grounds performance in a symbolic order of sexual norms that work with and through subjects, not objects (13–15). Here and throughout my argument, meaning emerges as external to

subject and to dress as actant: it is gestured at by both and inheres in the fraught assembly of humans and objects.

97. Miss Breton to Ottoline Morrell, n.d., quoted in Seymour, *Ottoline Morrell*, 70 (emphasis added).

98. T. S. Eliot, "Tradition and the Individual Talent," in *The Waste Land and Other Writings* (New York: Modern Library, 2002), 100–101.

99. Morrell Dress, Archive, BATMC 2000.312.

100. The profiles were published in 1923 and 1928. These two dates are significant, as Morrell appeared in the magazine under the auspices of two very different editors. In 1923, British *Vogue* was edited by Dorothy Todd, who wanted to fuse the magazine's traditional focus on women's fashion with coverage of the avant-garde. In 1928, *Vogue* was edited by Edna Woolman Chase, whose charge was to increase readership and, in her words, to "get our British edition back into the *Vogue* formula" of high fashion, celebrities, and society news (*Always in Vogue* [New York: Doubleday, 1954], 152). Chase occasionally included "features in line with the kind of thing Dorothy was promoting"; it is not clear whether Chase ran Morrell's picture because she was Todd's "kind of thing" or Chase's own.

101. My reading of Morrell's appearance in *Vogue* has been informed by Aurelia Mahood's analysis of the magazine's pursuit of a "double readership" ("Fashioning Readers: The *avant garde* and British *Vogue*, 1920–9," *Women: A Cultural Review* 13, no. 1 [2002]: 42).

102. In 1928, Paul Nystrom would note that "Spanish art has been the inspiration for several fashion motives during the last ten years, such as the use of rouge, certain types of hair dressing, softening the line of the feminine silhouette, and so on" (*Economics of Fashion* [New York: Ronald Press, 1928], 87–88).

103. *Ottoline: The Early Memoirs of Lady Ottoline Morrell*, ed. Robert Gathorne-Hardy (London: Faber and Faber, 1963), 176.

104. Ibid.

105. Morrell's dresses provide an example of Bruno Latour's concept of "interobjectivity," which dislocates "actions so much that someone else, from some other place and some other time, is still acting in it [an object] through indirect but fully traceable connections" (*Reassembling the Social: An Introduction to Actor-Network Theory* [Oxford: Oxford University Press, 2005], 196).

106. Virginia Woolf, "The New Dress," in *The Complete Shorter Fiction of Virginia Woolf*, ed. Susan Dick, 2nd ed. (San Diego, Calif.: Harcourt Brace Jovanovich, 1989), 171.

107. Ibid., 172.

108. Ibid., 171. "The New Dress" records the way that social anxiety is most keenly mediated by material possessions, as Bill Brown notes in "The Secret Life of Things (Virginia Woolf and the Matter of Modernism)," *Modernism/modernity* 6, no. 2 (1999): 12. Similarly, Jessica Burstein argues that "for Woolf, the dress means a way of relating, or a failure to relate. The story is driven by the character's cathexis onto the dress, and accordingly it is the dress that betrays her" (*Cold Modernism: Literature, Fashion, Art* [University Park: Pennsylvania State University Press, 2012], 129). Lisa Cohen observes that the dress is uniquely able to generate

social anxiety, writing that "there is a exhaustingly small space dividing proper femininity from its failure" ("'Frock Consciousness': Virginia Woolf, the Open Secret, and the Language of Fashion," *Fashion Theory* 3, no. 2 [1999]: 153).

109. Woolf, "New Dress," 175.

110. Ibid., 173. Readers may be tempted to regard Waring's reaction as simply a paralyzing form of self-consciousness. But the narrator is careful to include comments by other characters, who regard Waring as "absurdly dressed" and vow to "tell everyone about Mabel's fantastic appearance" (175). Such moments make it plain that the community in the drawing-room *does* criticize the new dress and Mabel for wearing it.

111. Burstein, *Cold Modernism*, 128.

112. Woolf, "New Dress," 174 (emphasis added).

113. Ibid.

114. Sean Latham, *The Art of Scandal: Modernism, Libel Law, and the Roman à Clef* (Oxford: Oxford University Press, 2009), 132. I am indebted to Latham's study, which identifies novels and characters based on Morrell and argues that she "bears a terrible burden, becoming the abject figure for the failure of aesthetic autonomy" in modernist romans à clef (141).

115. When Vanessa Bell first proposed the Omega Workshops dressmaking scheme, the idea was bound up with Morrell as client, patron, and source of material support. See Vanessa Bell to Roger Fry, April 9?, 1915, in *Selected Letters of Vanessa Bell*, ed. Regina Marler (New York: Pantheon, 1993), 173–74.

116. L. Woolf, *Beginning Again*, 199.

117. Virginia Woolf to Clive Bell, January 21, 1928, in *The Letters of Virginia Woolf*, ed. Nigel Nicolson and Joanne Trautmann, vol. 3, *1923–1928* (New York: Harcourt Brace Jovanovich, 1977), 448.

118. *The Diary of Virginia Woolf*, ed. Anne Olivier Bell and Andrew McNeillie, vol. 3, *1925–1930* (New York: Harcourt Brace Jovanovich, 1980), 36.

119. Vanessa Bell to Roger Fry, June 1916, in *Selected Letters of Vanessa Bell*, 199.

120. Aldous Huxley, *Crome Yellow* (New York: Harper, 1922), 16.

121. Ibid., 174.

122. Osbert Sitwell, *Triple Fugue* (1924; London: Penguin, 1940), 191.

123. Ibid., 195.

124. Evans chronicles the scandal created by the French designer Margaine Lacroix, who sent mannequins wearing evening styles to the Longchamp Racecourse in 1908, in *Mechanical Smile*, 60–62. The outrage that greeted the three women may be placed on a continuum with these representations of Morrell; even in the 1920s, it was scandalous to wear evening dress during the day.

125. W. J. Turner, *The Aesthetes* (London: Wishart, 1927), 40.

126. Ibid., 50.

127. Latour, *Reassembling the Social*, 239.

128. Roger Fry to Lady Mariabella Fry, December 14, 1913, in *The Letters of Roger Fry*, ed. Denys Sutton (New York: Random House, 1972), 2:375.

129. Cunnington, *Why Women Wear Clothes*, 188–89.

130. John Frow, "A Pebble, a Camera, a Man Who Turns into a Telegraph Pole," in "Things," ed. Bill Brown, special issue, *Critical Inquiry* 28, no. 1 (2001): 274.

131. Crane, *Fashion and Its Social Agendas*, 241.

132. Latour, *Reassembling the Social*, 28.

2. Wearable Memorials

1. C. Willett Cunnington, *Why Women Wear Clothes* (London: Faber and Faber, 1941), 239.

2. James Joyce, *Ulysses* (1922; New York: Vintage, 1990), 110.

3. Ibid., 254, 333, 427.

4. P. G. Wodehouse, "Jeeves and the Dog McIntosh," in *Very Good, Jeeves* (Garden City, N.Y.: Doubleday, Doran, 1930), 142.

5. For example, Jane Marcus argues that "the trench-coat is a class and gender mark covering the body of women at/in this war" (afterword to Helen Zenna Smith [Evadne Price], *Not So Quiet . . . Stepdaughters of War* [1930; New York: Feminist Press of CUNY, 1989], 291). Many scholars have also commented on the mackintoshes in *Ulysses* and *Mrs. Dalloway*. I will address these interventions more extensively later in the chapter.

6. *Oxford English Dictionary Online*, s.v. "mackintosh," http://www.oed.com/view/Entry/111902?redirectedFrom=mackintosh#eid.

7. Nancy Mitford, ed., *Noblesse Oblige: An Enquiry into Identifiable Characteristics of the English Aristocracy* (London: Hamish Hamilton, 1956), 30.

8. The spelling of the word "mackintosh" is varied; writers, perhaps following the spelling of the first manufacturer's name, regularly drop the *k*. I use the "mackintosh" spelling, as this is a standard version offered by the *OED*.

9. Sarah Levitt, "Manchester Mackintoshes: A History of the Rubberised Garment Trade in Manchester," *Textile History* 17 (1986): 51.

10. Ibid., 54.

11. Quoted in Christina Walkley and Vanda Foster, *Crinolines and Crimpling Irons: Victorian Clothes: How They Were Cleaned and Cared For* (London: Peter Owen, 1978), 138.

12. Levitt, "Manchester Mackintoshes," 56.

13. Quoted in ibid., 58.

14. Sarah Levitt, *Victorians Unbuttoned: Registered Designs for Clothing, Their Makers and Wearers, 1839–1900* (London: Allen & Unwin, 1986), 184.

15. Levitt, "Manchester Mackintoshes," 51.

16. Alison L. Goodrum, *The National Fabric: Fashion, Britishness, Globalization* (Oxford: Berg, 2005), 106.

17. *The Aquascutum Story* (London: Aquascutum, 1994), 8.

18. Georg Simmel, "Fashion," *American Journal of Sociology* 62, no. 6 (1957): 546.

19. Ibid., 558.

20. "Personal," *Punch*, May 6, 1925, 488–89.

21. Leonard de Vries, comp., *Victorian Advertisements*, text by James Laver (London: Murray, 1968), 126.

22. Nicola Shulman suggests that popular demand for clothed animals was fortunate for Beatrix Potter, as "many of her stories would have no plots if the animals had no clothes." As she notes, this is true of *The Tale of Mr. Jeremy Fisher*, in which a "mackintosh saves his life" ("Beatrix Potter's Tales of Escape," *Times Literary Supplement*, February 21, 2007). Carole Scott similarly notes that the mackintosh "serves to keep one from being eaten alive" ("Between Me and the World: Clothes as Mediator Between Self and Society in the Works of Beatrix Potter," *Lion and the Unicorn* 16 [1992]: 197).

23. Beatrix Potter, *The Tale of Mr. Jeremy Fisher* (1906; New York: Warne, 1987), 41, 45, 49.

24. *Sunday Pictorial*, November 21, 1926, 13.

25. Rebecca West, *The Return of the Soldier* (1918; New York: Penguin, 1988), 9, 48.

26. Ibid., 14, 16.

27. Ibid., 10.

28. Ibid., 68. It is this aspect of Grey's clothing that has received scholarly attention. As Wyatt Bonikowski writes, "Margaret's lower-class standing . . . can be read on her clothes and body" ("The Return of the Soldier Brings Death Home," *MFS: Modern Fiction Studies* 51 [2005]: 521).

29. West, *Return of the Soldier*, 64 (emphasis added).

30. As Barbara Johnson has argued, the "I–it" relationship is "a relation between a person and non-persons" (*Persons and Things* [Cambridge, Mass.: Harvard University Press, 2008], 9). Angela K. Smith notes that Grey is regarded as a cipher elsewhere in the novel, as Jenny casts her as "a draught-ox or a dog, rather than a fellow human being" (*The Second Battlefield: Women, Modernism and the First World War* [Manchester: Manchester University Press, 2000], 177).

31. West, *Return of the Soldier*, 88.

32. Ibid., 90.

33. Graham Green, *Brighton Rock* (1938; New York: Penguin, 2004), 183.

34. Ibid.

35. Johnson, *Persons and Things*, 6.

36. Greene, *Brighton Rock*, 184.

37. George Orwell, *Coming Up for Air* (1939; New York: Harcourt, Brace, 1950), 271.

38. Ibid., 278.

39. Annette Federico, "Making Do: George Orwell's *Coming Up for Air*," *Studies in the Novel* 37 (2005): 51. Federico argues that this reading ignores the novel's celebration of "faith in the existence of the ordinary as a repository of meaning" (51). While I find her reading of the body of Orwell's novel suggestive, it ignores the *conclusion* of the book, in which Bowling finds the ordinary more burden than pleasure.

40. Elizabeth Bowen, *The Last September* (1929; New York: Anchor, 2000), 106, 198.

41. Jed Esty, *Unseasonable Youth: Modernism, Colonialism, and the Fiction of Development* (New York: Oxford University Press, 2012), 193–94. Hermione Lee concurs, viewing the novel as "full of retarded overgrown juveniles . . . reckless innocents, characters who haven't found ways of compromising with adult society" (introduction to *The Mulberry Tree: Writings of Elizabeth Bowen*, ed. Hermione Lee [London: Virago, 1986], 3).

42. Bowen, *Last September*, 129.

43. Kathryn Klein has argued that Lois's "Sapphic feelings" for Marda "encourage Lois to question the 'pattern' of her existence" ("Writing Sapphism: Troubling Genre in Interwar Fiction" [Ph.D. diss., State University of New York at Stony Brook, 2013], 86 [ProQuest (3588126)], 86). I am in agreement with Klein's reading; the mackintosh in *The Last September* is thus aligned with the queer desires mobilized by other garments in this study.

44. Bowen, *Last September*, 42–43.

45. Ibid., 42. Enda Duffy observes that IRA terrorists, gunmen, and bomb carriers "were conventionally shown in trench-coats or macintoshes in photographs from the 1916–21 period." Bowen's novel thus represents the sartorial choices that mark the Irish "late-colonial context" (*The Subaltern Ulysses* [Minneapolis: University of Minnesota Press, 1994], 66).

46. Bowen, *Last September*, 120.

47. Ibid., 49, 80.

48. The trench coat was "a waterproofed overcoat worn by officers in the trenches" (*Oxford English Dictionary Online*, 2nd ed., s.v. "trench coat," http://www.oed.com/view/Entry/413383?redirectedFrom=trench+coat#eid). Although trench coats had what might seem to be signature details, including a gun flap, storm pockets, and a belt fastened with D-rings, these coats were produced by different manufacturers and in differing cuts, so any waterproof coat might be seen as a trench coat. The line between trench coats and mackintoshes was thus blurred.

49. Brent Shannon, *The Cut of His Coat: Men, Dress, and Consumer Culture in Britain, 1860–1914* (Athens: Ohio University Press, 2006), 58–59.

50. Jennifer Craik, *Uniforms Exposed: From Conformity to Transgression* (Oxford: Berg, 2005), 22.

51. Simmel, "Fashion," 554.

52. Derry & Toms, "Gentlemen's Raincoats" [advertisement], *Daily Mail*, April 11, 1916, 1.

53. Craik, *Uniforms Exposed*, 7.

54. Elizabeth Grosz, "The Thing," in *The Object Reader*, ed. Fiona Candlin and Raiford Guins (New York: Routledge, 2009), 125.

55. Douglas Mao argues that "the object world represented for modernists . . . a realm beyond the reach of ideology but not secure against the material consequences of ideological conflicts" (*Solid Objects: Modernism and the Test of Production* [Princeton, N.J.: Princeton University Press, 1998], 9). In the case of the mackintosh, however, the object does not seem beyond the reach of ideology so much as infused with it.

56. Aquascutum, advertisement, *Punch*, April 18, 1917.
57. Burberry, advertisement, *Daily Telegraph*, October 7, 1918, 3.
58. Smith, *Not So Quiet . . . Stepdaughters of War*, 218.
59. Ibid., 237.
60. Ibid., 238.
61. Burberry, advertisement, *Times* (London), July 1, 1915, 12.
62. Burberry, advertisement, *Times* (London), August 23, 1915, 11.
63. Because Dunlop's letter does not contain his full name, it is difficult to determine who, specifically, wrote it. One candidate is Major John Kinninmont Dunlop, a member of the Rangers (Twelfth London) Machine Gun Corps who served in France and was awarded the Croix de l'ordre de Sainte-Anne de Russie in 1916 for heroics at Delville Wood.
64. Quoted in Patrizia Calefato, "Signs of Order, Signs of Disorder: The Other Uniforms," in *Uniform: Order and Disorder*, ed. Francesco Bonami, Maria Luisa Frisa, and Stefano Tonchi (Milan: Charta, 2000), 201.
65. Aquascutum, advertisement, *Illustrated Sporting and Dramatic News*, June 7, 1919, 497.
66. Burberry, advertisement, *Times* (London), July 16, 1915, 15.
67. Ibid.
68. Burberry, advertisement, *Daily Telegraph*, July 2, 1917, 2.
69. *Harrods Weekly Price List* [advertisement circular], July 23–28, 1917, 32. These coats are also advertised in *Harrods Weekly Price List* [advertisement circular], February 5, 1917, 35.
70. Camilla Loew, "Miss Represented: Women at War, Propaganda vs. Autobiographical Writing," in *(Mis)Representations: Intersections of Culture and Power*, ed. Fernando Galván Bern, Jului Cañero Serrano, and José Santiago Fernández Vázquez (Bern: Lang, 2003), 124.
71. Vera Brittain, *Testament of Youth* (1933; New York: Penguin, 1978), 251.
72. Ibid., 252.
73. Classified advertisement, *Daily Telegraph*, January 5, 1917, 1.
74. This type of trade was so common that *Punch* depicted Kaiser Wilhelm running a secondhand shop after the war. In a series of sketches titled "The Hohenzollerns Under a German Republic," the former kaiser is depicted "in business as a second-hand wardrobe dealer." A trench-mac hangs in the doorway of his shop with the label "Uniforms slightly soiled" ("Winter Almanack," *Punch*, November 1917).
75. Marcus, afterword to Smith, *Not So Quiet . . . Stepdaughters of War*, 292.
76. I am here thinking of Grosz's assertion that "the stability of one, the thing, is the guarantee of the stability and on-going existence or viability of the other, the body" ("Thing," 132). The mackintosh suggests that such a model of the relationship between persons and things is optimistic; instead, the thing only guarantees its own existence. For more on Grosz's suggestion, see chapter 1.
77. For examples of the former, see J. Benjamin Cosgrove, "Macintosh and the Old Testament Character Joseph," *James Joyce Quarterly* 29, no. 3 (1992): 681–84; and John Gordon, *Joyce and Reality: The Empirical Strikes Back* (Syracuse, N.Y.:

Syracuse University Press, 2004). Other critics agree that, in Maria DiBattista's words, "there are certain mysteries that are, narratively as well as spiritually, best left unanswered" ("*Ulysses*'s Unanswered Questions," *Modernism/modernity* 15 [2008]: 270). Frank Kermode argues that "the appearances of MacIntosh lack coherence because they mime the fortuities of real life; a coherence related to another of our conventional expectations of narrative" ("The Man in the Macintosh," in *Pieces of My Mind: Essays and Criticism, 1958–2002* [New York: Farrar, Straus and Giroux, 2004], 124). Bernard Benstock concurs, writing that "the mysteries of *Ulysses* are those of an ordinary day in an extraordinary universe, and are only mysteries because they contain and present unsolved and unresolved dilemmas and possibilities" ("The Mysteries of *Ulysses*," in *International Perspectives on James Joyce*, ed. Gottlieb Ganser [Troy, N.Y.: Whitston, 1986], 43). Michael J. Sidnell's argument is the closest to my own in that he focuses on the figure's name and observes that "the garment stands forth as a man." His essay explores "whether *words* are convertible to persons, or whether language may construct, or *logos* create, them" ("Mac[k]intosh the Noun," *Joyce Studies Annual* 13 [2002]: 194, 195).

78. Sidnell, "Mac(k)intosh the Noun," 193.

79. Joyce, *Ulysses*, 254.

80. Ibid., 485.

81. As Stacy Gillis elegantly notes, poppies were part of a postwar "cult of remembrance" ("Consoling Fictions: Mourning, World War One, and Dorothy L. Sayers," in *Modernism and Mourning*, ed. Patricia Rae [Lewisburg, Pa.: Bucknell University Press, 2007], 186). Duffy argues that Joyce's man in the mackintosh is an IRA "proto-gunman," who wears the mac because it enables him to be inconspicuous (*Subaltern Ulysses*, 66). While I find Duffy's placement of *Ulysses* in a late-colonial context suggestive, M'Intosh fits less neatly in this framework given the cannons and poppies that mark the character's exit in "Circe."

82. Robert Spoo, "'Nestor' and the Nightmare: The Presence of the Great War in *Ulysses*," *Twentieth Century Literature* 32, no. 2 (1986): 151.

83. Joyce, *Ulysses*, 56.

84. John Blanford, advertisement, *Sunday Graphic*, September 9, 1928, 21.

85. Mattamac, advertisement, *Daily News*, June 7, 1920, 5. Such claims were contested by cartoons of the era, such as one that personifies coats on pegs and depicts expensive ones exclaiming, "UGH! And a yellow mackintosh!" ("Snobbery in the Cloak-Room," *Punch*, September 10, 1924, 301).

86. "Pearls and New Wraps," *Eve*, April 8, 1920, xiv.

87. "Vogues and Vanities," *Sunday Graphic*, August 4, 1929, 19.

88. "'Mosco' Mackintosh" [advertisement], *Vogue* (Britain), February 1932, 3.

89. Aquascutum, advertisement, *Vogue* (Britain), Early August 1923, iii.

90. Virginia Woolf, *Mrs. Dalloway* (1925; New York: Harcourt Brace Jovanovich, 1981), 12.

91. Ibid., 123.

92. Ibid., 126. As Laura Gwyn Edson writes, the mac becomes "an encapsulation of everything she [Clarissa] can't stand about Miss Kilman. The hostess figures the tutor as the coat." For Edson, what is most significant about the garment

is that "Woolf has submerged clothing into the substrata of multiple consciousness where clothing is claimed as cover or protection but also revealed as a projection of innermost secrets" ("Kicking Off Her Knickers: Virginia Woolf's Rejection of Clothing as Realistic Detail," in *Virginia Woolf and the Arts: Selected Papers from the Sixth Annual Conference on Virginia Woolf*, ed. Diane F. Gillespie and Leslie K. Hankins [New York: Pace University Press, 1997], 122, 123).While the coat certainly functions in this manner, I am interested in how Woolf engages the relationship between person and thing (and between thing and history) through Kilman's garment.

93. Doris Kilman's mackintosh in *Mrs. Dalloway* is uncannily similar to that of Margaret Grey in *The Return of the Soldier*. Woolf was almost certainly familiar with West's novel; in May 1918, the year it was published, she offered Vanessa Bell *Return of the Soldier* for her birthday (*The Letters of Virginia Woolf*, ed. Nigel Nicolson and Joanne Trautmann, vol. 2, *1912–1922* [New York: Harcourt Brace Jovanovich, 1976], 245), and on June 7, 1918, Woolf told Molly MacCarthy that she was going to read "Rebecca West's new novel" (247). Thanks to Mark Hussey for pointing me to the link between Woolf and West.

94. Woolf, *Mrs. Dalloway*, 12.

95. As Karen L. Levenback has argued, Clarissa's thoughts about Kilman suggest that her "emotions may, in fact, have seemed minor and trivial to Woolf herself" ("Clarissa Dalloway, Doris Kilman and The Great War," *Virginia Woolf Miscellany* 37 [1991]: 3). Levenback's larger point is that Kilman's character signals the lingering effects of World War I in the postwar period, an argument with which I am in complete agreement.

96. West, *Return of the Soldier*, 88.

97. Woolf, *Mrs. Dalloway*, 131, 132.

98. Ibid., 123.

99. Ibid., 128.

100. Ibid., 123.

101. Ibid., 14.

102. Ibid., 133.

103. As Christine Froula argues, "*Mrs. Dalloway* poses the great question of Europe's future . . . as the fate of collective mourning—a *historic* question of genre for a traumatized Europe poised between elegy and revenge tragedy" (*Virginia Woolf and the Bloomsbury Avant-Garde: War, Civilization, Modernity* [New York: Columbia University Press, 2005], 89).

104. Rita Felski, "Context Stinks!" *New Literary History* 42, no. 4 (2011): 585.

105. Daphne du Maurier, *Rebecca* (1938; London: Virago, 2003), 261.

106. Ibid., 262.

107. Graham Greene, *The Third Man* (1949; New York: Penguin, 1999), 24.

108. In this respect, Calloway is quite different from Greene's other main character, the popular author Rollo Martins; in *The Third Man*, Martins is famously unable to answer questions about James Joyce (ibid., 94). This scene serves as a sly dig that positions Greene himself as better read and more knowing than Martins.

109. Alison Clarke and Daniel Miller, "Fashion and Anxiety," *Fashion Theory* 6, no. 2 (2002): 193.

110. "Happiness," *Punch*, June 18, 1924, 661.

111. Dorothy L. Sayers, *Unnatural Death* (1927; New York: Avon, 1964), 116. Gillis argues that detective novels "encoded war narratives" and serve as a form of "witness to World War I" ("Consoling Fictions," 185, 194). In her words, Sayers's fiction depicts Wimsey as effecting "his own 'talking cure,'" as his cases require that he speak about the impact of the war on himself and others (192).

3. Aspiration to the Extraordinary

1. Terry Castle, *Masquerade and Civilization: The Carnivalesque in Eighteenth-Century English Culture and Fiction* (Sanford, Calif.: Stanford University Press, 1986), 341.

2. In addition to Castle, two writers on fancy dress bear mentioning. Historian Beverly Gordon examines early-twentieth-century costumes in the United States and reads them as important for group formation, in *The Saturated World: Aesthetic Meaning, Intimate Objects, Women's Lives, 1890–1940* (Knoxville: University of Tennessee Press, 2006). Her study focuses on the transformation of everyday experience through making and wearing costumes. Nicholas Foulkes offers a richly illustrated celebration of legendary international costume balls, emphasizing the craftsmanship that went into fancy-dress costumes and settings and observing that "it is possible to set these events in their cultural and social contexts and to appreciate them for what their hosts knew them to be: examples of a unique and fragile art form" (*Bals: Legendary Costume Balls of the Twentieth Century* [New York: Assouline, 2011], 43). His is a work of appreciation rather than analysis. There is little work on modernism and fancy dress. Kate McLoughlin writes that "party-going . . . is as much an art-form as party-giving. Appearance is the first consideration in preparing the performance" ("Introduction: A Welcome from the Host," in *The Modernist Party*, ed. Kate McLoughlin [Edinburgh: Edinburgh University Press, 2013], 5). Despite this important observation, the collection pays little attention to fancy dress.

3. Herbert Marcuse identifies such ontologies as those in which the "noncorporeal being of man is asserted as the real substance of the individual" (*Negations: Essays in Critical Theory*, trans. Jeremy J. Shapiro [Boston: Beacon Press, 1968], 104).

4. George J. Nicholls, *Bacon and Hams* (London: Institute of Certificated Grocers, 1917).

5. Daniel Miller, *Stuff* (Cambridge: Polity, 2010), 13. Miller's work at once underlines the promise of contemporary thing theory and articulates assumptions that would have been anathema in the period I address here. In *Stuff*, for example, his "starting point is that we too are stuff, and our use and identification with material culture provides a capacity for enhancing, just as much as for submerging, our humanity" (6).

6. Such representations reflect middle-class opinion, which often took "the form of hostility to the aristocracy and the rich as profiteers from the First World War, a criticism that lingered well into the 1920s in journalism and popular literature" (Simon Gunn and Rachel Bell, *Middle Classes: The Rise and Sprawl* [London: Phoenix, 2003], chap. 3).

7. Castle, *Masquerade and Civilization*, 332.

8. Anthea Jarvis and Patricia Raine, *Fancy Dress* (Aylesbury: Shire, 1984), 14.

9. Nannette Thrush, "Clio's Dressmakers: Women and the Uses of Historical Costume," in *Clio's Daughters: British Women Making History, 1790–1899*, ed. Lynette Felber (Newark: University of Delaware Press, 2007), 273.

10. Jarvis and Raine, *Fancy Dress*, 23.

11. Ibid.

12. "Fancy Dress Ball for Germans," *Illustrated Sunday Herald*, April 11, 1915, 7. The prevalence of American-themed costumes in this list is remarkable and suggests that Hollywood films influenced fancy-dress choices quite early. British prisoners of war in Holland seemed more eclectic in their choices when photographed in fancy dress as Pierrette and a geisha. See "Interned Sailors in Fancy Dress," *Sunday Pictorial*, June 6, 1915, 8. For discussion of cross-dressing on the British front lines, see David Boxwell, "The Follies of War: Cross-Dressing and Popular Theatre on the British Front Lines, 1914–18," *Modernism/modernity* 9, no. 1 (2002): 1–20.

13. "Through the Eyes of a Woman," *Illustrated Sunday Herald*, June 20, 1915, 19.

14. Jarvis and Raine, *Fancy Dress*, 24.

15. "Our Lives from Day to Day," *Vogue* (Britain), July 25, 1928, 45.

16. "By Their Fruits and Flowers Ye Shall Know Them," *Vogue* (Britain), January 1923, 40–41.

17. Jarvis and Raine, *Fancy Dress*, 25.

18. Geoffrey D'Egville, *How and What to Dance* (London: Pearson, 1919), 24–25.

19. Mrs. Charles J. Ashdown, *British Costume During XIX Centuries (Civil and Ecclesiastical)* (London: Nelson, [1910?]), 75.

20. Ardern Holt, *Fancy Dresses Described; or, What to Wear at Fancy Balls* (London: Debenham & Freebody, 1887), 9.

21. Ashdown, *British Costume During XIX Centuries*, viii.

22. "Our Lives from Day to Day," 45.

23. Holt, *Fancy Dresses Described*, 254.

24. *Fancy Dresses at Harrods* [catalog], November 1927, 1. It seems clear that some costumes, such as "Merry and Bright," were intended for holiday parties.

25. Jarvis and Raine, *Fancy Dress*, 16.

26. Ibid., 20.

27. Thrush, "Clio's Dressmakers," 258. Less lavish but still remarkable (and well-documented) fancy-dress balls were the Victory Ball, held to celebrate the end of World War I, which was covered by the *Sunday Pictorial*, December 1, 1918 (Viola Tree attended as Winged Victory and was, according to the reporter, "greatly impeded by her vast wings" [13]), and, in 1919, the Chelsea Arts Club Dazzle Ball,

which "took the inspiration of wartime camouflage" (Tim Newark, *Camouflage* [New York: Thames and Hudson, 2007], 88).

28. *Vogue* (Britain), August 22, 1928, 18.

29. Ibid.

30. *Fancy Dresses at Harrods*, 2.

31. Faye Hammill writes, "The word 'unpretentious' is a key term in the definition of the English middlebrow, which is characterized by a resistance to pretension in all its forms" (*Women, Celebrity, and Literary Culture Between the Wars* [Austin: University of Texas Press, 2007], 186). While there was not a complete correspondence between middle-class writers and readers and the middlebrow, the latter's treatment of pretension is reflected in widespread middle-class "cultural disapproval of conspicuous consumption," a form of economic pretension, according to Ross McKibbin, *Classes and Cultures: England, 1918–1951* (Oxford: Oxford University Press, 1998), 72.

32. E. M. Delafield, *Diary of a Provincial Lady* (1931; Chicago: Academy Chicago, 2002), 382.

33. Ibid.

34. Ibid., 383.

35. Ibid. References to "carnival" in twentieth-century works underline the difference between the festivals analyzed by Mikhail Bakhtin and modern fancy-dress parties. Fancy dress, frankly, was too aspirational and uptight to embrace the grotesque qualities that made carnival transgressive before and during the Renaissance. Twentieth-century costumes tilted toward the classical. Peter Stallybrass and Allon White clearly outline the distinction in their introduction to *The Politics and Poetics of Transgression* (Ithaca, N.Y.: Cornell University Press, 1986), 1–26.

36. The reference is to Philippians 3:21, which promises that God "shall change our vile body, that it may be fashioned like unto his glorious body, according to the working whereby he is able even to subdue all things unto himself."

37. Evelyn Waugh, *Vile Bodies* (1930; Boston: Little, Brown, 1958), 170–71.

38. Ibid., 66.

39. Ibid., 72.

40. Ibid., 74.

41. Ibid., 76.

42. Jarvis and Raine, *Fancy Dress*, 24.

43. Evelyn Waugh, "Cruise (Letters from a Young Lady of Leisure)," in *The Complete Stories of Evelyn Waugh* (Boston: Little, Brown, 1999), 124.

44. Examples of a body's imperviousness to costuming are rare but occasionally surface, especially in cartoons. In one, an overweight middle-aged lady tells a clerk, "I'm going to a fancy-dress dance, and I want you to make me up as one of those 'Vamps' one sees on the pictures" (*Punch*, December 21, 1921, 485). This woman wants the impossible and grants almost limitless power to things through her faith that a costume can transform her weighty body.

45. D. J. Taylor, *Bright Young People: The Lost Generation of London's Jazz Age* (New York: Farrar, Straus and Giroux, 2007), 79.

46. Lindsay Cable, "Carnival Week" [cartoon], *Punch*, September 9, 1936, 303.
47. G. L. Stamps, cartoon, *Punch*, January 5, 1938, 7.
48. P. G. Wodehouse, *Right Ho, Jeeves!* (1934), Project Gutenberg, http://www.gutenberg.org/ebooks/10554.
49. Ibid.
50. Ibid.
51. Arthur Moreland, "Simple Stories: The Fancy-Dress Dance," *Punch*, June 12, 1929, 654.
52. Ibid., 655.
53. Ibid.
54. Ibid.
55. As Nina Auerbach puts it, "Throughout the novel she is a docile companion to the overbearing rich." Moreover, she "cringes before the servants" in a way that demonstrates that she is not of Maxim's class (*Daphne du Maurier: Haunted Heiress* [Philadelphia: University of Pennsylvania Press, 2000], 102, 117).
56. See, for example, Gina Wisker's argument that "du Maurier's writing exposes the hollowness of the decadence of an upper class while drawing us wholesale into the dream—it is an imaginative lie we need but can see through" ("Dangerous Borders: Daphne du Maurier's *Rebecca*: Shaking the Foundations of the Romance of Privilege, Partying and Place," *Journal of Gender Studies* 12, no. 2 [2003]: 85–86).
57. Daphne du Maurier, *Rebecca* (1938; London: Virago, 2003), 239.
58. Ibid., 227.
59. Ibid.
60. Ibid., 230.
61. Ibid., 236.
62. Ibid., 238.
63. Ibid., 237.
64. Ibid., 238.
65. Ibid., 239–40.
66. Ibid., 242.
67. Ibid., 248.
68. Ibid., 292.
69. Ibid., 262.
70. Ibid., 336.
71. Ibid., 338.
72. Ibid., 339.
73. Wisker, "Dangerous Borders," 84.
74. du Maurier, *Rebecca*, 316.
75. Miller, *Stuff*, 10.
76. The evidence for this claim can only be indirect, but it is significant to note that successful industrialists in the period seldom accepted knighthoods. Such "trappings" were unwelcome to men who continued to identify as middle class despite their wealth. For examples, see Gunn and Bell, *Middle Classes*, chaps. 2 and 4.

77. George Rylands, interview, in *Recollections of Virginia Woolf by Her Contemporaries*, ed. Joan Russell Noble (London: Peter Owen, 1972), 140.

78. Ibid., 141.

79. Woolf's novel has been understood in relation to costuming since Sandra Gilbert's monumental "Costumes of the Mind: Transvestism as Metaphor in Modern Literature," *Critical Inquiry* 7 (1980): 391–417. In an article that highlights differing attitudes toward costuming among male and female modernists, Gilbert asserts, "Woolf's view of clothing implied that costume is inseparable from identity—indeed, that costume creates identity" (391). While my reading of Woolf's novel is indebted to Gilbert's work, I build on her argument by moving beyond a focus on sex and gender identity *and* by attending to the specific sartorial form that encouraged Woolf's experimentation. Gilbert's treatment of costuming is less material than metaphorical, an approach that serves to highlight Woolf's difference from her male counterparts but occludes the author's immersion in a cultural practice of literal, not figurative, costuming.

80. *Ottoline: The Early Memoirs of Lady Ottoline Morrell*, ed. Robert Gathorne-Hardy (London: Faber and Faber, 1963), 180.

81. Virginia Woolf, "Old Bloomsbury" in *Moments of Being*, ed. Jeanne Schulkind, 2nd ed. (San Diego, Calif.: Harcourt Brace Jovanovich, 1985), 200.

82. Virginia was recruited into the hoax after it had been planned; in her brother Adrian Stephen's words, he "got hold of my sister" (*The "Dreadnought" Hoax* [London: Hogarth Press, 1983], 31). As Georgia Johnston has documented, Virginia herself said she "signed on 'at the last moment' when two of the planners had withdrawn, because 'Either they were ill; or they were afraid; or they had urgent business elsewhere'" ("Virginia Woolf's Talk on the *Dreadnought* Hoax," *Woolf Studies Annual* 15 [2009]: 1). While scholars have argued that her participation in the hoax constituted a political act, she presented her actions as a joke. In her disguise, she felt that "I became another pseroen [sic]" and noticed that others "didnt seem to see that was a young lady [sic]" (15).

83. Woolf, "Am I a Snob?" 200.

84. *The Diary of Virginia Woolf*, ed. Anne Olivier Bell and Andrew McNeillie, vol. 2, *1920–1924* (New York: Harcourt Brace Jovanovich, 1978), 223.

85. Ibid.

86. Virginia Woolf to Clive Bell, January 18, 1930, in *The Letters of Virginia Woolf*, ed. Nigel Nicolson and Joanne Trautmann, vol. 4, *1929–1931* (New York: Harcourt Brace Jovanovich, 1978), 128.

87. Ibid., 129.

88. Ibid.

89. At a costume party in 1931, Vanessa asked guests to wear masks and noted that "Virginia came as Sappho I believe, at any rate a most voluptuous lady casting her eyes up to heaven" (Vanessa Bell to Quentin Bell, January 26, 1931, in *Selected Letters of Vanessa Bell*, ed. Regina Marler [New York: Pantheon, 1993], 357). And in 1933, Woolf described yet another fancy-dress party for which "I dressed up as Queen Victoria on her wedding night and fell into the arms of the Prince Consort," who was of course Leonard (Virginia Woolf to Elizabeth Bowen,

January 3, 1933, in *The Letters of Virginia Woolf*, ed. Nigel Nicolson and Joanne Trautmann, vol. 5, 1932–1935 [New York: Harcourt Brace Jovanovich, 1979], 145).

90. *The Diary of Virginia Woolf*, ed. Anne Olivier Bell and Andrew McNeillie, vol. 5, 1936–1941 (New York: Harcourt Brace Jovanovich, 1984), 203.

91. See, for example, Nancy Cervetti, "In the Breeches, Petticoats, and Pleasures of *Orlando*," *Journal of Modern Literature* 20, no. 2 (1996): 165–75; George Piggford, "'Who's That Girl?': Annie Lennox, Woolf's *Orlando*, and Female Camp Androgyny," *Mosaic* 30, no. 3 (1997): 39–58; and Talia Schaffer, "Posing Orlando," in *Sexual Artifice: Persons, Images, Politics*, ed. Ann Kibbey, Kayann Short, and Abouali Farmanfarmaian (New York: New York University Press, 1994), 26–63. Schaffer's argument is closest to my own, as she observes that *Orlando* "is about costuming, precisely because costuming is what gender is all about" (36). I argue more broadly that the novel is "all about" *identity* writ large.

92. Virginia Woolf, *Jacob's Room* (1922; New York: Harcourt, Brace & World, 1960), 122.

93. Ibid., 124.

94. *Diary of Virginia Woolf*, 5:203.

95. Although they do not look at Woolf's novel through the lens of fancy dress, I am in accord with R. S. Koppen and Christy L. Burns, who are interested in the ways in which *Orlando* challenges models of essential selfhood. Koppen reads Woolf's presentation of history "as a sequence of fashions, and sexual identity as mutable and performative" against "a nineteenth-century idealist discourse of authenticity and *Geist*" (*Virginia Woolf, Fashion and Literary Modernity* [Edinburgh: Edinburgh University Press, 2009], 57); Burns notes that "Woolf's conception of Orlando's identity holds within it the possibility for participation in social and self construction" by means of the clothing the character chooses for herself ("Re-Dressing Feminist Identities: Tensions Between Essential and Constructed Selves in Virginia Woolf's *Orlando*," *Twentieth Century Literature: A Scholarly and Critical Journal* 40 [1994]: 346, 351). Koppen and Burns see Woolf as working through and against (different) theorists of biography and identity; I am instead interested in the way that a specific sartorial form encouraged the author to see selfhood as less essential than put on.

96. Virginia Woolf to Vita Sackville-West, November 11, 1927, in *The Letters of Virginia Woolf*, ed. Nigel Nicolson and Joanne Trautmann, vol. 3, 1923–1928 (New York: Harcourt Brace Jovanovich, 1978), 435.

97. Koppen, *Virginia Woolf, Fashion and Literary Modernity*, 51.

98. Ibid., 53. Schaffer writes that in this photograph, Sackville-West "resembles nothing so much as a woman dressed for a fancy dress ball" ("Posing Orlando," 52), which is precisely my point.

99. Virginia Woolf, *Orlando* (1928; New York: Harcourt, Brace, 1956), 138.

100. Ibid.

101. Ibid., 187.

102. Ibid., 188.

103. Ibid.

104. Miller, *Stuff*, 40.

105. Woolf, *Orlando*, 189.
106. Ibid., 220.
107. Ibid., 221.
108. *Diary of Virginia Woolf*, 5:203.
109. Woolf, *Orlando*, 221.
110. Ibid.
111. Ibid.
112. Ibid., 236.
113. Ibid.
114. Ibid., 188.
115. Ibid., 308.
116. Ibid., 309.
117. Ibid., 310

118. Lisa Rado, for example, sees *Orlando* as "a novel about identity crisis" and asserts that Woolf's character is "unable to register reality, distinguish between objects, or presuppose any pure and stable singularity" at the end of the book (*The Modern Androgyne Imagination: A Failed Sublime* [Charlottesville: University of Virginia Press, 2000], 161, 169). Rado comes to this conclusion through a framework that posits the androgyne as in tension with Orlando's physical body. Her approach, like that of many other critics, focuses on the relationship between Orlando's sex and identity; here, I want to argue that we parse the novel's experiment with identity too narrowly if we attend to Orlando's "identity" only through gender, the character's sexed body, or sexuality.

119. Woolf, *Orlando*, 313.
120. Ibid., 314.
121. Ibid., 315.
122. Ibid., 324.
123. Ibid., 329.
124. *Diary of Virginia Woolf*, 5:203.

125. Djuna Barnes's *Nightwood* offers one of the other rare examples of a fictional character who becomes what she wears. Frau Mann's circus costume pervades her body and being: "She seemed to have a skin that was the pattern of her costume: a bodice of lozenges, red and yellow, low in the back and ruffled over and under the arms, faded with the reek of her three-a-day control, red tights, laced boots—one somehow felt they ran through her as the design runs through hard holiday candies" (*Nightwood* [New York: New Directions, 1961], 13). In contrast to Woolf, Barnes's challenge to depth ontology stems from her contact with actors, circus performers, and the Baroness Elsa (who made dress into a form of street art).

126. Dorothy Sayers to Her Parents [Henry Sayers and Helen Mary Leigh Sayers], October 27, 1912, in *The Letters of Dorothy L. Sayers, 1899–1936: The Making of a Detective Novelist*, ed. Barbara Reynolds (New York: St. Martin's Press, 1996), 65.

127. Barbara Reynolds, *Dorothy L. Sayers: Her Life and Soul* (New York: St. Martin's Griffin, 1997), 45–46.

128. Ibid., 62, 50.

129. Dorothy Sayers to Her Parents, October 1913, in *Letters of Dorothy L. Sayers*, 81.

130. Robert McGregor and Ethan Lewis argue that Wimsey's talents in *Murder Must Advertise* are "merely a collection of things" that "do not make him a superior, or even a better, human being" (*Conundrums for the Long Week-End: England, Dorothy L. Sayers, and Lord Peter Wimsey* [Kent, Ohio: Kent State University Press, 2000], 144). Such desires for the character miss the point that, through things, Wimsey questions the very nature of what it means to be human. Sean Latham is much nearer the mark when he argues that characters in Sayers's early Wimsey novels adopt "a series of poses" and that "the substance of subjectivity is replaced by the sign of style" (*"Am I a Snob?" Modernism and the Novel* [Ithaca, N.Y.: Cornell University Press, 2003], 180, 194). I believe that such arguments occlude the fact that *Murder Must Advertise* questions whether subjectivity *has* a substance.

131. Dorothy L. Sayers, *Murder Must Advertise* (1927; New York: Avon, 1964), 107.

132. Ibid.

133. Ibid., 69.

134. Ibid., 60.

135. Ibid., 70.

136. Ibid., 84.

137. Ibid., 69.

138. Reynolds notes that a story by G. K. Chesterton, whom Sayers admired, includes a criminal dressed as Harlequin. In "The Flying Stars" (1911), Chesterton's character wears this costume to perform in a Christmas play. Reynolds calls Sayers's use of the same costume "part of a literary game" ("G. K. Chesterton and Dorothy L. Sayers," *Chesterton Review* 9, no. 2 [1984]: 151).

139. Sayers, *Murder Must Advertise*, 71.

140. Ibid., 72.

141. Ibid., 160.

142. Ibid., 187.

143. Ibid., 189.

144. Ibid., 201.

145. Ibid., 248.

146. Ibid., 267.

147. Ibid., 284.

148. Ibid., 296–97.

149. Ibid., 291.

150. Ibid., 340.

151. Wimsey continues to use his full name in later novels, including *Gaudy Night*, and thus continues to be "Death Bredon" long after the conclusion of *Murder Must Advertise*. For a different reading of the novel's conclusion, see McGregor and Lewis, *Conundrums for the Long Week-End*, 150.

152. Sayers, *Murder Must Advertise*, 333.

153. Dorothy L. Sayers, *Gaudy Night* (1936; New York: HarperCollins, 1995), 314.

154. Matthew Levay, "Remaining a Mystery: Gertrude Stein, Crime Fiction and Popular Modernism," *Journal of Modern Literature* 36, no. 4 (2013): 4.

212   3. ASPIRATION TO THE EXTRAORDINARY

155. Sayers, like others who wrote detective fiction in the period, had both middlebrow and highbrow readerships. The author herself once wrote that "I can't write for low-brows. It's the merry high-brows who like my books, those who feel . . . that 'the detective story is the normal recreation of noble minds'" (Dorothy Sayers to John Cournos, February 3, 1925, in *Letters of Dorothy L. Sayers*, 229). Although Sayers does not mention her vast middlebrow readership in this letter, middlebrow and highbrow tastes overlapped in detective fiction, as Nicola Beauman argues in *A Very Great Profession: The Woman's Novel, 1914–39* (London: Virago, 1983), 173. Indeed, interwar debates about detective fiction were continuous with debates about modernism, according to Victoria Stewart, "Defining Detective Fiction in Interwar Britain," *Space Between* 9 (2013): 102.

156. T. S. Eliot, "Tradition and the Individual Talent," in *The Waste Land and Other Writings* (New York: Modern Library, 2002), 107.

157. Woolf, *Orlando*, 309.

158. Jarvis and Raine, *Fancy Dress*, 30.

159. Ibid.

160. Ibid.

161. Castle, *Masquerade and Civilization*, 341.

162. P. G. Wodehouse, *Joy in the Morning* (New York: Doubleday, 1946), 36.

163. Ibid., 51.

4. Serialized Selves

1. Rachel Ferguson, *Alas, Poor Lady* (1937; London: Persephone, 2006), 390.

2. Ibid., 391.

3. As Marilyn Strathern notes in her foundational analysis of Melanesian anthropology, in Western formulations a person is "axiomatically 'an individual' who . . . derives an integrity from its position as somehow prior to society" (*The Gender of the Gift* [Berkeley: University of California Press, 1988], 93). This individual works throughout his or her life to master the physical world, a process that takes in consumption, relationships with others, and additional acts of self-definition. Secondhand clothing disrupts this process because garments highlight a decidedly non-Western model of the self, one in which "items flow between persons, creating their mutual enchainment. The items carry the influence that one partner may have on another" (178). I am not alone in viewing the early twentieth century as a moment when serialization was perceived as a threat to human individuality. Caroline Evans argues that the mannequin and fashion shows came to be seen as carrying the taint of mass production and the loss of individualism, in *The Mechanical Smile: Modernism and the First Fashion Shows in France and America, 1900–1929* (New Haven, Conn.: Yale University Press, 2013), especially chaps. 3 and 6.

4. Ross McKibbin, *Classes and Cultures: England, 1918–1951* (Oxford: Oxford University Press, 1998), 70.

5. Although many of these texts are humorous, I use the term "comedy" in its broader sense of a text that has a positive understanding of human experience that is particularly reflected in a happy conclusion.

6. Beverly Lemire, "Consumerism in Preindustrial and Early Industrial England: The Trade in Secondhand Clothes," *Journal of British Studies* 27 (1988): 21.

7. Stanley Chapman, "The Innovative Entrepreneurs in the British Ready-Made Clothing Industry," *Textile History* 24 (1993): 5.

8. George R. Sims, "The Londoner out and at Home," in *Living London: Its Work and Its Play, Its Humor and Its Pathos, Its Sights and Its Scenes* (London: Cassell, 1903), 303.

9. The jumble sale (or, in the United States, rummage sale)—defined as "a sale of miscellaneous cheap or second-hand articles at a charitable bazaar" (*Oxford English Dictionary Online*, s.v. "jumble sale," http://www.oed.com/view/Entry/102009?rskey=3BoblL&result=1#eid40237844)—dates to the 1890s but became popular during World War I as a means of raising funds. For an example, see "Page Mainly for Women," *Sunday Pictorial*, October 14, 1917, 10. Although the columnist asserts that "you would have laughed a few years ago at these girls [munitions workers] buying Paquin and Lucille gowns," she later concludes that "now—well, I think gowns should only be sold to women producing certification of war-work."

10. Lady Sempill was quoted as saying that "fashions in wartime are wicked" (*Sunday Pictorial*, November 11, 1917, 10), and it was reported that "Mrs. Waldorf Astor, the wife of Major Astor, M.P., is so depressed by the sad sights she has witnessed among the wounded men at Marlow that she has turned her back on fashion" (*Illustrated Sunday Herald*, June 6, 1916, 9).

11. Simon Gunn and Rachel Bell, *Middle Classes: The Rise and Sprawl* (London: Phoenix, 2003), chap. 3.

12. Quoted in Christopher Breward, *The Culture of Fashion: A New History of Fashionable Dress* (Manchester: Manchester University Press, 1995), 201.

13. "Every Woman Her Own Chimney Sweep," *Lady*, June 24, 1920, 744. Such sentiments point to a powerful affective state that did not entirely reflect economic circumstances. McKibbin has argued that while it was "widely believed that much of the middle class had been pauperized after the war" (*Classes and Cultures*, 52), the "new poor" were generally only declassed temporarily: "For two or three years after the war many middle-class families suffered an appreciable loss of real earnings and the social disappointment that comes with frustrated expectations" (53), but the losses were mostly made up by 1923. Nevertheless, he notes that "the 'crisis' left long memories" (54) and inculcated frugality.

14. *Vogue* (Britain), Late May 1924, 97.

15. *Vogue* (Britain), October 31, 1928, 79. A sampling across issues of *Vogue* points to a steady uptick in classified advertisements for secondhand dealers during the 1920s: the Late June 1924 edition has fourteen (ix); by Early November 1924, there are fifteen (xviii); and the May 2, 1928, issue has twenty-two ads for dress agencies (99).

16. *Vogue* (Britain), June 1923, x.

17. *Vogue* (Britain), May 1925, xiv.
18. *Vogue* (Britain), January 6, 1932, 6.
19. Ibid., 4.
20. Some women were willing to buy and sell used clothes directly. In the 1920s, the *Gentlewoman in Town and Country* operated "The 'G' Private Exchange," and the *Lady* organized the "Private Exchange and Sale" for its readers.
21. Lemire, "Consumerism in Preindustrial and Early Industrial England," 1. Christopher Breward concurs: "There are, unsurprisingly, no retailers' guides or trade publications to help reconstruct the appearance, stock and profile of selling practices that lay at the peripheries of legal and social acceptability" (*The Hidden Consumer: Masculinities, Fashion and City Life, 1860–1914* [Manchester: Manchester University Press, 1999], 123).
22. Robina Wallis's business records are held at Blythe House, the Victoria and Albert Museum's off-site storage facility. The archive contains letters written to Wallis by her clients as well as ledgers. Unfortunately, Wallis's letters to her clients are not part of the collection. I have explored the significance of this archive at greater length in "Smart Clothes at Low Prices: Gendered Alliances, Class Divisions in the Interwar Secondhand Clothing Trade," in *Cultures of Femininity in Modern Fashion*, ed. Ilya Parkins and Elizabeth Sheehan (Lebanon, N.H.: University Press of New England, 2011), 71–86.
23. Barbara Armstrong to Robina Wallis, no date, Archive of Art and Design, AAD/1989/8/1/7, Victoria and Albert Museum, London.
24. Barbara Armstrong to Robina Wallis, June 28, no year, Archive of Art and Design, AAD/1989/8/1/5.
25. Mrs. Alderson Archer to Robina Wallis, March 26, no year, Archive of Art and Design, AAD/1989/8/1/2.
26. A. Bailey to Robina Wallis, no date, Archive of Art and Design, AAD/1989/8/1/15/.
27. G. Birch to Robina Wallis, January 5, 1935, Archive of Art and Design, AAD/1989/8/1/24.
28. In his analysis of Karl Marx's coat, Peter Stallybrass noted, "In the language of nineteenth century clothes-makers and repairers, the wrinkles in the elbows of a jacket or a sleeve were called 'memories.' Those wrinkles recorded the body that had inhabited the garment. They memorized the interaction, the mutual constitution, of a person and thing. But from the perspective of commercial exchange, every wrinkle or 'memory' was a devaluation of the commodity" ("Marx's Coat," in *Border Fetishisms: Material Objects in Unstable Places*, ed. Patricia Spyer [London: Routledge, 1998], 196). While, as Igor Kopytoff writes, there is a section of most economies "in which the selling strategy rests on stressing that the commoditization of goods bought for consumption need not be terminal," worn, stained, or unfashionable clothing appeared to all but the most penurious consumers as in terminal condition ("The Cultural Biography of Things: Commoditization as Process," in *The Social Life of Things: Commodities in Cultural Perspective*, ed. Arjun Appadurai [Cambridge: Cambridge University Press, 1986], 75).

29. Lesley Paul to Robina Wallis, no date, Archive of Art and Design, AAD 1989/8/1/155.

30. A. Linton to Robina Wallis, no date, Archive of Art and Design, AAD/1989/8/1/122.

31. For example, someone requested "a tennis frock and a mackintosh" but stipulated that they "must be inexpensive as I have very little money" (Jones to Robina Wallis, no date, Archive of Art and Design, AAD/1989/8/1/115). Since, as chapter 2 demonstrated, new mackintoshes were available at inexpensive prices (and some makers even offered financing plans), this consumer was obviously of quite limited means.

32. M. A. Smith to Robina Wallis, no date, Archive of Art and Design, AAD/1989/8/1/168.

33. *Encyclopaedia Britannica*, 14th ed., s.v. "dress."

34. C. Willett Cunnington, *English Women's Clothing in the Present Century* (London: Faber and Faber, 1952), 19.

35. Gilles Lipovetsky, *The Empire of Fashion; Dressing Modern Democracy*, trans. Catherine Porter (Princeton, N.J.: Princeton University Press, 1994), 60. As Lipovetsky writes, "New signs, more subtle and more nuanced, particularly in the realm of labels, shapes, and fabrics, ensured that dress would continue to mark social distinctions and social excellence" (61).

36. Breward, *Culture of Fashion*, 187.

37. I emphasize this point because only recently have scholars challenged the democracy of dress thesis. Rosy Aindow argues that "a real democratisation of clothing was not achieved during this period (and never has been)" (*Dress and Identity in British Literary Culture, 1870–1914* [Farnham: Ashgate, 2010], 22). By investigating the trade in secondhand clothing between the wars, which has been ignored to date, I want to suggest that scholars must consider more than periodical culture, the rise of department stores, and the expansion of designer brands in their assessments of modern fashion.

38. Elizabeth C. Pilkington, "Milly's Old Lavender Gown," *Windsor* 10, no. 4 (1899): 419.

39. Ibid., 420.

40. Ibid.

41. Ibid., 422–23.

42. Ibid., 424.

43. I am here thinking through Alfred Gell's model of distributed personhood: "[A]s social persons, we are present, not just in our singular bodies, but in everything in our surroundings which bears witness to our existence, our attributes, and our agency" (*Art and Agency: An Anthropological Theory* [Oxford: Clarendon Press, 1998], 103). For more on Gell, see the introduction.

44. Molly Keane, *Devoted Ladies* (1934; London: Virago, 1984), 79.

45. Ibid., 80.

46. Ibid., 79.

47. L. B. Martin, cartoon, *Punch*, August 19, 1925, 168.

216   4. SERIALIZED SELVES

48. Gell argues that human agents are "not just where their bodies were, but in many different places (and times) simultaneously" (*Art and Agency*, 21). While clothing represents a much softer technology than the landmines that Gell uses as his particular example, the shock on the face of sellers in *Punch* cartoons makes quite clear that their cast-offs remain "components of their identities" (21).

49. Norman Pett, cartoon, *Punch*, April 30, 1924, 468.

50. E. M. Delafield, *Diary of a Provincial Lady* (1931: Chicago: Academy Chicago, 2002), 138–39.

51. Ibid., 141.

52. Critics disagree on how to characterize Thompson's tone. Richard Mabey asserts, "*Lark Rise to Candleford* is remarkable for its celebratory realism. It neither romanticises poverty nor underplays it" ("Diary of a Country Woman," *Guardian*, December 12, 2008, http://www.guardian.co.uk/books/2008/dec/13/lark-rise-candleford-flora-thompson). Ruth Collette Hoffman, author of a rare book-length study of Thompson's work, concurs in calling the novels "sensitive but not sentimental" (*Without Education or Encouragement: The Literary Legacy of Flora Thompson* [Madison, N.J.: Fairleigh Dickinson University Press, 2009], 81). In contrast, Barbara English calls Thompson's work an "optimistic view of rural poverty" ("*Lark Rise* and Juniper Hill: A Victorian Community in Literature and in History," *Victorian Studies* 29, no. 1 [1985]: 10).

53. Flora Thompson, *Lark Rise to Candleford* (London: Oxford University Press, 1957), 19.

54. Ibid., 101.

55. Ibid. Diana Crane documents a similar fashion lag in both rural France and the United States, although she suggests that the lag shortened earlier than Thompson's novel represents, in *Fashion and Its Social Agendas: Class, Gender, and Identity in Clothing* (Chicago: University of Chicago Press, 2000), chaps. 2 and 3.

56. Thompson, *Lark Rise to Candleford*, 497.

57. Ibid., 523.

58. Ferguson, *Alas, Poor Lady*, 390.

59. Thompson, *Lark Rise to Candleford*, 171–72.

60. As Gillian Lindsay, one of Thompson's biographers, writes, the timing of the Candleford trilogy "was fortuitous. A few decades earlier, Flora would have been telling her readers about things which many of them would have preferred to forget; . . . but in the uncertain world of 1939 the 1880s had stability which held great appeal" (*Flora Thompson: The Story of the "Lark Rise" Writer* [Bordon: John Owen Smith, 2007], 145).

61. Ferguson, *Alas, Poor Lady*, 390.

62. Garry Leonard has argued that "subjectivity in modernity is the state of being transfixed before or amidst or among a constellation of objects" ("Holding on to the Here and Now: Juxtaposition in Modernity and in Joyce," in *James Joyce and the Fabrication of an Irish Identity* [Amsterdam: Rodopi, 2001], 42). I agree with Leonard's formulation but want to extend it: the constellation of secondhand clothes that confront modernist characters are not inert materials but the presence of subjects in (and as) objects.

63. James Joyce, *Ulysses* (1922; New York: Vintage, 1990), 268–69.

64. Don Gifford, with Robert J. Seidman, *"Ulysses" Annotated* (Berkeley: University of California Press, 1989), 299.

65. As Judith Walkowitz observes, "Since the eighteenth century, the Jewish old clothes' pedlar appeared in literary texts and illustrations as an iconic symbol of ethnic difference and degraded commerce" (*Nights Out: Life in Cosmopolitan London* [New Haven, Conn.: Yale University Press, 2012], 147).

66. Joyce, *Ulysses*, 268.

67. Ibid., 270.

68. Ibid., 774.

69. James Joyce, *A Portrait of the Artist as a Young Man* (1916; New York: Penguin, 1993), 275.

70. Roy Gottfried writes that the diary "suggests that Stephen can never flee the absurdity of the language which is his," and specifically calls the "new secondhand" construction "a comic contradiction, even if an expression of the economic reality in Ireland" (*Joyce's Comic Portrait* [Gainesville: University Press of Florida, 2000], 81). I agree that Stephen's language is absurd but want to think more carefully about the types of secondhand clothing Stephen confronts in both *Portrait of the Artist* and *Ulysses*.

71. Joyce, *Portrait of the Artist*, 275.

72. Ibid., 276.

73. Joyce, *Ulysses*, 6.

74. Ibid.

75. Ibid., 49.

76. R. J. Schork, *Latin and Roman Culture in Joyce* (Gainesville: University Press of Florida, 1997), 99.

77. Leonard, "Holding on to the Here and Now," 42.

78. Leonard further writes that "the loss of belief in transcendental certitude—God—does not eliminate the need to believe in the presumed individual coherency of identity" (ibid., 48). I wholeheartedly agree with this diagnosis of Stephen's problem; by recovering the way in which specific garments interfere with a coherent identity, I am working in harmony with Leonard's call to historicize "subjectivity within the physical environment generated by modernity" (43).

79. Joyce, *Ulysses*, 49.

80. Ibid.

81. Christine Froula discusses this passage as an example of Stephen's identification with both men and women; Buck, she writes, in "obliviously handing down cast-off boots, fails to see [Stephen] 'as I am'" (*Modernism's Body: Sex, Culture, and Joyce* [New York: Columbia University Press, 1996], 114). Here, I argue, part of Stephen's problem is that he also sees himself as Buck through the mediation of his secondhand shoes.

82. Stephen's many refusals of mutual dependence or responsibility are too numerous to mention, but notable examples include his tacit decision not to aid his sisters (and specifically Dilly) in "The Wandering Rocks" and his refusal to stay with the Blooms in "Ithaca." As Catherine Driscoll argues, Stephen uses his

vocation as artist to declare "his place outside social fixities and responsibilities" and thus his "social mobility" (*Modernist Cultural Studies* [Gainesville: University Press of Florida, 2010], 57). What Froula calls Joyce's "technology of resistance" (*Modernism's Body*, 17) emerges, I argue, not only in his rejection of Church, state, and family but also in his desire to reject material forms of connection and assistance.

83. Jean Rhys, *After Leaving Mr. Mackenzie* (1930; New York: Norton, 1997), 58.

84. "A Solid House" was published in *Tigers Are Better Looking, with a Selection from The Left Bank Stories* (London: Deutsch, 1968); although the precise date of its composition remains unknown, it was probably drafted by 1945. See Jean Rhys, *Letters, 1931–1966*, ed. Francis Wyndham and Diana Melly (London: Penguin, 1985), 40n.2.

85. Jean Rhys, "A Solid House," in *The Collected Short Stories* (New York: Norton, 1987), 226.

86. Ibid., 227.

87. Delafield, *Diary of a Provincial Lady*, 241.

88. Frank Whitburn, cartoon, *Punch*, September 22, 1926, 319.

89. Virginia Woolf, *Three Guineas* (1938; New York: Harcourt, Brace & World, 1966), 159.

90. Ibid., 41.

91. Ibid., 50.

92. Ibid., 40.

93. Elizabeth Wilson, *Adorned in Dreams: Fashion and Modernity* (1985; New Brunswick, N.J.: Rutgers University Press, 2003), 12.

94. Joyce, *Portrait of the Artist*, 194.

95. It is illuminating to compare Joyce's *Portrait of the Artist* with George Orwell's *Keep the Aspidistra Flying*, which depicts a character who regards used books and secondhand clothing as equivalent. The protagonist's employer, Mr. Cheeseman, runs a bookstore but "had been brought up in the old-clothes trade": "Over this dustheap Mr. Cheeseman had presided . . . presently it was borne in upon him that books, properly handled, are worth money. As soon as he had made this discovery he developed an astonishing flair for book-dealing. To him a book was as purely an article of merchandise as a pair of second-hand trousers" (*Keep the Aspidistra Flying* [1936; New York: Harcourt, Brace, 1956], 205). While this passage expresses sentiments at odds with those of Stephen Dedalus, it is important to note that Orwell's narrator regards Cheeseman with irony; *Keep the Aspidistra Flying* critiques romanticized ideals about artists and literature, but it does not endorse Cheeseman's entirely commercial view of the written word.

96. Faye Hammill, *Women, Celebrity, and Literary Culture Between the Wars* (Austin: University of Texas Press, 2007), 6.

97. The autobiographical elements of the fiction of Joyce, Rhys, and Woolf are too well known to need comment here. Even when some of their characters—like Rhys's Teresa—are not explicitly identified as artists, the parallels between author and character suggest that, as Oscar Wilde once quipped, "every portrait is a portrait of the artist."

98. Fredric Jameson, "Postmodernism and Consumer Society," in *The Anti-Aesthetic: Essays on Postmodern Culture*, ed. Hal Caine (New York: New Press, 2002), 114.

99. Le Corbusier, *Precisions: On the Present State of Architecture and City Planning*, trans. Edith Schreiber Aujame (Cambridge, Mass.: MIT Press, 1991), 12.

100. Anne Anlin Cheng, *Second Skin: Josephine Baker and the Modern Surface* (Oxford: Oxford University Press, 2011), 92.

101. Sax Rohmer, *The Orchard of Tears* (1918; Holicong, Pa.: Wildside Press, 2003), 26.

102. William Butler Yeats, "The Circus Animals' Desertion," in *Selected Poems and Four Plays*, ed. M. L. Rosenthal (New York: Scribner, 1996), 40.

103. Ibid., 39.

Coda

1. "Clothing and Footwear Rationed," *Times* (London), June 2, 1941, 5.

2. Geraldine Howell, *Wartime Fashion: From Haute Couture to Homemade, 1939–1945* (London: Bloomsbury, 2013), 26.

3. Ibid., 57.

4. Ibid., 58.

5. Ibid., 44.

6. The government's "Clothing Coupon Quiz" included a table that indicated that macs could require as many as eighteen coupons; thus it was the most costly garment of them all. According to Howell, each person was allotted sixty-six coupons in 1941/1942 and forty eight coupons in 1942/1943 (ibid., 95–96). These numbers are adjusted to reflect coupons per calendar year. See also "Clothing Coupon Quiz," in *Make Do and Mend: Keeping Family and Home Afloat on War Rations* (London: Michael O'Mara Books, 2007), 69–92.

7. Ministry of Supply, *How to "Make-Do-and-Mend,"* YouTube, http://www.youtube.com/watch?v=f4RpJcVs1VI.

8. Ministry of Information, *Clothing Coupons Trailer*, 1943, YouTube, https://www.youtube.com/watch?v=RgPlf2Pjm2A.

9. E. Baxter to Robina Wallis, May 1945, Archive of Art and Design, AAD1989/8/1/23, Victoria and Albert Museum, London.

10. Howell details the manner in which the coupon/points value for used clothing was determined, in *Wartime Fashion*, 134–35.

11. Angela Thirkell, *Marling Hall* (New York: Knopf, 1942), 106.

12. Howell, *Wartime Fashion*, 112–13.

13. By 1914, "wages had almost doubled from their level of 1851," and the social historian Harold Perkin's work demonstrated that "real wages increased between 1880 and 1913 by 34%" (Rosy Aindow, *Dress and Identity in British Literary Culture, 1870–1914* [Farnham: Ashgate, 2010], 17).

14. Angela Thirkell, *Northbridge Rectory* (1941; New York: Carroll & Graf, 1991), 241.

15. Ibid., 283.

16. Lou Taylor, *The Study of Dress History* (Manchester: Manchester University Press, 2002), 102.

17. Jane Bennett, *Vibrant Matter: A Political Ecology of Things* (Durham, N.C.: Duke University Press, 2010), 99.

18. As Ilya Parkins observes, Christian Dior and Walter Benjamin describe fashion as both the "*coupling* of the organic with the inorganic" and the "momentary *triumph* of the inorganic—the garment itself" (*Poiret, Dior and Schiaparelli: Fashion, Femininity and Modernity* [London: Berg, 2012], 140 [emphasis in original]). It is the triumph of the inorganic world, generally with a negative outcome, that surfaces most often in British literature of the early twentieth century.

19. "Mrs. Miniver and the New Car," *Times* (London), October 22, 1937, 19.

20. "The New Engagement Book," *Times* (London), January 7, 1938, 15.

21. Board of Trade, "Extension of the Life of Clothing—A Preliminary Investigation into Possibilities," July 2, 1941, BT64/3023, National Archives, Kew.

Bibliography

Abravanel, Genevieve. *Americanizing Britain: The Rise of Modernism in the Age of the Entertainment Empire*. New York: Oxford University Press, 2012.
Aindow, Rosy. *Dress and Identity in British Literary Culture, 1870–1914*. Farnham: Ashgate, 2010.
The Aquascutum Story. London: Aquascutum, 1994.
Ashdown, Mrs. Charles J. *British Costume During XIX Centuries (Civil and Ecclesiastical)*. London: Nelson, [1910?].
Auerbach, Nina. *Daphne du Maurier: Haunted Heiress*. Philadelphia: University of Pennsylvania Press, 2000.
A Ballroom Tragedy. New York: American Mutoscope and Biograph Company, 1905.
Beauman, Nicola. *A Very Great Profession: The Woman's Novel, 1914–39*. London: Virago, 1983.
Bell, Quentin. *On Human Finery*. 1976. New York: Schocken, 1978.
Bell, Vanessa. *Selected Letters of Vanessa Bell*. Edited by Regina Marler. New York: Pantheon, 1993.
Benjamin, Jessica. *The Bonds of Love: Psychoanalysis, Feminism, and the Problem of Domination*. New York: Pantheon, 1988.
Benjamin, Walter. "The Paris of the Second Empire in Baudelaire." 1937. In *The Writer of Modern Life: Essays on Charles Baudelaire*. Edited by Michael W. Jennings, 46–133. Cambridge, Mass.: Belknap Press of Harvard University Press, 2006.

Bennett, Jane. *Vibrant Matter: A Political Ecology of Things.* Durham, N.C.: Duke University Press, 2010.
Benstock, Bernard. "The Mysteries of *Ulysses.*" In *International Perspectives on James Joyce,* edited by Gottlieb Ganser, 32–43. Troy, N.Y.: Whitston, 1986.
Bonikowski, Wyatt. "The Return of the Soldier Brings Death Home." *MFS: Modern Fiction Studies* 51 (2005): 513–35.
Borch-Jacobsen, Mikkel. *Lacan: The Absolute Master.* Stanford, Calif.: Stanford University Press, 1991.
Bowen, Elizabeth. *The Last September.* 1929. New York: Anchor, 2000.
Breward, Christopher. *The Culture of Fashion: A New History of Fashionable Dress.* Manchester: Manchester University Press, 1995.
———. *The Hidden Consumer: Masculinities, Fashion and City Life, 1860–1914.* Manchester: Manchester University Press, 1999.
Brittain, Vera. *Testament of Youth.* 1933. New York: Penguin, 1978.
Brown, Bill. "The Secret Life of Things (Virginia Woolf and the Matter of Modernism)." *Modernism/modernity* 6, no. 2 (1999): 1–28.
———. "Thing Theory." In "Things," edited by Bill Brown. Special issue, *Critical Inquiry* 28, no. 1 (2001): 1–22.
———, ed. "Things." Special issue, *Critical Inquiry* 28, no. 1 (2001).
———. *A Sense of Things: The Object Matter of American Literature.* Chicago: University of Chicago Press, 2003.
Brown, Judith. *Glamour in Six Dimensions: Modernism and the Radiance of Form.* Ithaca, N.Y.: Cornell University Press, 2009.
Burns, Christy L. "Re-Dressing Feminist Identities: Tensions Between Essential and Constructed Selves in Virginia Woolf's *Orlando.*" *Twentieth Century Literature: A Scholarly and Critical Journal* 40 (1994): 342–64.
Burstein, Jessica. *Cold Modernism: Literature, Fashion, Art.* University Park: Pennsylvania State University Press, 2012.
Butler, Judith. *Bodies That Matter: On the Discursive Limits of "Sex."* New York: Routledge, 1993.
Calefato, Patrizia. "Signs of Order, Signs of Disorder: The Other Uniforms." In *Uniform: Order and Disorder,* edited by Francesco Bonami, Maria Luisa Frisa, and Stefano Tonchi, 155–204. Milan: Charta, 2000.
Castle, Terry. *Masquerade and Civilization: The Carnivalesque in Eighteenth-Century English Culture and Fiction.* Sanford, Calif.: Stanford University Press, 1986.
Chandler, Katherine R. "Thoroughly Post-Victorian, Pre-Modern Beatrix." *Children's Literature Association Quarterly* 32 (2007): 287–307.
Chapman, Stanley. "The Innovative Entrepreneurs in the British Ready-Made Clothing Industry." *Textile History* 24 (1993): 5.
Chase, Edna Woolman. *Always in Vogue.* New York: Doubleday, 1954.
Cheng, Anne Anlin. *Second Skin: Josephine Baker and the Modern Surface.* Oxford: Oxford University Press, 2011.
Clarke, Alison, and Daniel Miller. "Fashion and Anxiety." *Fashion Theory* 6, no. 2 (2002): 191–214.

"Clothing Coupon Quiz." In *Make Do and Mend: Keeping Family and Home Afloat on War Rations*, 69–92. London: Michael O'Mara Books, 2007.

Cohen, Lisa. "'Frock Consciousness': Virginia Woolf, the Open Secret, and the Language of Fashion." *Fashion Theory* 3, no. 2 (1999): 149–74.

Conor, Liz. *The Spectacular Modern Woman: Feminine Visibility in the 1920s*. Bloomington: Indiana University Press, 2004.

Cooley, Charles Horton. *Human Nature and the Social Order*. New York: Scribner, 1902.

Coppard, A. E. "The Fancy Dress Ball." In *The Black Dog and Other Stories*, 173–87. New York: Knopf, 1923.

Cosgrove, J. Benjamin. "Macintosh and the Old Testament Character Joseph." *James Joyce Quarterly* 29, no. 3 (1992): 681–84.

Craik, Jennifer. *Uniforms Exposed: From Conformity to Transgression*. Oxford: Berg, 2005.

Crane, Diana. *Fashion and Its Social Agendas: Class, Gender, and Identity in Clothing*. Chicago: University of Chicago Press, 2000.

Cunnington, C. Willett. *English Women's Clothing in the Present Century*. London: Faber and Faber, 1952.

———. *Why Women Wear Clothes*. London: Faber and Faber, 1941.

D'Egville, Geoffrey. *How and What to Dance*. London: Pearson, 1919.

Delafield, E. M. *Diary of a Provincial Lady*. 1931. Chicago: Academy Chicago, 2002.

De la Haye, Amy, Lou Taylor, and Eleanor Thompson. *A Family of Fashion: The Messels: Six Generations of Dress*. London: Wilson, 2005.

DiBattista, Maria. "*Ulysses*'s Unanswered Questions." *Modernism/modernity* 15 (2008): 265–75.

Doan, Laura. *Fashioning Sapphism: The Origins of a Modern English Lesbian Culture*. New York: Columbia University Press, 2001.

Driscoll, Catherine. *Modernist Cultural Studies*. Gainesville: University Press of Florida, 2010.

Duffy, Enda. *The Subaltern Ulysses*. Minneapolis: University of Minnesota Press, 1994.

du Maurier, Daphne. *Rebecca*. 1938. London: Virago, 2003.

Edson, Laura Gwyn. "Kicking Off Her Knickers: Virginia Woolf's Rejection of Clothing as Realistic Detail." In *Virginia Woolf and the Arts: Selected Papers from the Sixth Annual Conference on Virginia Woolf*, edited by Diane F. Gillespie and Leslie K. Hankins, 119–24. New York: Pace University Press, 1997.

English, Barbara. "*Lark Rise* and Juniper Hill: A Victorian Community in Literature and in History." *Victorian Studies* 29, no. 1 (1985): 7–34.

Esty, Jed. *Unseasonable Youth: Modernism, Colonialism, and the Fiction of Development*. New York: Oxford University Press, 2012.

Evans, Caroline. *The Mechanical Smile: Modernism and the First Fashion Shows in France and America, 1900–1929*. New Haven, Conn.: Yale University Press, 2013.

"Every Evening Occasion Has Its Appropriate Style of Dress." *Vanity Fair*, March 1923, 8–9.

Federico, Annette. "Making Do: George Orwell's *Coming Up for Air*." *Studies in the Novel* 37 (2005): 50–63.
Felski, Rita. "Context Stinks!" *New Literary History* 42, no. 4 (2011): 573–91.
Ferguson, Rachel. *Alas, Poor Lady*. 1937. London: Persephone, 2006.
Flügel, J. C. *The Psychology of Clothes*. London: Hogarth Press, 1930.
Foulkes, Nicholas. *Bals: Legendary Costume Balls of the Twentieth Century*. New York, Assouline, 2011.
Freedgood, Elaine. *The Ideas in Things: Fugitive Meaning in the Victorian Novel*. Chicago: University of Chicago Press, 2006.
Frost, Laura. *The Problem with Pleasure: Modernism and Its Discontents*. New York: Columbia University Press, 2013.
Froula, Christine. *Modernism's Body: Sex, Culture, and Joyce*. New York: Columbia University Press, 1996.
———. *Virginia Woolf and the Bloomsbury Avant-Garde: War, Civilization, Modernity*. New York: Columbia University Press, 2005.
Frow, John. "A Pebble, a Camera, a Man Who Turns into a Telegraph Pole." In "Things," edited by Bill Brown. Special issue, *Critical Inquiry* 28, no. 1 (2001): 270–85.
Fry, Roger. *The Letters of Roger Fry*. Vol. 2. Edited by Denys Sutton. New York: Random House, 1972.
Gell, Alfred. *Art and Agency: An Anthropological Theory*. Oxford: Clarendon Press, 1998.
Giddens, Anthony. *Modernity and Self-Identity: Self and Society in the Late Modern Age*. Stanford, Calif.: Stanford University Press, 1991.
Gilbert, Sandra M. "Costumes of the Mind: Transvestism as Metaphor in Modern Literature." *Critical Inquiry* 7 (1980): 391–417.
Gillis, Stacy. "Consoling Fictions: Mourning, World War One, and Dorothy L. Sayers." In *Modernism and Mourning*, edited by Patricia Rae, 185–97. Lewisburg, Pa.: Bucknell University Press, 2007.
Goodrum, Alison L. *The National Fabric: Fashion, Britishness, Globalization*. Oxford: Berg, 2005.
Gordon, Avery E. *Ghostly Matters: Haunting and the Sociological Imagination*. Minneapolis: University of Minnesota Press, 1997.
Gordon, Beverly. *The Saturated World: Aesthetic Meaning, Intimate Objects, Women's Lives, 1890–1940*. Knoxville: University of Tennessee Press, 2006.
Gordon, John. *Joyce and Reality: The Empirical Strikes Back*. Syracuse, N.Y.: Syracuse University Press, 2004.
Gordon, Lady Duff ("Lucile"). *Discretions and Indiscretions*. New York: Stokes, 1932.
Gottfried, Roy. *Joyce's Comic Portrait*. Gainesville: University Press of Florida, 2000.
Greene, Graham. *Brighton Rock*. 1938. New York: Penguin, 2004.
———. *The Third Man*. 1949. New York: Penguin, 1999.
Grosz, Elizabeth. "The Thing." In *The Object Reader*, edited by Fiona Candlin and Raiford Guins, 124–38. New York: Routledge, 2009.

Gunn, Simon, and Rachel Bell. *Middle Classes: The Rise and Sprawl*. London: Phoenix, 2003.
Habermas, Jürgen. *The Philosophical Discourse of Modernity: Twelve Lectures*. Translated by Frederick Lawrence. Cambridge, Mass.: MIT Press, 1987.
Haig, Margaret. *This Was My World*. London: Macmillan, 1933.
Hammill, Faye. *Women, Celebrity, and Literary Culture Between the Wars*. Austin: University of Texas Press, 2007.
Heglund, Jane E. "Evening Dress." In *Encyclopedia of Clothing and Fashion*, edited by Valerie Steele, 1:428–30. Farmington Hills, Mich.: Scribner, 2005.
Hoffmann, Ruth Collette. *Without Education or Encouragement: The Literary Legacy of Flora Thompson*. Madison, N.J.: Fairleigh Dickinson University Press, 2009.
Holt, Ardern. *Fancy Dresses Described; or, What to Wear at Fancy Balls*. London: Debenham & Freebody, 1887.
Howell, Geraldine. *Wartime Fashion: From Haute Couture to Homemade, 1939–1945*. London: Bloomsbury, 2013.
Humble, Nicola. *The Feminine Middlebrow Novel, 1920s to 1950s: Class, Domesticity, and Bohemianism*. New York: Oxford University Press, 2001.
Hussey, Mark. *Virginia Woolf A to Z: A Comprehensive Reference to Her Life, Works, and Critical Reception*. Oxford: Oxford University Press, 1996.
Huxley, Aldous. *Crome Yellow*. New York: Harper, 1922.
Jameson, Fredric. "Postmodernism and Consumer Society." In *The Anti-Aesthetic: Essays on Postmodern Culture*, edited by Hal Caine, 111–25. New York: New Press, 2002.
Jarvis, Anthea, and Patricia Raine. *Fancy Dress*. Aylesbury: Shire, 1984.
Johnson, Barbara. *Persons and Things*. Cambridge, Mass.: Harvard University Press, 2008.
Johnston, Georgia. "Virginia Woolf's Talk on the *Dreadnought* Hoax." *Woolf Studies Annual* 15 (2009): 1–45.
Joyce, James. *A Portrait of the Artist as a Young Man*. 1916. New York: Penguin, 1993.
———. *Ulysses*. 1922. New York: Vintage, 1990.
Keane, Molly. *Devoted Ladies*. 1934. London: Virago, 1984.
Kermode, Frank. "The Man in the Macintosh." In *Pieces of My Mind: Essays and Criticism, 1958–2002*, 119–42. New York: Farrar, Straus and Giroux, 2004.
Kershner, R. Brandon. *The Culture of Joyce's "Ulysses."* New York: Palgrave Macmillan, 2010.
Klein, Kathryn. "Writing Sapphism: Troubling Genre in Interwar Fiction." Ph.D. diss., State University of New York at Stony Brook, 2013. ProQuest (3588126).
Koppen, R. S. *Virginia Woolf, Fashion and Literary Modernity*. Edinburgh: Edinburgh University Press, 2009.
Kopytoff, Igor. "The Cultural Biography of Things: Commoditization as Process." In *The Social Life of Things: Commodities in Cultural Perspective*, edited by Arjun Appadurai, 64–91. Cambridge: Cambridge University Press, 1986.
Lacan, Jacques. *Écrits: A Selection*. Translated by Alan Sheridan. New York: Norton, 1982.

Laing, Kathryn S. "Addressing Femininity in the Twenties: Virginia Woolf and Rebecca West on Money, Mirrors and Masquerade." In *Virginia Woolf and the Arts: Selected Papers from the Sixth Annual Conference on Virginia Woolf*, edited by Diane F. Gillespie and Leslie K Hankins, 66–75. New York: Pace University Press, 1997.

Latham, Sean. "*Am I a Snob?*" *Modernism and the Novel*. Ithaca, N.Y.: Cornell University Press, 2003.

———. *The Art of Scandal: Modernism, Libel Law, and the Roman à Clef*. Oxford: Oxford University Press, 2009.

Latour, Bruno. *Reassembling the Social: An Introduction to Actor-Network Theory*. Oxford: Oxford University Press, 2005.

Leader, Darian. *Freud's Footnotes*. London: Faber and Faber, 2000.

Le Corbusier. *Precisions: On the Present State of Architecture and City Planning*. Translated by Edith Schreiber Aujame. Cambridge, Mass.: MIT Press, 1991.

Lee, Hermione. Introduction to *The Mulberry Tree: Writings of Elizabeth Bowen*. Edited by Hermione Lee. London: Virago, 1986.

Lemire, Beverly. "Consumerism in Preindustrial and Early Industrial England: The Trade in Secondhand Clothes." *Journal of British Studies* 27 (1988): 1–24.

Leonard, Garry. "Holding on to the Here and Now: Juxtaposition in Modernity and in Joyce." In *James Joyce and the Fabrication of an Irish Identity*, edited by Michael Patrick Gillespie, 39–51. Amsterdam: Rodopi, 2001.

Levay, Matthew. "Remaining a Mystery: Gertrude Stein, Crime Fiction and Popular Modernism." *Journal of Modern Literature* 36, no. 4 (2013): 1–22.

Levenback, Karen L. "Clarissa Dalloway, Doris Kilman and the Great War." *Virginia Woolf Miscellany* 37 (1991): 3–4.

Levitt, Sarah. "Manchester Mackintoshes: A History of the Rubberised Garment Trade in Manchester." *Textile History* 17 (1986): 51–70.

———. *Victorians Unbuttoned: Registered Designs for Clothing, Their Makers and Wearers, 1839–1900*. London: Allen & Unwin, 1986.

Lindsay, Gillian. *Flora Thompson: The Story of the "Lark Rise" Writer*. Bordon: John Owen Smith, 2007.

Lipovetsky, Gilles. *The Empire of Fashion: Dressing Modern Democracy*. Translated by Catherine Porter. Princeton, N.J.: Princeton University Press, 1994.

Loew, Camilla. "Miss Represented: Women at War, Propaganda vs. Autobiographical Writing." In *(Mis)Representations: Intersections of Culture and Power*, edited by Fernando Galván Bern, Jului Cañero Serrano, and José Santiago Fernández Vázquez, 123–33. Bern: Lang, 2003.

Lyon, Janet. "Sociability in the Metropole: Modernism's Bohemian Salons." *ELH* 76, no. 3 (2009): 687–712.

Mabey, Richard. "Diary of a Country Woman." *Guardian*, December 12, 2008. http://www.guardian.co.uk/books/2008/dec/13/lark-rise-candleford-flora-thompson.

Mahood, Aurelia. "Fashioning Readers: The *avant garde* and British *Vogue*, 1920–9." *Women: A Cultural Review* 13, no. 1 (2002): 37–47.

Mao, Douglas. *Solid Objects: Modernism and the Test of Production*. Princeton, N.J.: Princeton University Press, 1998.

Marcus, Jane. Afterword to *Not So Quiet . . . Stepdaughters of War*, by Helen Zenna Smith, 241–300. New York: Feminist Press of CUNY, 1989.
Marcuse, Herbert. *Negations: Essays in Critical Theory*. Translated by Jeremy J. Shapiro. Boston: Beacon Press, 1968.
Marshik, Celia. "Smart Clothes at Low Prices: Alliances and Negotiations in the British Interwar Secondhand Clothing Trade." In *Cultures of Femininity in Modern Fashion*, edited by Ilya Parkins and Elizabeth Sheehan, 71–86. Lebanon, N.H.: University Press of New England, 2011.
Maugham, W. Somerset. *The Painted Veil*. 1925. New York: Vintage, 2004.
McGregor, Robert Kuhn, and Ethan Lewis. *Conundrums for the Long-Weekend: England, Dorothy L. Sayers, and Lord Peter Wimsey*. Kent, Ohio: Kent State University Press, 2000.
McKibbin, Ross. *Classes and Cultures: England, 1918–1951*. Oxford: Oxford University Press, 1998.
McLoughlin, Kate. "Introduction: A Welcome from the Host." In *The Modernist Party*, edited by Kate McLoughlin, 1–24. Edinburgh: Edinburgh University Press, 2013.
Miller, Daniel. *Stuff*. Cambridge: Polity, 2010.
Mitford, Nancy, ed. *Noblesse Oblige: An Enquiry into Identifiable Characteristics of the English Aristocracy*. London: Hamish Hamilton, 1956.
Morrell, Lady Ottoline. *Ottoline: The Early Memoirs of Lady Ottoline Morrell*. Edited by Robert Gathorne-Hardy. London: Faber and Faber, 1963.
Mullin, Katherine. *James Joyce, Sexuality and Social Purity*. Cambridge: Cambridge University Press, 2003.
Newark, Tim. *Camouflage*. New York: Thames and Hudson, 2007.
Nicholls, George J. *Bacon and Hams*. London: Institute of Certificated Grocers, 1917.
Nicolson, Juliet. *The Perfect Summer: England 1911, Just Before the Storm*. New York: Grove Press, 2006.
Noble, Joan Russell, ed. *Recollections of Virginia Woolf by Her Contemporaries*. London: Peter Owen, 1972.
Nystrom, Paul H. *Economics of Fashion*. New York: Ronald Press, 1928.
Orwell, George. *Coming Up for Air*. 1939. New York: Harcourt, Brace, 1950.
——. *Down and Out in Paris and London*. 1933. New York: Harcourt, Brace, 1961.
——. *Keep the Aspidistra Flying*. 1936. New York: Harcourt, Brace, 1956.
Outka, Elizabeth. *Consuming Traditions: Modernity, Modernism, and the Commodified Authentic*. New York: Oxford University Press, 2009.
Parkins, Ilya. *Poiret, Dior and Schiaparelli: Fashion, Femininity and Modernity*. London: Berg, 2012.
Pilkington, Elizabeth C. "Milly's Old Lavender Gown." *Windsor* 10, no. 4 (1899): 419–24.
Potter, Beatrix. *The Tale of Mr. Jeremy Fisher*. 1906. New York: Warne, 1987.
Price, Julius M. *Dame Fashion*. London: Sampson Low, Marston, 1913.
Rado, Lisa. *The Modern Androgyne Imagination: A Failed Sublime*. Charlottesville: University of Virginia Press, 2000.
Reed, Christopher. *Bloomsbury Rooms: Modernism, Subculture, and Domesticity*. New Haven, Conn.: Yale University Press, 2004.

Reynolds, Barbara. *Dorothy L. Sayers: Her Life and Soul*. New York: St. Martin's Griffin, 1997.

——. "G. K. Chesterton and Dorothy L. Sayers." *Chesterton Review* 9, no. 2 (1984): 136–57.

Rhys, Jean. *After Leaving Mr. Mackenzie*. 1930. New York: Norton, 1997.

——. *The Collected Short Stories*. New York: Norton, 1987.

——. *Letters, 1931–1966*. Edited by Francis Wyndham and Diana Melly. London: Penguin, 1985.

Rohmer, Sax. *The Orchard of Tears*. 1918. Holicong, Pa.: Wildside Press, 2003.

Ross, John J. *Shakespeare's Tremor and Orwell's Cough: The Medical Lives of Great Writers*. New York: St. Martin's Press, 2012.

Roux, Dominique. "Am I What I Wear? An Exploratory Study of Symbolic Meanings Associated with Secondhand Clothing." *Advances in Consumer Research* 33 (2006): 29–35.

Sayers, Dorothy L. *Gaudy Night*. 1936. New York: HarperCollins, 1995.

——. *The Letters of Dorothy L. Sayers, 1899–1936: The Making of a Detective Novelist*. Edited by Barbara Reynolds. New York: St. Martin's Press, 1996.

——. *Murder Must Advertise*. 1933. New York: HarperCollins, 1993.

——. *Unnatural Death*. 1927. New York: Avon, 1964.

——. *Whose Body?* 1923. New York: Harper & Row, 1987.

Schaffer, Talia. "Posing Orlando." In *Sexual Artifice: Persons, Images, Politics*, edited by Ann Kibbey, Kayann Short, and Abouali Farmanfarmaian, 26–63. New York: New York University Press, 1994.

Schork, R. J. *Latin and Roman Culture in Joyce*. Gainesville: University Press of Florida, 1997.

Scott, Carole. "Between Me and the World: Clothes as Mediator Between Self and Society in the Works of Beatrix Potter." *Lion and the Unicorn* 16 (1992): 192–98.

Seymour, Miranda. *Ottoline Morrell: Life on the Grand Scale*. London: Hodder & Stoughton, 1992.

Shannon, Brent. *The Cut of His Coat: Men, Dress, and Consumer Culture in Britain, 1860–1914*. Athens: Ohio University Press, 2006.

Shulman, Nicola. "Beatrix Potter's Tales of Escape." *Times Literary Supplement*, February 21, 2007.

Sidnell, Michael J. "Mac(k)intosh the Noun." *Joyce Studies Annual* 13 (2002): 192–95.

Simmel, Georg. "Adornment." 1908. In *The Rise of Fashion: A Reader*, edited by Daniel Leonhard Purdy, 79–86. Minneapolis: University of Minnesota Press, 2004.

——. "Fashion." *American Journal of Sociology* 62, no. 6 (1957): 541–58.

Sims, George R. *Living London: Its Work and Its Play, Its Humor and Its Pathos, Its Sights and Its Scenes*. London: Cassell, 1903.

Sitwell, Osbert. *Triple Fugue*. 1924. London: Penguin, 1940.

Smith, Angela K. *The Second Battlefield: Women, Modernism and the First World War*. Manchester: Manchester University Press, 2000.

Smith, Helen Zenna [Evadne Price]. *Not So Quiet . . . Stepdaughters of War*. 1930. New York: Feminist Press of CUNY, 1989.

Spalding, Frances. *Vanessa Bell*. New Haven, Conn.: Ticknor & Fields, 1983.

Spencer, Herbert. *The Principles of Sociology*. Vol. 1. New York: Appleton, 1897.
Spoo, Robert. "'Nestor' and the Nightmare: The Presence of the Great War in *Ulysses*." *Twentieth Century Literature* 32, no. 2 (1986): 137–54.
Stallybrass, Peter. "Marx's Coat." In *Border Fetishisms: Material Objects in Unstable Places*, edited by Patricia Spyer, 183–207. London: Routledge, 1998.
Stallybrass, Peter, and Allon White. *The Politics and Poetics of Transgression*. Ithaca, N.Y.: Cornell University Press, 1986.
Steele, Valerie. *Fashion and Eroticism: Ideals of Feminine Beauty from the Victorian Era to the Jazz Age*. New York: Oxford University Press, 1985.
Stephen, Adrian. *The "Dreadnought" Hoax*. London: Hogarth Press, 1983.
Stewart, Victoria. "Defining Detective Fiction in Interwar Britain." *Space Between* 9 (2013): 101–18.
Strathern, Marilyn. *The Gender of the Gift*. Berkeley: University of California Press, 1988.
Taylor, D. J. *Bright Young People: The Lost Generation of London's Jazz Age*. New York: Farrar, Straus and Giroux, 2007.
Taylor, Lou. *Mourning Dress: A Costume and Social History*. London: Allen & Unwin, 1983.
——. *The Study of Dress History*. Manchester: Manchester University Press, 2002.
Thirkell, Angela. *Marling Hall*. New York: Knopf, 1942.
——. *Northbridge Rectory*. 1941. New York: Carroll & Graf, 1991.
Thompson, Flora. *Lark Rise to Candleford*. London: Oxford University Press, 1957.
Thrush, Nanette. "Clio's Dressmakers: Women and the Uses of Historical Costume." In *Clio's Daughters: British Women Making History, 1790–1899*, edited by Lynette Felber, 258–77. Newark: University of Delaware Press, 2007.
Turner, W. J. *The Aesthetes*. London: Wishart, 1927.
Tylee, Claire. *The Great War and Women's Consciousness: Images of Militarism and Womanhood*. New York: Palgrave Macmillan, 1989.
Vries, Leonard de, comp. *Victorian Advertisements*. Text by James Laver. London: Murray, 1968.
Walkley, Christina, and Vanda Foster. *Crinolines and Crimpling Irons: Victorian Clothes: How They Were Cleaned and Cared For*. London: Peter Owen, 1978.
Walkowitz, Judith. *Nights Out: Life in Cosmopolitan London*. New Haven, Conn.: Yale University Press, 2012.
Waugh, Evelyn. "Cruise: Letters from a Young Lady of Leisure." 1933. In *The Complete Stories of Evelyn Waugh*, 122–27. Boston: Little, Brown, 1999.
——. *Vile Bodies*. 1930. Boston: Little, Brown, 1958.
West, Rebecca. "I Regard Marriage with Fear and Horror." *Hearst's International Cosmopolitan Magazine*, November 1925, 66–68, 206–10.
——. *The Return of the Soldier*. 1918. New York: Penguin, 1988.
——. "The World's Worst Failure." 1916. In *The Gender of Modernism: A Critical Anthology*, edited by Bonnie Kime Scott, 580–83. Bloomington: Indiana University Press, 1990.
Wilson, Elizabeth. *Adorned in Dreams: Fashion and Modernity*. 1985. New Brunswick, N.J.: Rutgers University Press, 2003.

Wisker, Gina. "Dangerous Borders: Daphne du Maurier's *Rebecca*: Shaking the Foundations of the Romance of Privilege, Partying and Place." *Journal of Gender Studies* 12, no. 2 (2003): 83–97.

Wodehouse, P. G. *Joy in the Morning*. New York: Doubleday, 1946.

———. *Right Ho, Jeeves*. 1934. Project Gutenberg. http://www.gutenberg.org/ebooks/10554.

———. *Very Good, Jeeves*. Garden City, N.Y.: Doubleday, Doran, 1930.

Woodward, Sophie. "Looking Good, Feeling Right: Aesthetics of the Self." In *Clothing as Material Culture*, edited by Susanne Küchler and Daniel Miller, 21–40. Oxford: Berg, 2005.

Woolf, Leonard. *Beginning Again: An Autobiography of the Years 1911 to 1918*. New York: Harcourt Brace Jovanovich, 1972.

Woolf, Virginia. *The Complete Shorter Fiction of Virginia Woolf*. Edited by Susan Dick. 2nd ed. San Diego, Calif.: Harcourt Brace Jovanovich, 1989.

———. *The Diary of Virginia Woolf*. Edited by Anne Olivier Bell and Andrew McNeillie. 5 vols. New York: Harcourt Brace Jovanovich, 1977–1984.

———. *Jacob's Room*. 1922. New York: Harcourt, Brace & World, 1960.

———. *The Letters of Virginia Woolf*. Edited by Nigel Nicolson and Joanne Trautmann. 6 vols. New York: Harcourt Brace Jovanovich, 1975–1980.

———. *Moments of Being*. Edited by Jeanne Schulkind. 2nd ed. San Diego, Calif.: Harcourt Brace Jovanovich, 1985.

———. *Mrs. Dalloway*. 1925. New York: Harcourt Brace Jovanovich, 1981.

———. *Orlando*. 1928. New York: Harcourt, Brace, 1956.

———. *A Passionate Apprentice: The Early Journals, 1897–1909*. Edited by Mitchell A. Leaska. San Diego, Calif.: Harcourt Brace Jovanovich, 1990.

———. *Three Guineas*. 1938. New York: Harcourt, Brace & World, 1966.

Yeats, William Butler. "The Circus Animals' Desertion." In *Selected Poems and Four Plays*, edited by M. L. Rosenthal, 212–13. New York: Scribner, 1996.

Zimring, Rishona. "The Make-up of Jean Rhys's Fiction." *Novel* 33, no. 2 (2000): 212–34.

Index

Numbers in italics refer to pages on which illustrations appear.

Abdy, Lady, as "sea mist," 111–12, *113*
Abravanel, Genevieve, 186n.9
Adorned in Dreams (Wilson), 16–17, 173
advertising: aimed at men, 82; for Aquascutum, 82–83, *83*, *84*, 87, *95*, *96*; for Burberry, 84–85, *88*; for mackintoshes, 72, 88–89, *89*, 185n.3; for used-garment dealers, 149, 152–53, 154, 213n.1
advice manuals, on costumes, 108–9
Aesthetes, The (Turner), 62–63
aesthetic experimentation, 54
After Leaving Mr. Mackenzie (Rhys), 171
"After the Fancy-Dress Ball" (Watts; cartoon), *119*
agency: of clothing, 182; of evening gowns, 26–27, 50, 60; evening gowns and, 19, 37, 64; of humans, 100, 216n.48; locus of, 190n.10; mackintoshes and, 19, 72–73, 74, 77, 93; social relations, dependence on, 11–12; of used garments, 146–47; Woolf's lack of, 46
Aindow, Rosy, 215n.37
Alas, Poor Lady (Ferguson), 146, 163–64
"Alice in Wonderland" party, 128–29, *129*
All Quiet on the Western Front (Remarque), 85
Allen, Hugh Percy, 137
"Am I a Snob?" (Woolf), 44, 128
Amatt, W. G., 81, *81*
American Scene, The (James), 12–13, 14
animals, in human clothing, 52, 73–74, 195n.86, 199n.22
animation: conservation of subjectivity and, 14; of evening gowns, 50, 52, 64; of garments, 13, 158, 187n.18; of mackintoshes, 68, 78, 100; of modern garments, 9–10; of used garments, 172, 179–80

232 INDEX

anonymity, mackintoshes and, 79, 99–100
anthropomorphism, 52, 195n.86
Aquascutum (clothing manufacturer), 71, 82–85, *83*, 87, 90, 95, *96*
art, fancy-dress balls as, 204n.2
Art and Agency (Gell), 11–12
artists, highbrow, antipathy of, toward used garments, 176
Artists Revels (fancy-dress parties), 127
Ashdown, Mrs. Charles H., 109
assemblages, 30, 35–36, 92
Astor, Mrs. Waldorf, 213n.10
Auerbach, Nina, 207n.55

B., Lady (character; *Diary of a Provincial Lady*), 115, 117
backs (human), exposure of, in evening gowns, 32, 36
bacon, costume of, *104*, 104–5
Bacon and Hams (Nicholls), 105
Baldry, Chris (character; *The Return of the Soldier*), 74–75
Ballroom Tragedy, A (film), 35–36, 38, 42
Barnes, Djuna, 210n.125
Baroness Elsa (Elsa von Freytag-Loringhoven), 210n.125
Bast, Leonard (character; *Howards End*), 182
Baudelaire, Charles, 192n.41
Baudrillard, Jean, 87
Beaton, Cecil, 57–58, *58*
Beauchamp, Kenneth, 25–26, *26*
Beauman, Nicola, 212n.155
being, having vs., 29–30
Bell, Angelica, 128–29, *129*, 131
Bell, Clive, 129
Bell, Quentin, 29
Bell, Rachel, 152
Bell, Vanessa, 40–41, 44–45, 127–29, 131, 195n.89, 197n.115, 208n.82
Benjamin, Jessica, 193n.63
Benjamin, Walter, 10, 220n.18

Bennett, Jane, 183, 190n.10, 195n.86
Benny Hill Show, The, 7
Benstock, Bernard, 202n.77
biograph films, 35–36
Blimey (character; *Not So Quiet*), 85–86, 91
Bloom, Leopold (character; *Ulysses*), 93, 167–68
Bloom, Molly (character; *Ulysses*), 167–68
Bloomsbury, fancy dress and, 126–30
Board of Trade, on care of clothing, 184
bodies: alignment of military and civil, 83; body/self binary, 126; clothing's influence on, 210n.125; de-individuated, 100; of donors of used garments, 161, 171; exposure of, in evening gowns, 32, 36–38, *38*, *39*, 45, 191n.21; female, evening gowns as showcases for, 31–32; as ideas, 16–17; imperviousness of, to costuming, 206n.44; mackintoshes and, 97, 101; sexed, of Orlando, 131–32; of soldiers and officers, 87; things and, 43; used garments and embodiment, 157–58; used garments as marked by, 170
bohemianism, 195n.90
Bonikowski, Wyatt, 199n.28
books, used, 174, 218n.95
Boomer, Mr. (character; "Simple Stories"), 121–22
boots: used, in *Punch* cartoons, 161; used, in *Ulysses*, 2–3, 170, 172, 175, 217n.81; Wellingtons, 66
Borch-Jacobsen, Mikkel, 189n.55
Bowen, Elizabeth, 19, 77–79, 100
Bowling, George (character; *Coming Up for Air*), 77
Bredon, Death (character; *Murder Must Advertise*), 137–40
Brenton, Miss (dressmaker), 54–55
Breward, Christopher, 7, 157, 214n.21

INDEX 233

Bright Young Things, in Waugh, 115–16, 117
Brighton Rock (Greene), 75–77
British Army, mackintoshes for, 70
British Costume During XIX Centuries (Ashdown), 109
Brittain, Vera, 90
Brown, Bill, 12–13, 14, 187n.27, 187n.30, 188n.38, 196n.108
Brown, Judith, 185n.6
Brown family (characters; *Vile Bodies*), 116
Bruce, Miss (character; "Illusion"), 50–53
Burberry (clothing manufacturer), 69, 71, 85–88, 100–101
Burns, Christy L., 209n.95
Burstein, Jessica, 17, 60, 187n.19, 196n.108
Butler, Judith, 130, 195n.96
"By Their Fruits and Flowers Ye Shall Know Them" (*Vogue*), 108

Calloway, Major (character; *The Third Man*), 99–100, 203n.108
Candleford Green (Thompson), 164
Carlyle, Thomas, 7
carnivals, transgressive nature of, 206n.35
Carr, Patricia, 152–53
Castle, Terry, 35, 103, 107, 142
Chanel, Coco, 111, 149, 157
Chapman, Stanley, 149
Chase, Edna Woolman, 196n.100
Cheeseman, Mr. (character; *Keep the Aspidistra Flying*), 218n.95
Chelsea Arts Ball, 142
Chelsea Arts Club Dazzle Ball, 205n.27
Cheng, Anne Anlin, 175–76
choice. *See* agency
"Circe" (*Ulysses* episode), 93
"Circus Animals' Desertion, The" (Yeats), 177
Clarke, Alison, 100

Clarkson's (costume company), 109
class: class societies, fragmented societies vs., 65; depiction of, in *Punch* cartoons, 118–19, *119*; distinctions of, 30, 75, 97; evening dress as materialization of, 29, 32–33; identity, garments as constructors of, 147. *See also* lower (working) classes; middle classes; society; upper classes
classified advertisements, 90
Cleopatra: Lady Arthur Paget as, 111, *112*, Virginia Stephen as, 127–28
closed texts, open texts vs., garments as, 65
clothes and clothing: as chrysalis, 141; distinctiveness of British names for, 6; effects of, on wearers, 3–4, 5; futility of, 190n.6; gray, 169; identity and, 132–35; ordinary, social recognition and, 66–67; performing artists and, 167–68; power of, 8; rationing of, 8, 178–81; ready-to-wear, 70, 180; representations of, as social commentary, 4; snobbery of, 202n.85; social history and, 2; as things, 12–14. *See also* evening gowns; fancy dress; mackintoshes; objects; used garments; World War II
"Clothes Make the Man" (Keller), 189n.48
Clothing Coupon Quiz, 219n.6
Clothing Coupons Trailer (film), 179–80
cockleshell hat, 111, *113*
Cohen, Lisa, 196n.108
comedies, in popular culture, used garments and, 158–66
Coming Up for Air (Orwell), 77
commodities, 1, 190n.63
Conekin, Becky, 7
conservatism, of evening dress, 33–34
conspicuous consumption, middle-class disapproval of, 206n.31

contexts, problematic nature of, 11
Cooley, Charles Horton, 15–16, 174, 194n.67
costume balls and parties, 20, 107
costumes. *See* fancy dress
courtship rituals, evening gowns and, 31
Covent Garden Fancy Dress Ball, 104–5
Cowley, Father (character; *Ulysses*), 167
Cox, Caroline, 7
Craik, Jennifer, 82, 83
Crane, Diana, 44, 65, 216n.55
Crome Yellow (Huxley), 61
"Cruise (Letters from a Young Lady of Leisure)" (Waugh), 117
cultural phenomena, clothing as expressive of, 4–5
Cunnington, C. Willett: on day vs. evening clothes, 29; on decoration, traditional forms of, 64; on evening dress and evening gowns, 30, 32, 33; on fashion, democratization of, 156; reversal of process described by, 92; on social recognition, ordinary clothing and, 66–67

Daily Mail, promotion of men's raincoats in, 82
Daily Mirror, cartoons on aspirational fancy dress in, 119
Daily Telegraph: advertisements for used-garment dealers in, 90; Burberry advertisements in, 84–85, 88; on individuality, 17; Phosferine advertisement in, 81, 81–82
Dalloway, Clarissa (character; *Mrs. Dalloway*), 1, 8, 95–97, 98, 203n.95
Dalloway, Elizabeth (character; *Mrs. Dalloway*), 1, 96–97
Danvers, Mrs. (character; *Rebecca*), 123
daytime dress, evening dress vs., 29, 197n.124
de Meyer, Adolf, 57

de Winter, Caroline (character; *Rebecca*), 123–24, 125
de Winter, Maxim (character; *Rebecca*), 3, 99, 122–25
death: association of, with mackintoshes, 2, 85–86, 90–91, 91; representations of evening gowns through, 42, 43–54; of monarchs, 40
Debenham and Freebody (department store), 109
debutantes, evening gowns for, 31–32
Dedalus, Stephen (character; *Portrait of the Artist*, *Ulysses*), 2, 168–71, 174–76, 217nn.81–82
D'Egville, Geoffrey, 108–9, 121
dehumanization, 4, 8–9, 10
de-individuation, 72–73, 86–87
Delafield, E. M., 115, 161–62, 172
democracy of dress, thesis of, 21, 30, 215n.37
depth ontology: aspirational fancy dress and, 118, 125; Barnes on, 210n.125; challenges to, 117, 141, 145; costumes as reinforcing, 114; description of, 106; lack of interest in challenge to, post–World War II, 143; in *Orlando*, 130–37; *Punch*'s embrace of, 118; in Sayers, 21; Woolf on, 136
Derry & Toms (department store), 82
desires, of things vs. self, 53
detective fiction, 5, 101, 137–42, 212n.155
Devonshire House Ball, 111
Devoted Ladies (Keane), 160
Diary of a Provincial Lady (Delafield), 115, 161–62, 172
Diary of Virginia Woolf (Woolf), 47
DiBattista, Maria, 202n.77
Dior, Christian, 220n.18
discursive authority, 195n.96
disguises, 103–4
distributed personas (distribution of identity), 12, 170, 180, 215n.43
Doan, Laura, 194n.74

Dollard, Ben (character; *Ulysses*), 167–68
Down and Out in Paris and London (Orwell), 14
Dreadnought hoax, 128, 208n.82
dress: democratization of, 21, 30; design of, Morrell's attitude toward, 55; for evening, 28, 29, 33–34, 190n.8, 192n.41, 197n.124; history of, on clothing circulation, 7; ideology of democracy of, 180–81; literary representations of, 181. *See also* clothes and clothing; evening gowns; fancy dress; mackintoshes; used garments
dresses: black, 39–42; flapper, Constructivist, 188n.44
Driscoll, Catherine, 217n.82
du Maurier, Daphne, 3, 21, 99, 122–26
Duchamp, Marcel, 10
Duff Gordon, Lucy, Lady (Lucile), 32
Duffy, Enda, 200n.45, 202n.81
Dunlop, John Kinninmont, 87, 201n.63

early twentieth century: fancy dress in, 107–14; garments and process of individuation in, 3–4; on power of garments, 8; things in, preoccupation with ontological status of, 9–10
Edson, Laura Gwyn, 202n.92
Eliot, T. S., 55–56, 141–42
Elizabeth II (queen of England), 142
Elmer, Fanny (character; *Jacob's Room*), 130
Elverys (retailer), advertising of mackintoshes by, 185n.3
Encyclopaedia Britannica: on dress as marker of class distinctions, 156; on evening dress, democratization of, 30; on modern women's dress, evolution of, 34
English, Barbara, 216n.52
English Women's Clothing in the Present Century (Cunnington), 7
Englishness of English Dress, The (Breward, Conekin, and Cox), 7
Esty, Jed, 78
Evans, Caroline, 186n.12, 187n.18, 212n.3
Eve: advertisements for used-garment dealers in, 149; on modern mackintoshes, 94; on tango craze, 38–39
evening dress, 28, 29, 33–34, 59, 190n.8, 192n.41, 197n.124
evening gowns, 18, 25–65, 102; agency of wearer and, 19; bodily exposure in, 32, 36–38, *38*, *39*, 45, 191n.21; connectedness and, 60, 63; courtship rituals and, 31; for debutantes, 31–32; in films, 36–37; having vs. being and, 29–30; inappropriate, 12; incompatibility of, with intellectual achievement, 47–48; as locus of sorrow, 194n.70; mackintoshes and, 71; in mass-market fiction, 36–37; as materialization of temporality, 29, 32–33; Morrell's experiments with, 54–64; as particular things, 28–34; in popular culture, 34–43; representations of, through death and failure, 42, 43–54; as showcases for female body, 31–32; singularity and, 68, 82; wearers of, objectification of, 182; women's desires and, 64–65; World War II and, 23, 178–79; yearning and, 27
Evening News, cartoons on aspirational fancy dress in, 119
exercise/occupation, repose/sex attraction vs., 29
"Extension of the Life of Clothing" (Board of Trade), 184

failure, representations of evening gowns through, 43–54
families, as safe source of used garments, 163–65, 179

236   INDEX

fancy dress, 20–21, 102–44; as art, 204n.2; aspirational, 20, 105, 114, 118–26; Bloomsbury and, 126–30; in early twentieth century, 107–14; emergence of, 7; middlebrow representations of, 114–26; in *Murder Must Advertise*, 137–42; after 1939, 142–43; in *Orlando*, 130–37; power of, 3; in satire, 115–16; used garments and, 145, 176; World War II and, 23, 178–79
Fancy Dresses at Harrods (catalog), 109, 110, 112–13
Fancy Dresses Described (Holt), 109, 121
Farquar, Lois (character; *The Last September*), 77–78, 200n.43
fashion, 4; bodies and, 16–17; fashion industry, 2, 17–18, 34–35; as foreign sovereignty, 39–40; gender ideals of, vs. women's realities, 44; mackintoshes and, 72, 73, 94; as response to "Woman," 64; supposed democratization of, 156–57; in Thomson, 165. *See also* evening gowns
Fashion Museum (Bath), 54
fashionable women, as objects, 48
Federico, Annette, 199n.39
Felski, Rita, 99, 186n.11
female bodies, evening gowns as showcases for, 31–32
female volunteers, in World War I, wearing of mackintoshes by, 79–80, 80
feminist authors, 43–44, 98
femmes fatales, 193n.63
Ferguson, Rachel, 146, 163, 164, 166
fiction. *See* texts; *specific works*
film, women in evening gowns in, 36–37
Fink-Nottle, Gussie (character; *Right Ho, Jeeves!*), 119–21
Fisher, Jeremy (character; *The Tale of Jeremy Fisher*), 73–74

Flanders, Jacob (character; *Jacob's Room*), 130
flat ontology, location of, 17
Flügel, J. C., 13, 192n.30
Forster, E. M., 182
Foster, Hal, 1
Foulkes, Nicholas, 204n.2
Fourteenth International Psychoanalytical Congress, 15
France: fashion lag in, 216n.55; fashion trade, role in, 186n.12
Freedgood, Elaine, 9, 13
Freytag-Loringhoven, Elsa von (Baroness Elsa), 210n.125
friends, used garments procured from, 160
Froula, Christine, 203n.103, 217n.81, 218n.82
Frow, John, 64
Fry, Roger, 63–64

garment culture, 1–23; evening gowns, 25–65; fancy dress, 102–44; mackintoshes, 66–101; used garments, 145–77; World War II and, 178–84
Gaudy Night (Sayers), 141
Gell, Alfred, 10, 11–12, 13, 54, 215n.43
gender: evening dress as materialization of, 32–33; evening gowns and, 27; fancy dress, gender-bending through, 115; fashion ideals, vs. women's realities, 44; fluidity of, 133; gender roles, 4, 65; hyper-genderization, evening gowns as means of, 32; income gap and, 173. *See also* men; women
Gentleman's Magazine, on mackintoshes, 70
Gentlewoman, on black dresses, 39
Giddens, Anthony, 15
Gifford, Don, 167
Gilbert, Sandra, 208n.79
Gillian Lindsay, 216n.60
Gillis, Stacy, 202n.81, 204n.111

INDEX 237

Goodrum, Alison, 7
Goodyear Tire & Rubber Company, 70
Gordon, Avery E., 188n.41
Gordon, Beverly, 204n.2
Gottfried, Roy, 217n.70
Grant, Duncan, 195n.89
Green, Ivy, 54
Greene, Graham, 75–77, 99–100
Grey, Margaret (character; *The Return of the Soldier*), 74–75
Grosz, Elizabeth, 26, 42–43, 84
group identity, uniforms and, 82
"gumboot girls," 74
Gunn, Simon, 152

Habermas, Jürgen, 4
"Hades" (*Ulysses* episode), 67
Haig, Margaret (Viscountess Rhondda), 42
Hammill, Faye, 5, 114, 175, 186n.8, 186n.10, 206n.31
"Happiness" (poem), 100
Harlequin (character; *Murder Must Advertise*), 137–39
Harrods (department store), 72, 109, 110, 179, 185n.3
Harrods General Catalogue, advertisements for mackintoshes in, 69
Harrods Weekly Price List, advertisements for mackintoshes in, 88–89, *89*
"Harvest of Folly, The" (Rhodes), 37–38, *38*, *39*, 42
Haselden, W. K., 119
haunting, 188n.41
having, being vs., evening gowns and, 29–30
headgear, for fancy dress, 111, *113*
Heglund, Jane, 28, 31
Heidegger, Martin, 10
heterogeneous assemblages, 190n.10
heterosexuality, evening gowns as emphasizing, 31
high modernism, 141, 166–74

highbrow, 166, 176.
historical fiction, used garments in, 160
historical sense, Eliot on, 55–56
Hoffman, Ruth Collette, 216n.52
Hollywood, influence of, on fancy dress, 205n.12
Holt, Ardern, 109, 121
How and What to Dance (D'Egville), 108–9, 121
How to "Make-Do-and-Mend" (film), 179
Howards End (Forster), 182
Howell, Geraldine, 178, 219n.6, 219n.10
Humble, Nicola, 186n.8
Huxley, Aldous, 61
hyper-genderization, evening gowns as means of, 32

Ideal-*I*, 124
Ideal-*other*, 124
ideas, bodies as, 16–17
Ideas in Things, The (Freedgood), 9
identity: distribution of, 12, 170, 180, 215n.43; fancy dress and, 103–5, 128, 129–30, 131, 135–36; gender, 27; group, 82; individual, mackintoshes and erasure of, 86; locus of, 126; national, mackintoshes and, 70–71; stabilization of, through dress, 173; used garments and, 174, 180. *See also* depth ontology; individuality (individuation) and individualism; self
I–it relationship, 199n.30
"Illusion" (Rhys), 50–53, 194n.80, 195n.86
Illustrated London News, on black dresses, 41
Illustrated Sporting and Dramatic News, advertisements for mackintoshes in, 72, 87
Illustrated Sunday Herald: on fancy-dress parties for interned soldiers, 107–8; "Through the Eyes of a Woman" (column) in, 108

238   INDEX

inanimate objects, 183–84
India Rubber Journal, on mackintoshes, 70
individuality (individuation) and individualism: de-individuation, 72–73, 86–87; fashion industry on, 17; garments and difficulty of, 3–4, 71; mackintoshes and, 93; modernism and, 175; used garments and, 145–47, 166–67, 175; Western formulations of, 212n.3
industrial revolution, individualism and, 4
industrialists, identification of, with middle class, 207n.76
intentionality, of objects, 11
interned soldiers, fancy-dress parties of, 107–8
interobjectivity, 196n.105
intimate exchanges, used garments as, 165
IRA members, mackintoshes and, 200n.45

Jacob's Room (Woolf), 130–31
James, Henry, 12–13, 14
Jameson, Fredric, 175
Jarvis, Anthea, 107, 108, 142
Jeanneret-Gris, Charles-Édouard (Le Corbusier), 175–76, 177
Jeeves (character; "Jeeves and the Dog McIntosh," *Right Ho, Jeeves!*), 67, 120–21
"Jeeves and the Dog McIntosh" (Wodehouse), 67
Jenny (character; *The Return of the Soldier*), 74–75
Jews, association of, with used-garment trade, 167, 217n.65
John Blanford (mackintosh manufacturer), 93, 97
Johnson, Barbara, 8, 10, 76, 187n.22, 199n.30
Johnston, Georgia, 208n.82

Jones, Ann Rosalind, 188n.44
Joy in the Morning (Wodehouse), 143
Joyce, James, 177; mackintoshes in works of, 84, 92–93, 100, 181; Orwell and, 218n.95; on self, clothing's distribution of, 22; on used garments, 148, 176. See also *Ulysses*
jumble (rummage) sales, 213n.9

Keane, Molly, 160
Keep the Aspidistra Flying (Orwell), 218n.95
Keller, Gottfried, 189n.48
Kermode, Frank, 202n.77
Kiaer, Christina, 188n.44
Kilman, Doris (character; *Mrs. Dalloway*), 1–2, 6, 8, 95–98, 203n.95
Klein, Kathryn, 200n.43
Koppen, R. S., 131, 193n.56, 209n.95
Kopytoff, Igor, 214n.28

La Tour, Leda-Maria, 2, 185n.3
labels (on clothing), 31, *31*, 71, 85
Lacan, Jacques, 15, 16, 17, 124, 174, 189n.53
Lacroix, Margaine, 197n.124
Ladies Field, on mourning evening dresses, 40
Lady: advertisements for used-garment dealers in, 154; on "new poor," 152
Laing, Kathryn S., 50, 193n.61
language, facilitation of dehumanization by, 10
Lark Rise (Thompson), 163–64, 165, 179
Last September, The (Bowen), 77–79, 200n.43
Latham, Sean, 60, 211n.130
Latour, Bruno, 10, 11, 13, 63, 187n.30, 196n.105
Le Corbusier (Charles-Édouard Jeanneret-Gris), 175–76, 177
Leader, Darian, 15

Lee, Hermione, 200n.41
Lee, Joseph, 119
Lemire, Beverly, 149, 154
Leonard, Garry, 216n.62, 217n.78
lesbians, apparitional quality of, 35, 194n.74
Levay, Matthew, 141
Levenback, Karen L., 203n.95
Levitt, Sarah, 70
Lewis, Ethan, 211n.130
Lipovetsky, Gilles, 30–31, 157, 215n.35
literature. *See* texts; *specific works*
Loew, Camilla, 88
"Londoner Out and at Home, The" (Sims), 149
looking-glass self (mirror stage, reflected self), 15–16, 17, 174, 189n.55, 194n.67
lower (working) classes, 126, 143, 147
Lucile (Lady Lucy Duff Gordon), 32
Lukács, Georg, 10
Lusitania, sinking of, 42
luxe brands, 85
Lyon, Janet, 195n.90
Lyttleton, Oliver, 178
Lytton Strachey, Giles, 127, 195n.89

Mabey, Richard, 216n.52
Macintosh, Charles, 67, 69, 100–101
mackintoshes, 19–20, 66–102; anonymity and, 79, 99–100; arrested development and, 78–79; association of, with death, 2, 85–86, 90–91, 91; association of, with flashers, 7; association of, with violence, 2, 91, 92–93; children and, 1–2, 19, 72–74; commemoration and, 68; commercial history of, 69–72; by fashion designers, 2; IRA members and, 200n.45; legacies of, 98–101; murder and, 101; as *muséal* objects, 91; national identity and, 70–71; odors of, 70, 77, 94; patenting of, 7; postwar reflections on, and transformations of, 92–98; poverty and, 1, 72–79, 92, 96–97; tartan lining in, 70; in World War II, 23, 179; yachting and, 72; young adults and, 74

IN WORLD WAR I, 79–91; as "armor," 88; costs of militarism and, 87–89; female volunteers and, 79–80, 80; iconic status of, 81–82; manufacturers' marketing of, 82–87; names of, 88–89, 89; proliferation of, 79–80; as uniforms, 83–84; used, 90–91

Mahood, Aurelia, 196n.101
"Make-Do-and-Mend," 22–23, 179
malfunctions, prioritization of objects with, 13
Mann, Frau (character; *Nightwood*), 210n.125
mannequins (models), 187n.18
Mao, Douglas, 200n.55
Marcus, Jane, 91, 198n.5
Marcuse, Herbert, 190n.65, 204n.3
Marling Hall (Thirkell), 180
Martin, Julia (character; *After Leaving Mr. Mackenzie*), 171
Martins, Rollo (character; *The Third Man*), 203n.108
Marx, Karl, coat of, 214n.28
Mary (queen of England), 40
masculine character traits, privileging of, 52
masquerades, marginalization of, 103
masques, differentiation of, from fancy dress, 107
mass-market fiction, evening gowns in, 36–37
mass-production, 70
materials, reading of, 185n.6
Mattamac (mackintosh manufacturer), 93–94, 97
McGregor, Robert, 211n.130
McKibbin, Ross, 147, 213n.13
McLoughlin, Kate, 204n.2

240 INDEX

melon (pouf beret) sleeves, 55, 56
memento mori, 91
memories (wrinkles), 214n.28
men: advertising aimed at, 82; character traits of, privileging of, 52; evening wear for, 28–29, 36; great masculine renunciation, 192n.30
Messel, Maud, 31, 40, 41
Messel Family Dress Collection, 40
middle classes: clothing expenditures by, 147; disapproval of conspicuous consumption by, 206n.31; fancy dress and, 106, 114, 126, 138–39, 143; new clothing, expectation of, 165–66
middlebrow representations of fancy dress, 114–26; in *Diary of a Provincial Lady*, 115; in *Punch*, 118–19, 121–22; in *Rebecca*, 122–26; in *Right Ho, Jeeves!*, 119–21; in Waugh, 115–17
middlebrow texts (middlebrow fiction): characteristics of, 175, 177; modernist works and, 5, 182, 186n.8; used garments in, 147–49, 158, 159, 161–62, 183
militarism, 83, 84, 87–89
Miller, Daniel, 100, 105, 126, 204n.5
Mills, A. Wallis, 150, 151
"Milly's Old Lavender Gown" (Pilkington), 158–59
Miniver, Mrs. (character; *Mrs. Miniver*), 183–84
M'Intosh (character; *Ulysses*), 67, 92–93, 99–100, 202n.81
mirrors, 123–24, 189n.53
"Modern Gumboot Girls Don't Care" (photograph), 74
modernism (modernity): cold, 187n.19; high, 141, 166–74; literary, Jameson's description of, 175; middlebrow and, 5, 182, 186n.8; modern commerce, idealization of, 177; modern experiences, of used garments, 149–58; modern garments, animation of, 9–10; modern world, individualism in, 4; modernist texts (modernist fiction), 137, 147–49, 175, 177, 182; objects in, 187n.27; subjectivity in, 216n.62
Molly Strong Dress Agency, "new poor" and, 153
Momerie, Dian de (character; *Murder Must Advertise*), 139
Moreland, Arthur, 121–22, 143
Morrell, Ottoline, 18–19, 54–64; aesthetic failures of, 58–59; Beaton's photograph of, 57, 58; as caricature, 54; evening gowns of, 27–28, 54–55, 56, 56–57; Mabel Waring, comparison with, 59–60; nonconformity of style of, 55, 56, 61–62; queering of, 62–63; sartorial caricatures of, 60–62, 183, 197n.114; tradition, sense of, 55–56; vulnerability of, 63, 188n.37; on Woolf's and Bell's fancy dress, 127
mourning dress, 18, 40–42, 41, 44, 169, 192n.41
Mrs. Dalloway (Woolf), 1–2, 8, 20, 95–97, 203n.103
Mulligan, Buck (character; *Ulysses*), 2–3, 169–70, 175
murder, mackintoshes and, 101
Murder Must Advertise (Sayers), 21, 106, 137–42, 143, 182, 211n.130

names: for clothing, distinctiveness of British, 6; of mackintoshes, 88–89, 95; of ordinary clothing, 66–67
National Fabric, The (Goodrum), 7
national identity, mackintoshes and, 70–71
National War Savings Committee, 150, 151
negativity: of experiences, evening gowns as agents for, 27; of fancy dress, 20–21; mackintosh as shorthand for, 69

"Nestor" (*Ulysses* episode), 93
Neville, Mrs. (dressmaker), *31*, 40, *41*
new, used garments as, 168, 171, 217n.70
"New Dress, The" (Woolf), 59–60, 196n.108
"new poor": buying and selling of clothes by, 21; modernism's lack of treatment of, 5–6; standard of living of, changes in, 152; temporary nature of, 213n.13; used garments, modern experiences of, 149–58; used garments and, 147–48, 159, 161
"New Poor, The" (Thomas; cartoon), 152, *153*
Nicholls, George J., *104*, 104–5
Nicolson, Juliet, 40
Nightwood (Barnes), 210n.125
Noblesse Oblige: An Enquiry into Identifiable Characteristics of the English Aristocracy (Mitford), 69
Northbridge Rectory (Thirkell), 181
Norton, Marda (character; *The Last September*), 78, 200n.43
Not So Quiet . . . Stepdaughters of War (Smith), 19, 85–86, 181
nudity principle, 32
Nystrom, Paul, 196n.102

objectification: evening gowns and, 31, 48, 182; garments and, 4, 8–9; mackintoshes and, 76, 100; of people, 67–68, 75, 76; poverty and, 76–77; reversal of process of, 92; of self, 15
objects: agency of, 11–12; animated, 78; fashionable women as, 48; human sequentiality and, 99; ignoring of, 52–53; inanimate, 183–84; intentionality of, 11; liveliness conferred by, 123; in mirrors, 189n.53; modernists on, 200n.55; *muséal*, mackintoshes as, 91; things vs., 11, 13, 187n.30;

transformational nature of, 125. See also subjects; things
occupation/exercise, repose/sex attraction vs., 29
odors (smells), of mackintoshes, 70, 77, 94
"Old Bloomsbury" (Woolf), 44
old-clothes trade. *See* used garments: trade in
Omega Workshops, 60, 63–64, 197n.115
open texts, closed texts vs., garments as, 65
Orchard of Tears, The (Rohmer), 176, 182
ordinary clothing, social recognition and, 66–67
Orlando (Woolf): agency of clothing in, 182; fancy dress in, 21, 106, 127, 130–37, 142, 209n.95; on human–object relationships, 143; illustrations in, 131; Rado on, 210n.118
Orwell, George, 14, 77, 218n.95
Outka, Elizabeth, 190n.63
Oxford English Dictionary: on fancy dress, 20, 103; on mackintoshes, 69

Paget, Lady Arthur, 111, *112*
Pankerton, Miss (character; *Diary of a Provincial Lady*), 115
Paquin, Jeanne, 39–40
Parker, Charles (character; *Murder Must Advertise*), 140
Parkins, Ilya, 220n.18
Patou, Jean, 40, 111, 160
"Penelope" (*Ulysses* episode), 167–68
people, as things. *See* objectification
performatives, 195n.96
performing artists, clothing and, 167–68
Perkin, Harold, 219n.13
"Personal" (*Punch* story), 71
personas, distributed (distribution of identity), 12, 170, 180, 215n.43

personhood, garments and difficulty of attaining, 3–4. *See also* identity
Persons and Things (Johnson), 10
person/thing binary, 126
Philippians 3:21, 206n.36
Phosferine, advertisement for, *81*, 81–82
Pilkington, Elizabeth C., 158
Pinkie (character; *Brighton Rock*), 75–76
pleasure, 46, 50, 51, 53–54
Poiret, Paul, 17, 149
"Poor Clara" (Beauchamp; cartoon), 25–26, *26*, 65
poppies, 93, 202n.81
popular culture: comedies of, 158–66; evening gowns in, 34–43
Portrait of the Artist as a Young Man, A (Joyce), 168–69, 174, 218n.95
Potter, Beatrix, 19, 73–74
pouf beret (melon) sleeves, 55, *56*
Pound, Ezra, 10
poverty: mackintoshes and, 1, 72–79, 92, 96–97; objectification and, 76–77; used garments and, 2; of women, 173. *See also* lower (working) classes; "new poor"
power: of clothing, 183; dress as manifestation of, 100; of fancy dress, 3; sharing of, between people and garments, 53; of used garments, 14
Price, Evadne (Helen Zenna Smith), 19, 84, 85–86, 100, 181
Principles of Sociology, The (Spencer), 10
"Proteus" (*Ulysses* episode), 170
Psychology of Clothes, The (Flügel), 13
Punch: Aquascutum advertisements in, 84; on fancy dress, 21, 118–19, 121–22; on mackintoshes, 71, 100
 CARTOONS IN: on aspirational fancy dress, 118–19; by Beauchamp, 25–26, *26*, 65; on class, 118–19, *119*; on "new poor," 152, *153*; on used garments, 150, *151*, 160–61, 172; on Wilhelm II, 201n.74

Queen, 152
queering, 62–63, 75, 97, 134. *See also* sex and sexuality

Rado, Lisa, 210n.118
raincoats. *See* mackintoshes
Raine, Patricia, 107, 108, 142
Ramsay, Mr. and Mrs. (characters; *To the Lighthouse*), 182
rationing, of clothing, 8, 178–81
ready-to-wear clothing, 70, 180
Reassembling the Social (Latour), 11
Rebecca (du Maurier): fancy dress in, 3, 21, 122–26, 144; on human–object relationships, 143; mackintoshes in, 99
reflected self (looking-glass self, mirror stage), 15–16, 17, 174, 189n.55, 194n.67
Remarque, Erich Maria, 85
repose/sex attraction, exercise/occupation vs., 29
representation, subject–object distinctions and, 12
Return of the Soldier, The (West), 74–75, 99, 181
Reynolds, Barbara, 137
Rhodes, Kathlyn, 37–38
Rhondda, Viscountess (Margaret Haig), 42
Rhys, Jean: anti-feminist views of, 190n.2; conclusions on, 177; evening gowns in works of, 18, 27, 43, 50–53; on self, clothing's distribution of, 22; on used garments, 148, 176; used garments in works of, 171–72
Right Ho, Jeeves! (Wodehouse), 119–21, 143
Rohmer, Sax, 176, 177, 182
romans à clef, 61–62, 197n.114
Rose (character; *Brighton Rock*), 76

INDEX   243

rummage (jumble) sales, 213n.9
Runcible, Miss (character; *Vile Bodies*), 116, 117
rural working-class life, 163–64
Rylands, George "Dadie," 126–27

Sackville-West, Vita, 131
Salmon and Co. (used-garment dealer), 90
Sartor Resartus (Carlyle), 7
sartorial pleasure, 50, 53–54
satire, fancy dress in, 115–16
Sayers, Dorothy L.: agency of clothing in works of, 182; depth ontology in works of, 21; fancy dress, enjoyment of, 137, 143; fancy dress in works of, 127, 137–42; mackintoshes in works of, 20, 84, 101; readers of, 212n.155
Schaffer, Talia, 209n.91, 209n.98
Schiaparelli, Elsa, 2, 185n.3
Scott, Carole, 199n.22
Scrimgeour, Mary and Grace (characters; *Alas, Poor Lady*), 146
secondhand clothes. *See* used garments
secondhand style, threat of, 174–77
self: bodies, independence from, 131–32; construction of, class and, 21; dependencies of, 148; distribution of, 12, 22, 162–63; fancy dress and, 20, 127–28, 140–41; gaps in narrative of, 170; garments and construction of, 133–34, 135; garment-selves, 172; looking-glass (mirror, reflected), 15–16, 17, 174, 189n.55, 194n.67; materialization of, 105; nature of, 17; self-awareness, source of, 170; self/body binary, 126; self-consolidation and self-recognition, 16; selfhood, 14–15, 20, 130, 157; self-reflectivity of garments, impact of, 14–15; sex, relationship to, 133; surface, fancy dress and relationship to, 103
Selfridges (department store), 7, 17, 190n.63
Sempill, Lady, 213n.10
Sense of Things, A (Brown), 12
serialization (sequentiality), of individuals: as threat to individuality, 212n.3; through mackintoshes, 99, 182; through used garments, 147, 166, 170–71, 182–83
servants, clothing for, 71
sex and sexuality: clothing's construction of, 134; fluidity of, 133–34; orientation of, clothing's construction of, 134; postsubjective, evening gowns' role in, 27; queering, 62–63, 75, 97, 134; sex appeal/attraction, evening gowns and, 32, 35, 64; sex attraction/repose, exercise/occupation vs., 29; sexy women, 193n.63
Seymour, Miranda, 55
Shannon, Brent, 82, 192n.30
"Shoppers' and Buyers' Guide, The" (*Vogue*), 153
Shulman, Nicola, 199n.22
Sidnell, Michael J., 92, 202n.77
Simmel, Georg, 29–30, 47, 65, 71, 82, 191n.10
"Simple Stories: The Fancy-Dress Dance" (Moreland), 121–22, 143
Sims, George R., 149
"Sirens" (*Ulysses* episode), 167
Sitwell, Osbert, 61–62
"Sketch of the Past, A" (Woolf), 44, 45, 46, 57
Smith, Angela K., 199n.30
Smith, Helen Zenna (Evadne Price), 19, 84, 85–86, 100, 181
Smith, Septimus Warren (character; *Mrs. Dalloway*), 98
snobbery, of clothing, 202n.85

society: fragmented, class vs., 65; social classes, 2, 4; social commentary, clothing as, 4; social events, sartorial conformity of, 60; social history, garments' engagement with, 2; social position, mackintoshes and, 1–2; social recognition, ordinary clothing and, 66–67; social relationships, 11–12; socialization, dress as manifestation of, 100. *See also* lower (working) classes; middle classes; upper classes
soft technologies, thinginess of, 13
"Solid House, A" (Rhys), 22, 171–72
Somme, Battle of the, 88
Spearman, Mrs. (character; "A Solid House"), 172
Spencer, Herbert, 9–10
Spoo, Robert, 93
sports, 33–34, 65, 72
"Le stade du miroir" (Lacan), 15
Stallybrass, Peter, 188n.44, 206n.35, 214n.28
Standard (National) Dress, 33, 191n.22
Stein, Gertrude, 10
Stephen, Adrian, 208n.82
Stephen, George, 46
Stephen, Vanessa. *See* Bell, Vanessa
Stephen, Virginia. *See* Woolf, Virginia
Stewart, Victoria, 212n.155
Strathern, Marilyn, 212n.3
Struther, Jan, 183
Stuff (Miller), 204n.5
subjectivity, 14, 216n.62
subjects: agency of, 11–12; subject/object binary, 12, 48, 50, 53, 105–6, 181. *See also* objectification; objects
Sunday Graphic: on mackintoshes, 94; Rhodes's serial fiction in, 37–38, 38, 39; "Vogues and Vanities" (column) in, 94
Sunday Pictorial, photographs of mackintoshes in, 74, 80, 80
surface, self vs., fancy dress and, 103

Tale of Mr. Jeremy Fisher, The (Potter), 73–74, 199n.22
tango craze, 38–39
tartan cloth, as lining in mackintoshes, 70
Taylor, D. J., 118
technology of resistance, 218n.82
Telegraph, advertisements for used-garment dealers in, 90
Teresa (character; "A Solid House"), 171–72
Testament of Youth (Brittain), 90
texts: clothing in, 181; evening gowns as, 36; highbrow fiction, used garments in, 166; historical fiction, used garments in, 160; mass-market fiction, evening gowns in, 36–37; modernist, 137, 147–49, 175, 177, 182; open vs. closed, garments as, 65; romans à clef, 61–62; significance of, 99. *See also* middlebrow texts
things: affective response to, 53; becoming persons, 92; bodies and, 43; characters as, 60; evening gowns as animate, 64; garments as, 12; history of, 26; objects vs., 11, 187n.30; in *Orlando*, 131; people as, mackintoshes and, 67–68, 75, 76; potency of, 114; preoccupation with ontological status of, 9–10; social relationships, impact on, 11; thing theory, 10, 13–15; thing/person binary, 126. *See also* objectification; objects
Third Man, The (Greene), 99–100, 203n.108
Thirkell, Angela, 180, 181
This Was My World (Viscountess Rhondda), 42
Thompson, Flora, 163–65, 167, 179
Three Guineas (Woolf), 173
Thrush, Nanette, 107
Times (London): advertisements for used-garment dealers in, 90;

Burberry advertisements in, 86, 87; on mourning dress, 40
To the Lighthouse (Woolf), 182
Todd, Dorothy, 196n.100
"Tradition and the Individual Talent" (Eliot), 55–56
Traditional Weatherwear (brand), 71
transformations, 114, 121–26, 133–35, 142. *See also* serialization (sequentiality), of individuals
trap doors, 93
Tree, Viola, 205n.27
trench coats, 19, 78, 79, 200n.48. *See also* mackintoshes
Triple Fugue (Sitwell), 61–62
trotte-bébé (walker), 15
Turner, W. J., 62
"22 Hyde Park Gate" (Woolf), 44

Ulysses (Joyce): "Circe" episode in, 93; Dedalus in, 2, 168–71, 174–76, 217nn.81–82; "Hades" episode in, 67; mackintoshes in, 20, 99, 181; M'Intosh in, 67, 92–93, 99–100, 202n.81; "Nestor" episode in, 93; "Penelope" episode in, 167–68; "Proteus" episode in, 170; "Sirens" episode in, 167; used boots in, 2–3, 170, 172, 175, 217n.81; used garments in, 22, 167, 169
uniforms: armed forces' code of, 183; Baudrillard on, 87; Craik on, 83; group identity and, 82; mackintoshes as quasi-, 98; used, 90
United States: fashion lag in, 216n.55; fashion trade in, 186n.12
Unnatural Death (Sayers), 20, 101
upper classes: construction of self and, 21; dangers of fancy dress of, 116; depth ontology and, 106; evening gowns and, 37, 38; fancy dress of, 106, 107, 114–15, 126, 143; mackintoshes and, 75, 97; mourning dress of, 40; new clothing, expectation of, 165–66; news sources for, 94; trench coats for, 84–85
used books, 174, 218n.95
used garments, 21–22, 145–77; "dress agencies" for, 152–53; familiarity of, 163–64; from family, 163–65, 179; from friends, 160; high modernism and, 166–74; market for, 90; "new poor" and, 149–58; Orwell and, 14; popular culture comedies and, 158–66; poverty and, 2; as quasi-subjects, 172; self, impact of, on, 145; serialization of, by fictional characters, 147; in World War II, 23, 179
TRADE IN, 90, 149, 150, 152–54, 161–62, 165; direct seller–buyer transactions, 214n.20; frustrations of, 156; popular representations of, 166; in World War I, 150; in World War II, 180

values, clothing as expressive of, 4–5
Vanity Fair, on evening dress, 28
Vaughan, Emma, 44
Verdun, Battle of, 88
Victoria (queen of England), 40, 107, 111, 208n.82
Victorian era, advertising in, 82
Victory Ball, 205n.27
Vile Bodies (Waugh), 115–16
violence, association of, with mackintoshes, 2, 91, 92–93
Vogue: advertisements for used-garment dealers in, 149, 152–53, 213n.15; black dresses in, 40; clothing advice in, 6–7; on costume shops, 109; editors of, 196n.100; on fancy dress, 108; founding of, 7; Lady Abdy in, 111–12, *113*; mackintoshes in, 94–95; Morrell in, 57–58, *58*; Poiret in, 17
Vogue Pattern Book, on evening dress, 178
volt sorcery, 12

Walkowitz, Judith, 217n.65
Wallis, Robina, 7, 154–55, 157, 161, 180, 214n.22
war charities, fund-raisers for, 107
"War Economy" (Mills; cartoon), 150, *151*
Waring, Mabel (character; "The New Dress"), 59–60, 197n.110
waterproofs. *See* mackintoshes
Watts, Arthur, *119*
Waugh, Evelyn, 21, 115–17
We Have Never Been Modern (Latour), 11
wealth, display of, through fancy dress, *111*, *112*
wealthy individuals. *See* upper class
weather alls, weatherproofs. *See* mackintoshes
Weldon's Patterns, costume designs in, 108
Wellesley, Dorothy, 129
Wellington, Arthur Wellesley, first Duke of, 67
West, Rebecca: evening gowns in works of, 18, 27, 43, 47–50, 53; mackintoshes in works of, 19, 74–75, 181; self-description of, 194n.70
"What the Butler Saw" (biograph) machines, 35
White, Allon, 206n.35
Whose Body? (Sayers), 101
Why Women Wear Clothes (Cunnington), 66–67
Wilde, Oscar, 218n.97
Wilhelm II (kaiser of Germany), 201n.74
Williams, William Carlos, 10
Willis, Mr. (character; *Murder Must Advertise*), 138–39
Wilson, Elizabeth, 16–17, 31–32, 173
Wimsey, Peter (character; *Murder Must Advertise*), 21, 101, 106, 137–42, 211n.130, 211n.151
Windsor, stories on used garments in, 158–59
Wisker, Gina, 125, 207n.56
Wodehouse, P. G., 67, 119–21, 143
women: bodies of, evening gowns as showcases for, 31–32; desires of, evening gowns and, 64–65; evening dress for, 28–29; in evening gowns, modernist representations of, 27; fashionable, as objects, 48; feminist authors, 43–44, 98; femmes fatales, 193n.63; mackintoshes for, 72, 73, 79–80, *80*, 94; poverty of, 173; realities of, gender ideals of fashion vs., 44; sportswear for, 33–34; in World War I, 89. *See also* evening gowns; *specific women*
Women's Volunteer Reserve, 80, *80*
Women's Wear Daily, founding of, 7
Woodward, Sophie, 188n.44
Woolf, Leonard, 47, 60, 129, *129*, 195n.89
Woolf, Virginia Stephen: amethysts, as trope for evening dress in memoirs of, 45; on appearances, 47; conclusions on, 177; evening gowns in works of, 18, 27, 43; evening gowns of, 44–47, 53, 193n.56; fancy dress and, 106, 127–30, 136, 143, 208n.89; "frock consciousness" of, 44, 181; on getting dressed, 45; Gilbert on, 208n.79; mackintoshes in works of, 84; on Morrell, 60; on new vs. used garments, 173; on selfhood, 130; on used garments, 148, 176; West's works and, 203n.93; white satin, as trope for evening dress in memoirs of, 45
Wooster, Bertie (character; "Jeeves and the Dog McIntosh," *Right Ho, Jeeves!*), 119–21, 143
working classes. *See* lower (working) classes

World War I: effects of, clothing as commentary on, 4; evening gowns and, 33; fancy dress and, 107–8; mackintoshes and, 94–95, 98; mourning dress during, 40–41; used-garment trade during, 150. *See also* mackintoshes: during World War I

World War II: attitudes on clothing during, 22–23, 178–84; fancy dress and, 142; impact of, 7–8

"World's Worst Failure, The" (West), 47–50
Worth (couturier), 191n.22
wrinkles (memories), 214n.28

Yeats, William Butler, 177
Young, Sarah Fullerton Monteith (Sally Young), 193n.48

Zimring, Rishona, 190n.2, 194n.80, 195n.86

GPSR Authorized Representative: Easy Access System Europe, Mustamäe tee
50, 10621 Tallinn, Estonia, gpsr.requests@easproject.com

www.ingramcontent.com/pod-product-compliance
Lightning Source LLC
Chambersburg PA
CBHW021940290426
44108CB00012B/910